The McGraw-Hill Guide to

WORLD
LITERATURE

The McGraw-Hill Guide to

WORLD

LITERATURE

Volume Two
Molière to Beckett

DAVID ENGEL
RUTH HOBERMAN
FRANK PALMERI

McGRAW-HILL BOOK COMPANY

New York   St. Louis   San Francisco   Auckland   Bogotá
Guatemala   Hamburg   Johannesburg   Lisbon   London   Madrid
Mexico   Montreal   New Delhi   Panama   Paris   San Juan
São Paulo   Singapore   Sydney   Tokyo   Toronto

THE MCGRAW-HILL GUIDE TO WORLD LITERATURE

1 2 3 4 5 6 7 8 9 DOC DOC 8 7 6 5

ISBN 0-07-019526-9

LIBRARY OF CONGRESS CATALOGING IN PUBLICATION DATA (Revised for vol. 2)

Engel, David (date)
    The McGraw-Hill guide to world literature.

    Includes bibliographies and indexes.
    Contents: 1. Homer to Cervantes—v. 2. Moliere to Beckett.
    1. Literature—History and criticism—Miscellanea. I. Hoberman, Ruth. II. Palmeri, Frank. III. Guide to world literature.
IV. Title.
PN524.E54   1985   809   85-240
ISBN 0-07-019525-0 (pbk. : v. 1)
ISBN 0-07-019526-9 (pbk. : v. 2)

The editors for this book were Karl Weber and Barbara Brooks; the editing supervisor was Marthe Grice.

BOOK DESIGN BY PATRICE FODERO

PREFACE

The McGraw-Hill Guide to World Literature is a reader's companion to continental European literature, intended for students, teachers, and general readers. It appears in two volumes and follows the historical plan of most year-long college survey courses in world literature. Volume One, which covers authors from Homer through Cervantes, is divided into three parts: the Classical World, the Judeo-Christian Heritage, and the Middle Ages and Renaissance. Volume Two, which covers authors from Molière through Samuel Beckett, also is divided into three parts: the Neoclassical Age, Romantic and Realist, and the Modern World. Each chapter focuses on a single author. The centerpiece of each chapter is a discussion in question and answer format of a significant text. Also included are a biographical introduction to the author and suggestions for further reading. Each literary period is introduced with an essay that discusses the historical and cultural background of the literary works.

The McGraw-Hill Guide is unique in that it is largely a "how-to" book. It attempts to teach a strategy for reading and enjoying some of the classics of western literature. Such a strategy is made necessary, the authors feel, by the very idea of classic literature.

It is probably safe to say that nobody approaches a classic without some reluctance. The classics, we are told, are the best that has been thought and written. They have enriched numberless readers through the ages, and if we will only give them a chance, we too will be enlarged by the experience of reading them. As a consequence, most of us are likely to approach the classics with the grim dutifulness reserved for doing what is "good for us." If we do not like a classic novel, play, or poem, we are likely to think there is something wrong with us. While other books have readers, the classics, it sometimes seems, have victims.

We have attempted to make the classics less intimidating by using the question and answer format. Each question provides an occasion for the reader to think independently about the text under discussion. Our hope is that these questions will encourage you to encounter the texts more actively and spontaneously and with greater freedom to make up your own mind about them.

The best time to turn to the questions is after you have read the text once and want to consider more fully what you have read. The answers we have provided should not be thought of as the only "right" answers but merely as one way in which the authors, as informed readers, have tried to understand and organize their own experience of the texts. We hope you will formulate your own answers to the questions, and we fully expect that you will sometimes prefer your answers to ours. Furthermore, our questions are by no means the only ones that could be asked. We expect the answers, both ours and yours, to lead to further questions, and you are encouraged to ask them.

The process of question, answer, and further question is our strategy for reading the classics. While our application of this method may be unique, the method itself is by no means original. It is the way in which a demanding reader reads any book that is worth a second thought. It is, however, particularly useful when applied to authors of such intimidating renown as Aristotle, Dante, Dostoevsky, and Proust, because it helps put us on a par with them. After all, an author is essentially someone who is skilled at questioning his or her own experience, and the books that result may be considered the author's personal answers, although these answers are often complex, provisional, and ambiguous. When we in turn interrogate a book, we join the author in a common interpretive enterprise. We may adopt the author's questions as our own and test the answers the author suggests against both the experience represented in the text and our own experience of the world. Or we may find that our experience of the book troubles our own conclusions. When we cycle back and forth like this between reading the text and thoughtfully examining it, we are, like the author, moving back and forth between experience and the effort to represent it. Reading actively like this allows us to meet our authors, classic and otherwise, on common ground, where we are free to determine for ourselves the particular merits and pleasures of each.

There is, however, one further thing that is special about the context in which we encounter classic literature. Classics are by definition books which successive generations of readers have found meaningful. They thus have a history in two senses. First, they were written in the more or less distant past, and they take their distinctive identity from the time and place of their writing. Second, they have a history as texts. They have been appreciated and criticized through the years; they have been influenced by earlier books and have themselves influenced later books; their reputations have risen and fallen. Both these histories are described in the biographical introductions and period headnotes in *The McGraw-Hill Guide to World Literature*. Some readers will find this information useful and interesting. Those who do not should not be dismayed. These materials are intended as adjuncts, not prerequisites, to the interpretive experience we have been eager to recommend.

D.E.

R.H.

F.P.

CONTENTS

Part One

THE
NEOCLASSICAL
AGE

INTRODUCTION

Two revolutions frame the neoclassical period in European culture: the Puritan Revolution in England (1641–1660) and the French Revolution (1789). The storming of the Bastille and the execution of Louis XVI signaled the end of a century and a half of political continuity and cultural eminence in France. The parallel period in English culture and politics had begun with the end of the Puritan Revolution and the restoration of the monarchy under Charles II; it ended with the Napoleonic wars and the rise of romanticism at the close of the eighteenth century.

Especially in England, this period is sometimes called the Augustan age, by analogy with the first decades of the Roman Empire under Augustus, which Horace, Virgil, and Ovid made into a golden age of Latin literature. The parallel is a suggestive one. In the first decades of the Christian era, Rome was emerging from a century of debilitating civil wars and disorienting territorial expansion. In consequence, her citizens were grateful to Augustus for ushering in a period of peace, stability, and cultural consolidation. Seventeen hundred years later, Europe was emerging from over a century of religious civil wars and territorial struggles, and, like Augustan Rome, longed for a period of peace and tranquility. The similarity of circumstances accounts for many of the cultural values shared by Augustan Rome and eighteenth-century France and England. These values include a cosmopolitan tolerance of cultural differences, a suspicion of fanaticism of any sort, and a sense that civilization is an expensive human triumph in which elements of liberation and repression are necessarily bound together.

Augustus had brought an end not only to the self-destructive civil wars but

3

also to the republican form of government in Rome through the imposition of his personal rule as emperor. A similar concentration of power in the hands of central authority followed the ebbing of the European religious civil wars. In France, Louis XIV, who reigned from 1643 to 1715, consolidated all power and patronage in his own person, a state of affairs that his less capable successor, Louis XV, maintained for sixty years thereafter. Frederick II of Prussia (reigned 1740–1786) and Catherine II of Russia (reigned 1762–1796) are other examples of the eighteenth-century "enlightened despot": a ruler who wields absolute power but tolerates debate, patronizes art, and, prodded by thoughtful loyal subjects, institutes needed reforms. Thus, the idea of democracy was not central to the thinking of most philosophers of the Enlightenment. Only in England did national authority rest not in an individual ruler but in a body of elected officials, as a result of the bloodless Glorious Revolution of 1688, in which Parliament had replaced the Catholic-leaning monarch James II with the thoroughly Protestant rulers, William and Mary, and so firmly established the principle of parliamentary sovereignty.

The establishment of a national religion in each of the various countries of Europe brought to an end the shedding of blood over religious differences, but persecution, bigotry, and discrimination did not wither away as a result. In fact, whether the established church was Roman Catholic and the victims Protestant or vice versa, religious intolerance remained one of the distinguishing features of the time. As a Roman Catholic in England, for example, the poet Alexander Pope was taxed at twice the normal rate, barred from the major universities, and forbidden to live within ten miles of the capital or hold any public office. In Catholic France, on the other hand, the works of Montesquieu, Diderot, Voltaire, Rousseau, and other philosophers were regularly condemned by the authorities of church and state; most of these thinkers spent time either in prison or in exile for what they had written.

Against such alliances of secular and religious authority, many eighteenth-century thinkers moved to a philosophical position known as *deism*. The deists argued that the differences between religious denominations are unimportant, and that human reason, unaided by revelation and working only from the evidence of natural laws and the beauty of creation, would lead all people to acknowledge and revere God, conceived of rather impersonally as the deity, the creator, or simply a great spirit. The deists maintained that moral laws rest on a foundation not of revealed religion but of natural reason, and they perceived morality as natural and universal: in their view, people of very different racial, cultural, and religious backgrounds value generosity, loyalty, courage, and learning, and condemn selfishness, betrayal, cowardice, and ignorance.

The deists denied the doctrine of original sin with its implication of human depravity, and argued that the practice of virtue, rightly understood, is not a painful duty but a gratifying pleasure, and that the pursuit of virtue does not conflict with but complements the pursuit of happiness and self-interest. Stated baldly, such arguments may sound strange, but they underlie, for example, both Jefferson's Declaration of Independence and Adam Smith's defense of rational self-interest as the basis of capitalism. For these men, and for other deists, nature's reasonableness allows human beings to reconcile goodness and happiness, virtue and pleasure.

Thinkers in the neoclassical period generally turned away from the supernatural or mysterious, preferring to explore the certainties of science and the clarity of mathematics. It is this change that has led some historians to label the period the Enlightenment. The philosopher and essayist Sir Francis Bacon had earlier stressed the importance of the experimental method, and René Descartes had demonstrated the elegant explanatory powers of mathematics. Sir Isaac Newton, one of the preeminent scientists of all time, built on the insights of both of these predecessors in formulating his laws of gravity and motion. Newton's achievements brought him honor verging on veneration throughout the eighteenth century for the depth and lucidity of his insights. Pope was not alone in regarding Newton's mind as possessing a nearly God-like power:

> Nature and nature's laws lay hid in night;
> God said, "Let Newton be," and all was light.

Throughout the century, science, then called "natural philosophy," took on increasing importance. By 1800, Carolus Linnaeus had developed the modern system of biological classification; Antoine Lavoisier had laid the foundations of modern chemistry; and Newton and Gottfried Leibniz had developed the calculus. In the view of many, science was coming to replace religion as the source of ultimate certainty.

A similar focus on human affairs in the natural world led to the study and writing of history in a form that we would recognize as modern—not as a mere chronicle of events and dates nor as a record of religious prophecies confirmed, but as a pattern of events determined by human agents facing recognizable problems and responding with the best means available to them. The increased consciousness of secular history in turn laid the groundwork for modern notions of human progress. Utopias sprouted thickly in the soil of the Enlightenment; when the goal of human history is translated from religious to secular terms, the philosophical utopia replaces the Christian New Jerusalem.

However, strong countercurrents qualified the Enlightenment belief in the indefinite progress of history and the rationality of human beings. The dominance of tragedy and satire as literary forms in the neoclassical period suggests the pessimism underlying Enlightenment philosophy. Almost all of Racine's classic tragedies, for example, revolve around heroic conflicts between reason and passion; they are tragedies precisely because the characters' passions overpower and bring to nought the honorable strivings of their reason. Similarly, satire points out the gap between what is and what ought to be, between optimistic projections and disappointing realities, or, as in the works of Jonathan Swift, between an ideal rationality and an inescapable animality. Neither tragedy nor satire invites sweet reason to celebrate its own preeminence. When, in a survey of the period, philosopher Immanuel Kant called his own time an age of enlightenment, he meant the phrase not as a celebration but as a negative judgment. He went on to contrast his century with the ideal of a *truly* enlightened age, in which the work of intellectual emancipation and maturation would be complete. In Kant's view, the eighteenth century had barely begun the necessary unchaining and enlightening of the mind.

Many people mistakenly think of neoclassical art as grounded in a serene contemplation of beautiful, unchanging truths, far removed from the sweat and grime of the real world. It is, perhaps, more accurate to understand the neoclassical moment as a condition of tension in which strongly-felt competing claims are held in precarious balance, with the mental attitude of the artist determined by the sum of the countervailing forces affecting it.

In this view, James Madison's defense of the U.S. Constitution in the *Federalist Papers* can stand as a representative argument of the neoclassical mind. In response to the fear that even a partial democracy will encourage the growth of factions, parties, and other self-interested groups, Madison suggests that the solution is not to try to stamp out such growth—that would suffocate all freedom—but, paradoxically, to encourage it, so that competing interests will oppose, qualify, and even cancel one another. The work of representative government, Madison argues, can only be accomplished when the various self-interested parties are fighting at cross-purposes so that the resultant policies are determined by a kind of political "vector analysis." Such policies may not always be right, but, in Madison's view, they will at least represent the self-interest of some large portion of the populace. No other political system can guarantee even that much.

C H A P T E R 1

MOLIÈRE

Youth

Actor, playwright, and manager of theatrical companies, Molière was in the fullest sense a man of the theater, although nothing in his origins would have suggested such a career. He was born Jean-Baptiste Poquelin in 1622 to a Parisian family which for many years had been successful tradespeople. His father served as master upholsterer to King Louis XIII, an office to which Jean-Baptiste probably would have succeeded had he not chosen a more exciting and unpredictable life in the theater.

From 1632 to 1637, Jean-Baptiste studied at the Jesuit Collège de Clermont, where his friends included his later patron, the prince de Conti, and Cyrano de Bergerac, already a swaggering, larger-than-life figure, although rather different from the version of him in Rostand's nineteenth-century play. After leaving Clermont, Jean-Baptiste seems to have taken some halfhearted steps in the direction of a legal career, undoubtedly to placate his father, a solid burgher who hoped for a reasonable return on his investment in his son's education. During these years in Paris, he became well acquainted with the theater and its personalities, notably with Tiberio Fiorelli, known by the stage name Scaramouche (which Molière later used for the stock character he invented), the great Italian *farceur* from whom Jean-Baptiste is rumored to have taken lessons. In 1643, Jean-Baptiste Poquelin renounced his right to his father's court appointment, adopted the name Molière (of unknown origin), and, formalizing his decision to enter the theater, contracted with several members of the Béjart family and some other actors to create L'Illustre Théâtre.

Theatrical Career

The most important figure among the free-living Béjarts was Madeleine, who was throughout Molière's life his capable partner in all things: fellow actor, codirector of their troupes, shrewd manager of their messy business affairs, and, it is supposed, his mistress. Their first theatrical venture was a rapid and resounding failure. Unable to match the fierce competition of the two reigning Parisian theater companies, the Hôtel de Bourgogne and the Théâtre du Marais, L'Illustre collapsed within a year amid rising debt and the desertion of its best actors. Throughout his career, Molière and Molière's theater would be one and the same; when things went well, he was usually stage front in the best role to take the applause, and when things went badly, he paid the penalty himself. Upon L'Illustre's bankruptcy, Molière was imprisoned for the theater's debt to a supplier of candles; only the generosity of a friend allowed Molière to purchase his freedom.

Having failed in the capital, Molière and what remained of the company moved to the provinces, where for the next fourteen years they lived the harum-scarum life of itinerant players. Although there are few reliable details about the company in this period, the general tenor of their adventures is clear: run-ins between bohemian actors and offended locals, dust-ups with rowdy audiences, and amours, quarrels, and general mayhem within the company as they traveled the roads to Bordeaux, Nantes, Toulouse, Angoulême, Carcassonne, and a dozen other towns. Their typical stage was a tennis court, converted with the aid of chandeliers and tapestries into the semblance of a theater. Here they entertained a heterogeneous audience with varied fare: farces from the Italian, fables from the French folk tradition, borrowings from the classics, pantomime, music, ballet—in short, anything to amuse an audience that tended to show its displeasure crudely. In these circumstances, Molière mastered the skill that is equally apparent in both his slightest and his most sophisticated plays: the ability to entertain. His playwriting, which he undertook only after years of acting and then primarily to provide the company with suitable material, is preeminently a theatrical art. It took its life from the stage, and it plays as brightly and amusingly today as it did 300 years ago. Every line Molière wrote was meant to be performed; to be fully appreciated, his plays must be seen as well as read. The years on the road played a crucial role in the education of Molière the dramatist.

The company's routine of travel was sometimes interrupted by a longer residence at the establishment of some local notable for whom they would provide *divertissements* on commission. For a time, the company was located in Languedoc under the patronage of the prince de Conti, who later expelled the company after his conversion to a strenuously puritanical religiosity. (Conti had joined the Society of the Blessed Sacrament, a group devoted to religious reformation, which, along with Conti himself, is thought to be among Molière's objects of satire in *Tartuffe*.)

During a residence at Lyons (1655), Molière staged *L'Étourdi* (*The Blunderer*), the first comedy he can be said to have written. Of course, *L'Étourdi*, like many of his later plays, borrowed liberally from the dramas of other nations and authors, in this case from the Italian theater. The wily servant Mascarille is a stock character from the Italian *commedia dell'arte* and the first of Molière's numerous servant-pranksters, who typically outwit the doddering head of the family to help the young master marry the girl he loves.

The Italian *commedia dell'arte* was perhaps the single most important influence on Molière's comedies. It featured stock characters, such as Pierrot the melancholy clown and Harlequin the rascal, in stock situations. Sketchy scripts allowed considerable freedom for improvisation and put a premium on virtuosity in comic timing and slapstick. The appeal of this popular theater lay in its energy and cheerful vulgarity, its willingness to do anything—if possible, several things at once—for a laugh. In his mature comedies, Molière added to these lively elements psychological verisimilitude, satirical bite, and poetic composition to create an appealing combination of robustness and complexity.

Although Molière's second comedy, *Dépit amoureux* (*Lover's Quarrels*, 1656), was not as well received as the first, the company prospered well enough under Molière's leadership to be able to return to Paris in 1658, armed with some capital and the theatrical expertise gained in their long provincial apprenticeship, and resume its battle for a share of the Parisian audience. The key to success in this battle was the favor of the young Louis XIV, who had ascended to the throne in 1642. The strategies used by the competing companies included, beyond direct attempts to woo the Sun King, various ploys to ruin the reputation of their theatrical rivals. No attack was considered too scurrilous, and blows were regularly directed not only at the dramaturgy of one's enemies but at their appearance, religion, morality, and sexual habits. The knockabout of farce was not confined to the Parisian stage; the backstage maneuverings of the time were equally undignified.

In 1658, Molière's troupe performed for the first time before the king, at the Louvre. Although Louis seems not to have enjoyed the main production, Corneille's *Nicomède* (as a producer, Molière never succeeded with tragedy),

Molière's comic sketch *Docteur amoureux* (*The Doctor in Love*) delighted the king and his court. With the king's approval and under the patronage of his brother, the company was able to make its home in the Théâtre du Petit-Bourbon and begin its Parisian career in earnest.

Early Comic Successes

Molière's first great comic success was *Les Précieuses ridicules* (*The Precious Damsels*, 1659), a satire on contemporary manners, in particular, snobbery and affectation. Although the moral intention of the play is serious in its way, Molière saw no reason to sacrifice any of the comic potential of theater for the sake of seriousness. In *Les Précieuses ridicules*, Molière typically has things both ways, combining social critique with all the lively stuff of farce: disguises, comic plots of revenge, slapstick, characters of monumental absurdity, trickster servants, and to top it all off, a sound drubbing for the offenders. The play was a great success with the public, but for this Molière had to pay the usual price of retaliation from his two perennial enemies: those jealous of his talents and those who felt the barbs of his satire directly. In this case, the accusation was plagiarism. Hardly a play of Molière's was not greeted with this charge, which was in most cases both true and irrelevant. The charge was irrelevant because his borrowings were from plays which had themselves dipped into the universal stock of classic comic characters and situations and because the comic stew he brewed of these borrowings was a concoction all his own.

In 1660, on the instigation of one of Molière's competitors, the home theater of his company was demolished without warning by the royal surveyor, an incident which suggests as well as any the maliciousness of Parisian theatrical relations. The company moved, on the king's invitation, to the Great Hall of the Palais Royal, where they staged their next success, Molière's *Sganarelle, ou le cocu imaginaire* (*The Imaginary Cuckold*, 1660), followed in the same year by *Dom Garcie de Navarre*, *L'École des maris* (*The School for Husbands*), and *Les Fâscheux* (*The Nuisances*). In 1662, Molière presented *L'École des femmes* (*The School for Wives*), which included a comic sermon against infidelity placed in the mouth of a sententious old fool, thus calling down the wrath of the *dévots*, the hidebound religionists and moralists who were to hound Molière for the rest of his life.

The battle with the *dévots* was joined in earnest over *Tartuffe* (first performed in 1664), which was almost immediately placed under interdiction by irate divines, perhaps with the aid of the queen mother. *Tartuffe* offended church conservatives and reformers alike, and both factions competed for the right to claim that the satire was directed against themselves. Molière was branded an enemy of religion, a blasphemer, and "a demon clad in human flesh."

Although Louis, who had his own arguments with the *dévots,* seems to have been on Molière's side in this quarrel, he allowed the play to remain banned for five years, during which time it was rewritten in several versions and occasionally read by Molière for private audiences. When, after years of sally and countersally, ploy and counterploy, Molière finally won the right to perform the play in public in 1670, it was an extraordinary success.

Marital Woes

In 1662, Molière had married Armande Béjart, his junior by twenty years, an act which brought him the double misery of an unhappy marriage and vulnerability to a new and vicious slander. Molière's numerous enemies lost no time spreading the rumor that Armande was the daughter of Madeleine Béjart, thus making Molière guilty of an incestuous marriage to his own illegitimate progeny, a charge recorded in a famous 1688 pamphlet *Les Intrigues de Molière et celles de sa Femme; ou la fameuse comédienne* (*The Intrigues of Molière and His Wife; Or, The Famous Comedienne*). (The study of the voluminous contemporary literature contra Molière is a discipline in its own right.) It now seems fairly certain that Armande was Madeleine's young sister, not her daughter, although the legality of the marriage did nothing to alter the misery of it.

People generally like clowns to have a melancholy side, and Molière found much ground for unhappiness in his relationship with Armande. She was an incurable flirt and, as Molière felt with pain, essentially indifferent to her husband, while he was infatuated with her and distressed by the rumors, perhaps accurate, that she was playing him false.

This unfortunate match had at least one happy result, however: *Le Misanthrope* (1666), considered by many to be Molière's best play, in which he both played out and transformed his feelings about Armande. Alceste, originally played by Molière, is one of Molière's monomaniacs; like Harpagon the miser (*L'Avare*) and Orgon the true believer (*Tartuffe*), he is dominated by a single idea: in this case, an inflexible commitment to candor. Society, in Alceste's opinion, is a vast system of deceit, from its casual forms of politeness to its dealings with the most serious emotions. Alceste will have none of it anymore, even if this means offending others right and left and becoming a pariah in the process. Célimène is both Alceste's adversary and his heart's desire, a coquette whose life revolves around the gossip, casual deceit, and triviality Alceste abhors. Nonetheless, Alceste is hopelessly in love with her, and the play evolves as a battle between Alceste's desire to have both the world and Célimène on his terms and her wittily defended desire to continue to live as she lives, between Alceste's inflexibility and her own more supple and tolerant relation to the world.

Alceste, like all Molière's extremists, must lose. His final proposition to Célimène is characteristically absolute: Will she leave everything to live alone in the desert with him? Célimène refuses, with a phrase that is a vindication of both nature and society, imperfect as it is: "but I'm only twenty years old." Alceste is left to stalk off to his chosen exile alone. In equal measure heroic and absurd, Alceste demonstrates how complicated and subtle Molière's characters can be. Not the least attractive aspect of the play is the generosity of spirit which allowed Molière to step back from himself and lampoon, in Alceste, the impatience and absolutism he no doubt often directed at his young wife and to sketch a sympathetic portrait of Célimène, a woman not unlike Armande.

Later Works

Molière's mature achievements include *Dom Juan* (1665), which, like *Tartuffe*, was a matter of public dispute and was withdrawn from production; *Le Médecin malgré lui* (*The Doctor in Spite of Himself*, 1666); *Amphitryon* (1668), an extravaganza in the mythological mode; *George Dandin* (1668), a rather cruel farce at the expense of a foolish cuckold; *L'Avare* (*The Miser*, 1668), a treatment of obsession which has been known to provoke horror as well as laughter; *Le Bourgeois Gentilhomme* (*The Bourgeois Gentleman*, 1670), a satire on the socially ambitious parvenu Monsieur Jourdain, one of Molière's greatest roles; *Les Fourberies de Scapin* (*The Rascalities of Scapin*, 1671), a helter-skelter farce featuring another wily servant; *Les Femmes savantes* (*The Learned Ladies*, 1672); and *Le Malade imaginaire* (*The Hypochondriac*, 1673), a satire on, among other things, the medical profession, which was one of Molière's favorite targets.

On February 17, 1673, Molière went on stage in *Le Malade imaginaire* in the role of Argan despite an exacerbation of the consumption which plagued him during the last portion of his life. During Argan's last speech, as accounts have it, he was stricken with a paroxysm, but he carried on until the play's end. He collapsed backstage and shortly thereafter died, it is said, calling unavailingly for a priest. Only the king's personal intervention prevented the Church from barring Molière's body from consecrated ground. At his death, Molière left not only an extraordinary body of comic drama but the company which, upon its amalgamation with its rivals in 1680, became the Comédie-Française, to this day a great national institution.

Style

Molière's plays were written in a variety of forms, including prose (*Les Précieuses ridicules*, *Le Médecin malgré lui*), free verse (*Amphitryon*), and rhymed couplets in the twelve-syllable lines known as *alexandrines* (*Tartuffe*, *Le Misanthrope*). The characteristic virtue of Molière's writing, visible in all these styles, is the vitality and flexibility with which it renders conversation. Molière is equally adept at capturing the flavor of everyday speech, the linguistic pretensions of the savant, and the witty repartee of a lover's quarrel. The liveliness and humor of Molière's writing owe a great deal to his unerring sense of pace and rhythm— in a word, his timing, the essential instinct of the comic artist in any form.

ESSAY QUESTIONS WITH ANSWERS

Tartuffe, or The Impostor

1.1 Is Tartuffe's imposture subtle or difficult to see through?

Answer In his "Preface" to *Tartuffe*, which was written to defend himself against the charge of having lampooned true piety, Molière states that he took every precaution to make Tartuffe a blatant fraud whose imposture could not possibly be mistaken for genuine Christian faith. To this end, Molière writes, he used the play's first two acts, with their reports of Tartuffe's deceit, to forewarn the audience of Tartuffe's villainy. By the time Tartuffe makes his entry in Act III, ostentatiously calling over his shoulder to his servant to hang up his hair shirt and his scourge, we know all about this hypocrite and how he has bamboozled Orgon. We unhesitatingly recognize him for the fraud he is, and in all likelihood we wonder how anybody *could* be fooled by him. As his opening lines indicate, he is not very subtle. He plays the part broadly, exaggerating his piety beyond all belief, and at the same time he is too reckless to moderate or conceal the entirely profane appetites—for food, women, and power—that motivate him. Would a truly artful deceiver move so boldly to marry his protector's daughter and seduce his wife? Of course, much of the play's humor lies in the fact that Tartuffe can get so far with such a shoddy disguise and the way that Orgon remains blissfully deceived despite evidence which all but slaps him in the face.

Tartuffe's hypocritical pretense of piety is so transparent that Orgon's unshakable faith in him amounts to much more than an innocent mistake. It is a monstrous obsession, a gross abnormality. The play forces the question, Why does Orgon persist in believing this absurd fake? How can he be so completely fooled by so obvious a fraud?

Since so much of the play is involved with the peculiar nature of Orgon's delusion, we need not rush toward an explanation of it; any overly simple answer is not likely to do the play justice. We might begin by recognizing that like Tartuffe, Orgon does not appear on stage until the play is well under way. If the first two acts help prepare our understanding of Tartuffe, might not the first few scenes help us understand Orgon when he appears? Since the energetic first scene centers on Mme Pernelle, Orgon's mother, who is the only other character to be taken in by Tartuffe, we may understand something about the folly of the son by examining the folly of the mother.

1.2   What is the characteristic sentiment or habit of mind which animates Mme Pernelle?

Answer   Mme Pernelle is marked most of all by her suspiciousness. She has an accusation or insinuation to direct at everyone. Her granddaughter, Mariane, is not so innocent as she seems; such shyness, Mme Pernelle implies, often conceals impurity. Her daughter-in-law Elmire—and Mme Pernelle makes sure to remind her that she is Orgon's second wife and no match for her predecessor in virtue or economy—is far too worldly and, she intimates, less than wholly faithful: "I'm distressed/To see you so elaborately dressed./When it's one's husband that one aims to please/One has no need for costly fripperies."* Elmire's brother, Cléante, Mme Pernelle declares, is an improper presence in the house of the married couple; his counsels to his sister come close, she hints, to pandering. For Mme Pernelle, Tartuffe is a rod to scourge the family's immorality. The more they protest against his hypocrisy and insist on their innocence, the more she feels confirmed in her suspicions: "You all regard him [Tartuffe] with distaste and fear/Because he tells you what you're loath to hear,/Condemns your sins, points out your moral flaws,/And humbly strives to further Heaven's cause" (I, i; references are to act and scene).

Mme Pernelle darts her suspicious glance everywhere. She seems to follow some rule of mistrust by which every appearance is assumed to conceal its opposite: Mariane's demureness argues that she is secretly a slut; Cléante's forthrightness cloaks an intriguer's wiles; Elmire's modesty is the perfect adulterer's disguise. The joke, of course, is that Mme Pernelle has gotten everything backwards. These good people are exactly what they seem, and her shrewdness fails her utterly when it comes to Tartuffe. One wonders whether it is the sheer obviousness of his crimes which allows them to elude her prying investigations. Mme Pernelle is keen enough to know that people often are not what they seem and that the world is as fond of lies as of truth, only she cannot tell which is which.

Tartuffe, Act I, Scene i. Translated by Richard Wilbur, New York, Harcourt, Brace & World, 1963. All references to *Tartuffe* in this chapter are to the Wilbur translation.

1.3 Like her son, Mme Pernelle combines the qualities of mistrust and absolute credulity, a seemingly odd combination of opposites. What is the relationship between these antithetical traits in Mme Pernelle's psychology?

Answer Mme Pernelle's mistrust predisposes her to precisely the kind of gullibility which blinds her to Tartuffe. She believes that the world is corrupt and deceitful. This sense of evil and her pervasive skepticism make her want, even need, to believe in someone like Tartuffe; he offers the certainty of absolute moral authority ("all he reprehends is reprehensible," she says of him) in a world she finds devious and menacing. His spiritual counsel provides a sure guide to what to believe and how to think. By trusting him wholeheartedly Mme Pernelle can achieve a comforting certainty that allows her an escape from her usual doubts. Her absurd trust in Tartuffe is the result of her exaggerated mistrust of others. The fact that she is so egregiously wrong about Tartuffe suggests that there is something terribly wrongheaded about the habit of suspicion which sends her to him for relief.

Mme Pernelle's behavior demonstrates how a desire to see through appearances to the truth—in her case, her desire to unmask the family—can be betrayed to misperception by the need for certitude. Her eagerness to interpret and judge originates in a moral anxiety which makes her need to feel sure about people but doubt that she can. Her absolutely certain but absolutely wrong judgments about Tartuffe and Orgon's family embody one of the principles of delusion the reader finds at work throughout the play, where the desire to reach some reassuringly certain judgment, to understand the world in black and white, inevitably results in one's getting things very wrong indeed.

1.4 Is Mme Pernelle's error unwitting, a mere failure to perceive clearly, or is it more active and willful? Is it merely blindness or is it a delusion that twists the world into the shape she wishes? Which description more aptly characterizes the nature of folly in *Tartuffe*?

Answer Mme Pernelle embodies a psychological principle that animates many of Molière's characters, in which the fool or bigot invariably creates a world in the image of his or her folly. The erotic intrigue which Mme Pernelle fancies she detects in the family originates nowhere but in her imagination. But remarkably, her imagining it virtually makes it so, as Elmire is forced to turn seducer in Act IV not because she is unfaithful but in order to expose Tartuffe and save the family from the delusions in which Mme Pernelle and Orgon have involved it. This is an extreme, literal version of the act of imagination which enables the puritan, for example, to create a world of sin by projecting his or her unacknowledged prurient fantasies onto others.

In much the same way, the promiscuity which Tartuffe sees all around him originates in his own salacious imagination, as demonstrated when he asks Dorine to cover the bit of bosom exposed above her blouse. She neatly points out that it is not her immodesty but only his prurient mind which is revealed by such exaggerated prudishness: "Your soul, it seems, has very poor defenses,/ And flesh makes quite an impact on your senses./It's strange that you're so easily excited;/My own desires are not so soon ignited" (III, i). Indeed, Dorine's flesh is not indecent until Tartuffe, titillated, imagines it so.

Tartuffe's prudery demonstrates the extent to which one encounters the world not only passively but actively, bringing into being out of one's private desires and obsessions a certain kind of world—an eroticized world for the prude, an untrustworthy world for the cynic—which for some reason we choose to believe in. *Tartuffe* suggests that what we call "reality" might best be understood as an active collaboration between our own quirky, willful minds and the materials—people, things, and events—given to us by experience.

This sheer willfulness of the mind is well illustrated in Orgon's first speech, his dialog with Dorine in Act I, Scene iv, which is also one of the funniest moments in the play. To Orgon's question about the welfare of his family while he has been away, Dorine replies with an account of Elmire's illness. But Orgon cannot restrain his true sympathies. He follows each detail of his wife's indisposition with the anxious query, "And Tartuffe?" To each of Dorine's affirmations of Tartuffe's good health and hearty appetite, he replies with superb incongruity, "Poor fellow!" The perfect form of their exchange—the tempo of question, reply, and repetition—contrasted with the extravagant absurdity of what Orgon is actually saying makes this scene an inspired piece of comic staging.

The improbability of anybody acting as Orgon does identifies this scene as farce, the kind of comedy that sacrifices realism and psychological subtlety for broad and obvious humor. Yet the scene reiterates a serious truth that already has been suggested in connection with Mme Pernelle, that is, the sheer power of the mind, its ability to see and hear what it wants. While Orgon's behavior may seem mechanical, almost beyond his conscious control, his comic automatism also constitutes an act of will. Orgon refuses to acknowledge what he would rather ignore. No matter if it is Elmire who has been sick; Orgon insists, "Poor Tartuffe!"

That the mind can be an instrument of power is an insight at the very heart of *Tartuffe*. There can be no doubt that Tartuffe's ruse is a strategy of power when, toward the end of the play, his manipulation of Orgon becomes a battle for outright domination in which the stakes are Orgon's authority, property, and even freedom. The significant conflict is not only over who is true and who is false but over who is boss. Orgon finally can recognize Tartuffe for what he is, but can he stop him from taking over?

1.5   If Orgon's deluded faith in Tartuffe can be seen as a kind of power, against whom does Orgon assert it?

Answer   At the start of the play, Mme Pernelle arraigns Orgon's entire family, which defends itself as one against her intrusion and her slanders. When Orgon arrives, he also takes his family as his antagonist. Elmire, Cléante, Damis, Mariane, and their outspoken maid Dorine all see through Tartuffe and protest, rather temperately considering the situation, against Orgon's imposing this saintly fraud on them. Orgon views this as rebellion not only against the holy truth that Tartuffe represents but against his own authority as father and head of the household. The more the family protests, the more autocratically Orgon reacts, until the family becomes in effect the victim of his belief in Tartuffe. He tries to break up Mariane's engagement to Valère and force her to marry Tartuffe. He disinherits Damis and banishes him from the house rather than listen to his testimony against the impostor. He exposes Elmire to Tartuffe's seductions and all but forces her into bed with him before he will believe that Tartuffe has acted improperly.

The plainspoken Dorine sees something unnatural, perhaps even an element of sexual inversion, in the way Orgon sides with Tartuffe against his family: "He calls him brother, and loves him as his life/Preferring him to mother, child, or wife. . . ./He pets and pampers him with love more tender/Than any pretty maiden could engender" (I, ii). Indeed, when Orgon explains that Tartuffe's religious guidance has helped him transcend all earthly attachments, he gives a rather extreme interpretation of Christ's command that one should love God above home and family: "Under his tutelage my soul's been freed/From earthly loves, and every human tie:/My mother, children, brother, and wife could die,/And I'd not feel a single moment's pain" (I, v). When Orgon banishes Damis in a rage and accuses the whole family of plotting against Tartuffe, he completes his undoing by making Tartuffe his sole heir, literally putting him in the family's place: "By making you my only son and heir/This very day I'll give to you alone/Clear deed and title to everything I own./A dear, good friend and son-in-law-to-be/Is more than wife or child or kin to me" (III, vii).

Orgon's advocacy of Tartuffe against his family's opposition to this lying, domineering intruder gives Orgon an excuse to play the tyrant, a role for which he has a natural affinity. He appears to enjoy bullying his family—"it pleases me to vex them," he admits. However, Orgon makes a rather incongruous autocrat; he is obviously not strong but terribly weak. After all, he has been subjugated by Tartuffe; his absolute faith in the hypocrite amounts to a surrendering of all responsibility for his own thoughts and actions. The impunity with which Dorine, who is not bound by the family's loyalty to the father, mocks him confirms how spineless he is.

The truism that inside every bully is a cringing coward describes Orgon quite well. The bully and the coward in Orgon complement each other perfectly, as the weakness which allows Tartuffe to dominate him also provides him with an excuse—Tartuffe himself—to dominate his family. Orgon's domination of his family is all the more cowardly for being disguised; Orgon's will to command is hidden and rationalized by his insistence that the real issue is obedience not to himself but to Tartuffe and the higher law he represents. With marvelous economy, Orgon's devotion to Tartuffe performs a double service for him. It allows him to indulge his weakness by capitulating to Tartuffe's authority and becoming his puppet, and at the same time it enables him to lord it over the family, bludgeoning them with his faith in the hypocrite. If Orgon's appalling loyalty to Tartuffe indicates weakness, it is weakness in the service of a devious desire for strength. Orgon believes in Tartuffe in part for the power it gives him.

1.6   Why does Orgon feel the need to dominate his family in this way? Elmire, Damis, and Mariane all seem, except for their justified animus against Tartuffe, devoted and properly deferential to Orgon. What incites Orgon against them?

Answer   In order to interpret any single aspect of a character's behavior, we have to draw on our general understanding of that character, which relies in turn not only on our sense of the character's actions throughout the play but on our general sense of what the play is about and how the play's broad themes and issues are expressed in this particular case. Accordingly, let us try to interpret Orgon's need to dominate his family by comparing two scenes against the background of the play as a whole. The two scenes, which may not immediately seem to have much in common, are Act II, Scene iv, in which Mariane and Valère quarrel, and Act IV, Scenes iii through vii, in which Elmire tricks Tartuffe into making sexual advances toward her while Orgon looks on from hiding. The emotional or psychological issues common to these two scenes help illuminate both Orgon's behavior toward his family and the general themes of the play.

Act II, Scene iv, presents a comic lover's quarrel between Mariane and Valère. The humorous aspect lies in the fact that although each begins the conversation desiring only reassurance of the other's love, they quickly find that they have unwittingly resolved to break off their marriage plans. Although this is the last thing they want, they stubbornly maintain their disaffection until Dorine energetically cajoles them back into each other's arms.

The scene begins with Valère asking Mariane what she proposes to do about Orgon's plan to marry her to Tartuffe. Instead of reiterating her love for him, as Valère had hoped, Mariane hesitates and asks in return for Valère's advice, meaning to test the strength of his commitment to her. At a standoff, unsure of Mariane's feeling for him and afraid to expose his own tender feelings, Valère blurts out, "Marry him!"

The emotional issue here is trust. The trust each feels toward the other is of an incomplete sort which demands some tangible proof or declaration. To this insecurity both prefer the bitter certainty of accomplished rejection. Valère finally says, "And I now see/That you were never truly in love with me." He is wrong, and we should recognize that he has arrived at his error in the same way that Mme Pernelle has come to her misjudgments of Orgon's family and of Tartuffe: by jumping hastily from mistrust and uncertainty to an exaggerated and quite mistaken certainty. Jealousy always finds something to be jealous about; for Mariane and Valère, the penalty of suspecting the worst about each other is, until Dorine saves them from themselves, to find it true.

The same issues of trust and proof also dominate Act IV, in which Elmire unmasks Tartuffe by encouraging him to resume his seductions while Orgon looks on from beneath a table. Orgon's problem is knowing whom to trust. How could the good and faithful Tartuffe be guilty of such a thing? But why would his wife lie? To believe one is to disbelieve the other, and Orgon is at first inclined to trust Tartuffe rather than his wife. This is tantamount to Orgon's accusing Elmire of lying about a very delicate matter. Not only Tartuffe's but Elmire's honor seems to be in question here. Orgon refuses to believe Elmire without evidence of some sort, and Elmire promises to provide tangible proof of Tartuffe's lechery. This scene constitutes the climax of the play and the moment when Orgon will at last be released from his stubborn unreason.

As Orgon looks on, Elmire's plan goes almost too well, as Tartuffe, overjoyed at the opportunity, presses for "palpable assurance" of Elmire's love. It seems that nothing but actual intercourse will satisfy him. As Tartuffe presses toward his goal, Elmire frantically signals to Orgon to leap out and apprehend him, now shamelessly revealed for what he is. But Orgon continues to hang back, peeking from beneath the table. As Elmire and Tartuffe grapple, their words take on extra meaning in relation to the hidden Orgon, who seems intent on observing his own cuckolding. When Tartuffe pleads for "palpable assurance" from Elmire because, he says, "with our doubts, mere words can never cope," Elmire tells him that "since you/Will not allow mere language to convince you/ And since you ask for concrete evidence, I/See nothing for it, now, but to comply" (IV, vi). The evidence they speak of refers not only to Tartuffe's fervent demand but also to Orgon's apparent desire for proof. Both men want proof; however, while Orgon wants to prove the loyalty of his friend and the chastity of his wife, the concupiscent proof that Tartuffe desires will demonstrate just the opposite and work Orgon's ruin.

But in a brilliant comic twist, Orgon does want, at least in part, exactly what Tartuffe does; this is why he delays so long. Orgon wants to prove the faithfulness of his friend and his wife, but faithfulness, by nature, cannot be proved. Faithfulness is a negative—the absence of adultery—and therefore is incapable of proof. Adultery, however, is easily proved. It is merely a matter of catching someone in the act.

Orgon wants the impossible, some concrete evidence to command his faith; ideally, he would like to catch Tartuffe and Elmire "in the act" of being faithful. In his benighted condition, he has made the further mistake of hoping to find this proof by spying on an act which must shake his faith. The scene is masterfully contrived to place in doubt Elmire's chastity and Orgon's faith in her as well as Tartuffe's uprightness and Orgon's belief in him, in short, to try the very bases of Orgon's existence. If Tartuffe is not what he seems, is Elmire? Is anybody?

As he watches this astounding scene, Orgon must desperately wish for some certainty which would allow him to put his world back together. He wants some proof of who is who, of who can be trusted and who cannot, but the only proof promised by the situation is the one act which will, with fierce finality, make his wife an adulteress, his friend a traitor, and himself a cuckold. No wonder Orgon remains hypnotized with horror and fascination beneath the table as he awaits a graphic demonstration of exactly what he does not want to know. When he finally comes out, Elmire mocks his ambivalent hesitation: "What, coming out so soon? How premature!/Get back in hiding, and wait until you're sure./Stay till the end, and be convinced completely;/We mustn't stop till things are proved concretely" (IV, vi).

Orgon's predicament constitutes a wonderful satire on those sentiments— jealousy, mistrust, suspicion—which lead us to crave certainty even if it means having our worst fears confirmed. By comparing this scene with Mariane and Valère's quarrel and with Mme Pernelle's behavior in the play's first scene, we can recognize that one of the persistent themes of *Tartuffe* is the penalties—

psychological, moral, and cognitive—of mistrust. Mme Pernelle's mistrust of the family embroils her in sexual fantasy. Mariane and Valère's mistrust of each other leads to their disaffection. Orgon's mistrust of his wife's testimony about Tartuffe brings her to the brink of adultery. In each case, the prime penalty for mistrust is an exaggerated and mistaken credulity: Mme Pernelle's belief in Tartuffe, her rock of certitude; Mariane and Valère's mutual certainty that "you never loved me at all"; and Orgon's credulity in mistaking Elmire's performance for actual infidelity.

Perhaps Orgon's extraordinary faith in Tartuffe, like Mme Pernelle's, also begins in some antecedent mistrust. Is it possible that Orgon's mistrust, like hers, is actually a matter of sexual suspicion? After all, the climax of the play is a classic scene of sexual jealousy, as Orgon beholds his wife in his best friend's embrace. We should remember that Elmire is Orgon's second wife and that the play is usually cast with a young woman in her role opposite an older, if not elderly, Orgon. This makes them, of course, the classic pair for a comedy of infidelity. With a new young wife and two children of marriageable age at home, Orgon might well be troubled by some of the same anxieties about sexual behavior which plague his mother.

Most suggestive in this respect is the scene immediately before Elmire's encounter with Tartuffe in which Orgon banishes Damis rather than credit his account of Tartuffe's lechery. In his rage, Orgon lets slip something which suggests that his wife's fidelity is very much at issue with him: "Madam, I know a few plain facts, and one/Is that you're partial to my rascal son" (IV, iii). This is the mistrusting mind working at a very high pitch. It is possible that Orgon believes in Tartuffe in part because this provides a way for him to cope with his secret anxieties about such uncomfortable, intimate matters. Chastity is, after all, one of Tartuffe's greatest virtues in Orgon's not very keen eyes, and it is chastity which, from his first encounter with Dorine, the hypocrite preaches.

Tartuffe brings into the house a moral authority which Orgon can wield against any of the sexual improprieties he half consciously fears, and to the same purpose, the family's opposition to Tartuffe gives Orgon the perfect excuse to dominate them and keep them more strictly in line. Too uncertain of their love to allow them to give it freely, Orgon must imperiously command it.

1.7   When *Tartuffe* was originally staged in the seventeenth century, Molière's enemies and offended divines charged that the play constituted an attack on religion as such. While modern audiences are less likely to mistake Molière's debunking of religious hypocrisy for an assault on Christianity, we may still wonder in what way *Tartuffe*, which does turn on a problem of religion and belief, may be a religious play. Can the play be seen to communicate some attitude about the issues of religious faith which it raises?

Answer Orgon's extravagant faith in Tartuffe is wrong not only because it is misplaced. The peculiar form of Orgon's faith makes it actually a kind of faithlessness. Tartuffe's lavish displays of holiness save Orgon the effort of summoning any genuine faith, that is, a trusting belief in things invisible. It is simply too easy to believe in Tartuffe. Orgon succumbs to his trickery the way one might find oneself buying a persuasively advertised product. He can believe in Tartuffe without undertaking the more difficult interior act of truly keeping faith.

Furthermore, Orgon's faith in Tartuffe also originates partially in faithlessness, that is, in a lack of faith in his family's loyalty. In this regard, Orgon's trust in Tartuffe merely compensates for his mistrust of others, and such mistrust is hardly a proper foundation for piety. Orgon's problem is that like Mme Pernelle, he thinks in terms of extremes. His excessive mistrust of others predisposes him to an equally exaggerated, inappropriate, and absolute trust in Tartuffe.

Cléante is the play's *raisonneur*, the voice of reason who pleads the case for common sense and moderation against Orgon's extremism. "Man," he counsels Orgon, "is a strangely fashioned creature/Who seldom is content to follow Nature,/But recklessly pursues his inclination/Beyond the narrow bounds of moderation,/And often, by transgressing Reason's laws,/Perverts a lofty aim or noble cause" (I, v). And, Cléante feels, when applied to matters of religion, reason should keep us from falling prey to "affected zeal and pious knavery" and those who "make a flashy show of being holy." Cléante favors a religion that is "moderate and humane" and whose hallmark is a generous trust in one's fellow human beings. Believers so enlightened do not use their belief in God as a weapon against others; instead, "They think censoriousness a mark of pride,/And therefore, letting others preach and rave,/They show, by deeds, how Christians should behave./They think no evil of their fellow man,/But judge him as kindly as they can" (I, v). Although Cléante's remarks are more relevant to matters human than divine, recommending as they do a way for people to conduct their daily lives and their relations with others, their spirit is one of Christian charity. It is precisely uncharitableness, his tendency to suspect the worst of his wife and family, which is Orgon's besetting sin.

Cléante claims, then, that true religious faith includes a charitable faith in humankind. But why should Orgon trust humankind when the race can produce a lying abomination such as Tartuffe? In fact, when Orgon finally sees through Tartuffe, he angrily swears that from now on he will mistrust all apparently pious men. Yet as Cléante notes, this is just another instance of Orgon's unfortunate tendency to go to extremes. Again, Cléante attempts to point out the path of moderation: "You've recognized your recent grave mistake/In falling victim to a pious fake;/Now, to correct that error, must you embrace/An even greater error in its place,/And judge our worthy neighbors as a whole/By what you've learned of one corrupted soul?" (V, i). Orgon must, Cléante feels, learn to make finer and more accurate distinctions. He concludes his advice about this difficult business of judging the sincerity of others on a familiar note: "It is best to err, if err one must,/As you have done, upon the side of trust" (V, i).

Although Cléante may appear unappealingly stiff and sober amid the play's frequent uproariousness, it is tempting to identify him as Molière's spokesperson, especially since the Christian charity he recommends is in fact much in evidence throughout the play, serving as an implicit rebuke to Orgon's habits of faithless belief and secret suspicion. Elmire is extraordinarily charitable to her foolish husband. She endures with hardly a reproof his infatuation with Tartuffe and his ungenerous treatment of her. At the end of all the trials to which Orgon has subjected her, her loyalty to this silly man, to whom she is superior in every way, seems entirely undiminished.

Likewise, Damis, Mariane, and Valère, whom Orgon has bullied and insulted, forgive him unreservedly and without hesitation. When he hears of Tartuffe's attempt to dispossess his father, Damis immediately returns home despite his father's furious banishment of him; he strides bravely into the house, swearing to defend Orgon: "Father, I hear that scoundrel uttered threats/Against you. . . . Leave it to me, Sir; let me trim his ears" (V, ii). Presented with the golden opportunity to say I told you so, Damis thinks only to return good for evil.

Orgon does in fact live in a world where people can be trusted. His family's loyalty to him and the charitableness with which they regard his folly reveal with embarrassing clarity how ungenerous his suspicions had been and how unnecessary his improper reliance on Tartuffe is. Thus Molière's play about hypocrisy and deceit recommends faith in others, a paradox only if we fail to recognize that a society which practiced a generous but reasonable trust in others would be less vulnerable to the fraudulent certainties promised by a Tartuffe.

Tartuffe uses the issue of faith to propound a kind of everyday politics of living with and understanding one another, and Molière's real concerns in the play tend more toward the worldly than the divine. But if the play is less concerned with God than with humankind, the trust and charity it recommends are traditional Christian values.

1.8 Near the close of *Tartuffe*, Orgon finds himself pushed to the brink of destruction. It seems that every bit of his error will unforgivingly be revenged upon him; he is about to lose his reputation, property, and freedom. At the last moment, Molière saves the poor man from disaster. How does he accomplish this last-minute rescue? How satisfactory an ending does this provide for the play?

Answer As Orgon's complaint against Tartuffe's perfidy indicates—he means "to drive me from my house, a ruined man,/And make me end a pauper, as he began" (V, iii)—Tartuffe threatens no less than to turn society upside down. And it is no less than the embodiment of society, the King, who personally intervenes to save Orgon and turn chaos to order, to punish the bad and reward the good. The King functions as a *deus ex machina* (Latin, "god from the machine"; the machine was the contraption which lowered a god onto the Roman stage), a special agency who intercedes and, with the aid of extraordinary powers, providentially resolves otherwise unresolvable problems. Indeed, the King seems possessed of a godlike wisdom and breadth of vision. Molière takes the opportunity to shamelessly flatter Louis XIV, whose good opinion was essential to any French dramatist's success. He is "A Prince who sees into our inmost hearts,/And can't be fooled by any trickster's arts./His royal soul, though generous and human,/Views all things with discernment and acumen" (V, vii). Given such powers, it's no wonder that, looking down from on high at Tartuffe, "With one keen glance, the King perceived the whole/Perverseness and corruption of his soul" (V, vii). One certainly could lead a confident and trusting life in a world ruled over by such a benevolent and percipient authority.

This godlike authority sanctions comedy as the appropriate mode in which to understand experience, since it guarantees that all wrongs will be righted, that justice will triumph, and that endings will be happy. *Tartuffe* concludes with the happy ending traditional to comedy: the proclamation of a marriage (Valère and Mariane's), the rite which celebrates the defeat of the abnormal and threatening and affirms society's continued ability to thrive and prosper through its usual forms.

The keynote of the last scene, struck resonantly by the King, is the power of society to maintain itself, to defend its notions of the good and the true against intruders who threaten it. This vision of power focused in the absolute power of the King represents a qualification of the play's ethos of trust, since it reveals something of the political and institutional nature of a society which seemingly can lend its official sponsorship to such an ethos. It is no accident that the idea of a community of charitable, common understanding of which Molière gives the reader a glimpse in *Tartuffe* is the imaginative product of a culture that was at its best moments supremely confident of itself.

The certitude of this culture depended in turn on the stability of a society envisioned as a fixed hierarchy of classes, ruled by an absolute monarch. The criticism of social foibles that the play undertakes never extends to this base of society, and in this respect *Tartuffe* is indeed, as Molière claims in his "Preface," a moral play. It is moral in the sense that it offers no offense to the fundamental nature of the society whose capacity for order and continuity it ultimately celebrates.

D.E.

SUGGESTED READINGS

Auerbach, Erich, *Mimesis* (1974). See the chapter on Molière.

Gossman, Lionel, *Men and Masks: A Study of Molière* (1963).

Guicharnaud, Jacques (ed.), *Molière: A Collection of Critical Essays* (1963).

Hubert, J. D., *Molière and the Comedy of Intellect* (1962).

Lewis, D. B. Wyndham, *Molière: The Comic Mask* (1959).

Mander, Gertrud, *Molière* (1973).

Moore, W. G., *Molière: A New Criticism* (1962).

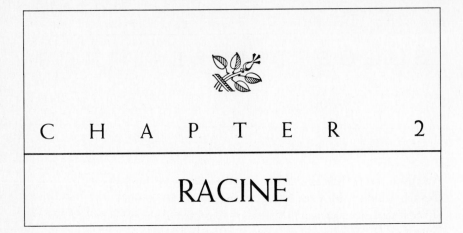

C H A P T E R   2

RACINE

Racine and the Jansenists

Jean Racine, the great French tragedian, was born in 1639 in the small town
of La Ferté-Milon, about fifty miles from Paris. His mother died only a year
later, and his father, a minor official in the local government, two years after
that. Racine was then sent to live with his maternal grandparents. In 1649, at
the Collège de Beauvais, he began a thorough classical education, which was
continued in 1655 at the Jansenist center at Port Royal des Champs, near
Versailles.

Much has been made of the influence of Jansenism on Racine's life and art.
A Roman Catholic reform movement condemned as heretical by the Church
and always at violent odds with the Jesuits, Jansenism held that a person is
predestined by God to either salvation or damnation. According to this pre-
destinarianism, people are both entirely unable to attain grace by their own
deeds, merit, or faith and unable even to know whether they are saved or
damned. Although we bear the indelible mark of God's judgment, it is unin-
telligible to us. The Jansenist God appears, accordingly, as always present in
his determination of our immortal fate but immeasurably distant from our com-
prehension. In his masterly analysis of the influence of Jansenism on the writings
of Racine and Pascal, Lucien Goldmann has tellingly named the incomprehensible but ever-watching deity of the Jansenists "the Hidden God."

More than an abstract body of theology, seventeenth-century Jansenism was a way of life and a fully elaborated world view. For the Jansenist, because our actions have no bearing on the single desideratum of salvation, the everyday world is a realm of senseless vanity in which no valid activity is possible. Consequently, the devout Jansenist would refuse the world and become a *solitaire*, withdrawing to the monastic precincts of Port Royal to dwell on the awful truths of human ignorance, sinfulness, and helplessness before God.

As Goldmann has demonstrated, Jansenism articulated a tragic vision of life, and this vision was elaborated with great fidelity and power in Racine's mature tragedies. The Jansenist rejection of the world is repeated in the tragic hero's recognition that the world cannot accommodate an individual's passionate aspiration. The Jansenists' strict either-or morality, which classifies everything as either godly or worldly, appears in Racine in the form of the hero's insoluble tragic conflict which opposes one absolute to another, as in Phaedra's conflict between love and honor. The Jansenists' sense of powerlessness before a humanly incomprehensible, punitive God is duplicated in the tragic hero's helplessness and the inevitability of the hero's defeat. Finally, the Jansenists' conviction of the spiritual superiority of resignation is mirrored in the nobility of Racine's tragic heroes, who sometimes seem to have consciously chosen the tragic life and by so doing have transcended a paltry, meaningless world.

Early Ambitions

The Jansenists of Port Royal seem to have treated Racine more than kindly, and their beliefs clearly made a lasting impression on him. But the ascetic regime of the cloister placed severe restraints on Racine's energies and ambitions, and in 1658 he left it for the profane world. Almost immediately upon leaving Port Royal for Paris, he turned his hand to an activity entirely antipathetic to the puritanical Jansenists: literature. He then compounded this sin with the even greater vice of worldly ambition. He wrote an ode celebrating the recent marriage of Louis XIV, campaigned to push his first dramatic efforts into production, and set about pursuing fame in the theater and preferment at court. Racine's failure to achieve any notable progress, along with the pleas and reproaches sent him from Port Royal, soon put an end to this first Parisian adventure.

In 1661, Racine did a sudden about-face and set off toward what now seemed to be his main chance. He traveled to Uzès in Languedoc to live with a clergyman uncle who, he hoped, would be able to help him attain a sinecure with the Church. Racine was cold-bloodedly aware of his lack of a pastoral calling, and his letters of this time reveal a cynicism which reminds one of that classic climber of nearly two centuries later, Stendhal's Julien Sorel in *The Red and the Black* (1830). These plans also fell through, perhaps fortunately, since Racine's entry into the Roman Catholic clergy would very likely have caused a final, irreconcilable break with his Jansenist friends.

First Literary Successes

In 1663, Racine returned to Paris, and this time he progressed quickly in the two careers of courtier and playwright in which he was to be almost equally successful. An ode celebrating King Louis's recovery from a mild illness earned Racine the king's favor, which he maintained through most of his life and which eventually drew him into the highest circles of life at court. In 1664, he mounted his first theatrical production, *La Thébaïde*, which, like many of his later plays, drew on classical themes and borrowed from the work of an earlier playwright (in this case, Euripides). *La Thébaïde* was followed in 1665 by *Alexandre le grand.*

The events surrounding the production of *Alexandre* show Racine at his most unflatteringly opportunistic. He originally gave the play to Molière's company, which made a considerable success of it. But after only a half dozen performances, Racine, perhaps displeased with the style of Molière's players and clearly determined to make the most of his valuable property, secretly brought the play to the Hôtel de Bourgogne, the leading Parisian company and Molière's perennial rival. What is worse, he also took with him to the Bourgogne Mlle du Parc, Molière's leading lady and mistress. The play quickly closed at Molière's Palais Royal but went on with the other company to establish Racine's reputation. Needless to say, this was the end of amicable relations between the two greatest French playwrights of the day. Nearly all of Racine's subsequent plays were staged by the Hôtel de Bourgogne.

A second incident from this period does little to raise one's estimation of Racine's character. In 1666, Nicole, one of the leading lights of Port Royal, published his *Lettres son les visionnaires,* a pamphlet attacking drama as cheap, immoral dissemblance and dramatists as "poisoners of the public." Although it contained no explicit reference to him, Racine was sensitive to the implied censure of his new and much-desired theatrical success. He sent off a stinging reply that defended his art, but unfortunately he directed the nastiest sort of *ad hominem* arguments at the Port Royalists who had been his friends and protectors. This outburst marked a low point in Racine's relationship with Port Royal, which throughout his life evoked alternating feelings of gratitude, resentment, rebellion, and contrition.

Apex of Success

In 1667, Racine staged *Andromaque*, his first thoroughly "Racinian" play, in which he found his great theme—monumentally tragic passion—and his characteristic mode—a single-minded concentration of all the play's energies around one central conflict. This was followed in 1668 by his only comedy, *Les Plaideurs* (based on Aristophanes's *The Wasps*) and by two plays set in imperial Rome, *Britannicus* (1669) and *Bérénice* (1670). *Bérénice* was written in competition with *Tite and Bérénice* by Racine's great contemporary Pierre Corneille. The public judged Racine's the better of the two plays, marking not only Racine's decisive triumph over Corneille but a general shift in dramatic taste away from the baroque complexities of Corneille's plays and toward the relative simplicity and dramatic unity of Racine's.

Bajazet, a "Turkish" melodrama, was performed in 1672; *Mithridate* followed in 1673; and the hugely successful *Iphigénie* was produced in 1674. During those years, Racine's star had been constantly rising. He had been granted numerous pensions and sinecures, elected to membership in the Academie Française in 1672, and ennobled and granted a lucrative position at the national treasury in 1674. Racine had traveled far from both his early days as a penniless orphan and the unworldly ideals of Port Royal.

Phèdre (*Phaedra*, 1677), the last of Racine's secular plays and the last he wrote before withdrawing from the theater for ten years, has been the subject of considerable biographical speculation. Some have seen a *rapprochement* between Racine and Jansenist thought in the utter solitariness of *Phaedra*'s characters and the malevolence of its gods. In any case, Racine's life changed radically at this time. He married a placid, thoroughly colorless woman from outside the theater, fathered several children in quick succession, and generally retreated from the hectic life of the theater. He also took on added duties at court, becoming official historiographer to Louis, a post shared with Nicolas Boileau (1636–1711), the greatest critic of the day and Racine's longtime friend.

Last Years

In 1689, upon the urging of the marquise de Maintenon (secretly Louis's wife), Racine returned to the theater with *Esther*, an Old Testament drama. He followed this in 1691 with *Athalie*, another biblical drama. In many ways, the central character of *Athalie* is God himself, who, although he displays much of the harshness of the Jansenist deity, seems to extend a hope of redemption and reconciliation to humanity. While Racine's life at court in these last years prevented any wholehearted participation in Jansenist activities, throughout this time he used his considerable influence to help the beleaguered Port Royalists. His early spiritual education seems to have been much on his mind in these last years, as evidenced not only by his two biblical plays but by the history of Port Royal he composed in 1697. When Racine died in 1699, he was buried, as he had requested, at Port Royal.

Racine and Neoclassicism

Racine and Corneille were the two great practitioners of neoclassicism in French drama. The essence of neoclassicism, which dominated French literary theory and practice in the seventeenth century, was imitation of the formal qualities of Greek and Roman literature as these were understood, not always correctly, at that time.

Aristotle's *Poetics* was the lodestar for neoclassical drama. From Aristotle, French dramatists took the interlocking formal concepts of imitation of nature, or verisimilitude, and regularity of form. The playwright was to strive for verisimilitude by depicting universal elements of human moral nature and psychology as they might plausibly be brought to light by means of dramatic conflict. According to the principle of regularity, each subject has its appropriate literary form with its own rules. Thus, the fate of a great individual can be treated properly only in tragedy. Tragedy had to obey the three so-called classical unities of time, place, and action (only the last is actually found in Aristotle). These unities required that the action of the drama unfold in a single, continuous span of time (usually one day), take place in one location, and focus primarily on the hero's motivation, progress, and fate. Tragedy, like all other forms, had to follow the principle of decorum or propriety, according to which, for example, a character's language should be suited to that character's station in society. A Racinian king will display the hallmarks of kingliness, often exaggeratedly, in every detail of speech, bearing, and action.

Taken together, these dramatic principles were intended to serve the goals of dramatic illusion and psychological verisimilitude. However, they were often followed strictly, to the detriment of these very goals.

The influence of French neoclassicism extended well beyond seventeenth-century France. German and English literature of the eighteenth century, notably the writings of John Dryden, Alexander Pope, and Joseph Addison, was strongly influenced by French neoclassicism, especially as formulated in Boileau's *Art poétique* (1674). This influence was not entirely beneficial, since it exported not only the aesthetic theory of French neoclassical literature but the idiosyncratic interpretations of Greek and Roman literature on which it was based.

Racine's Style

Racine's eminence in French literature derives as much from his poetic style as from his skill as a tragedian. Racine's tragedies were written in *alexandrines*, the twelve-syllable line that had been the established meter for French poetry since the sixteenth century. His language employs a highly restricted vocabulary, sometimes said to consist of as few as 2000 words. The level of diction is refined and abstract. This eloquent language is well suited to express the grand passions and exalted concerns of Racine's noble characters, and it contributes to the feeling that the action of his tragedies takes place at a vast remove from ordinary life.

Further contributing to the intense stylization of Racine's language is his use of a broad range of poetic devices such as stichomythia (the alternation of single lines of dialog, often in argument), periphrasis (naming by describing, as in the use of "finny tribe" to mean "fish"), repetition for emphasis, symmetry, and figures of speech such as metaphor, metonymy (naming by substituting a related object, as in "scepter" for "king"), and synecdoche (suggesting the whole by naming the part, or vice versa, as in "hand" for "worker"). Racine's frequent use of alliteration and assonance adds to the musicality of his language. Racine's style has long been held in high regard for its purity of sound and eloquence, and the choruses from his religious dramas are considered to be among the greatest achievements of French lyric poetry.

ESSAY QUESTIONS WITH ANSWERS

Phaedra

2.1 In ordinary speech, among the words used to describe the experience of adversity, "tragic" seems appropriate on only the rarest occasions. In the idea of the tragic one recognizes an exceptional kind of experience and grants it a special weight and magnitude. What kind of characters and actions does Racine portray in order to create a world which allows him to convey the distinctive experience of the tragic?

Answer *Phaedra* is set in ancient Greece, and its characters are the royalty of Athens. With the exception of the few members of their retinue, there are no "low" characters in the play. Theseus is king of Athens. Phaedra, his wife, is descended from the royal family of Crete. Hippolytus, Phaedra's stepson, is doubly royal, since his father is Theseus and his natural mother was Antiope, queen of the Amazons. Aricia is a princess in the line of Athenian succession whose claim to the Athenian throne conflicts with that of Theseus.

The nobility of these characters is more than a matter of titles. They seem to take their identities from their exalted status, manifesting grandeur in every aspect of their behavior. Instead of speaking, they declaim. Their long speeches unfold imposing tapestries of narrative that bring the great events of the past—the deeds of heroes, the turbulent histories of families and cities—into the present. They address the gods and the noble dead who are their ancestors as familiars whose stature they share.

The pronoun constantly on the lips of these outsized characters is "I." Each is preoccupied with the characteristics and vicissitudes of selfhood; they speak endlessly of "my honor," "my guilt," "my passion." It is possible to see them as monstrous egoists. But to make too much of their titanic self-absorption is to miss the point that tragedy is precisely that literary form which invites us to sympathize imaginatively with the self at its peak of aspiration and its extreme limits of endurance.

As her fate unfolds, Phaedra's troubled psyche comes to seem virtually coextensive with the realm she inhabits; her passion shakes her world as violently as it wracks her body, destroying the lives of every member of her family and of virtually every character in the play. If the tragedy of Phaedra begins in her tortured heart, it creates a world in its own image, a tragic world in which no happier possibility exists.

We can measure the degree to which the world of *Phaedra* is tragic by recognizing the sorts of things which do *not* appear in it. The broad midground of everyday life—the familiar round of work, family, and friends that makes up most of a person's days—is entirely absent. No practical activity of any sort takes place. Even Theseus, whom one would expect to see performing some of the business of kingly statecraft, is entirely unencumbered by such mundane duties. *Phaedra's* characters are freed from everyday affairs, almost as if to make them purer conduits for feeling. The feelings which dominate them are in turn purified of any but the most extreme and exalted kinds of moral and psychological experience. While some kinds of tragedy can accommodate comedy, as in Shakespeare, *Phaedra* is untinctured by humor of any sort. Racine has imagined in *Phaedra* a world in which every aspect of life has been raised to the heightened realm of the tragic. The play seems to have a climate all its own. If, in everyday life, tragedy is the rare and unexpected bolt from the blue, the world of *Phaedra* is perpetually storm-riven and lightning-blasted.

To summarize, Racine has created a drama which strives to convey the extraordinary experience of tragedy by imagining a world that is itself extraordinary, with sublime figures taken from myth and history, their orotund speech, and their all-absorbing trials of self.

2.2 The action of tragedy has been described, following Aristotle, as the hero's "movement of spirit." It is often broken down into three stages: (1) the hero's initial motivation or ambition, (2) a complicating encounter with the conditions, concrete or intangible, which frustrate this ambition, and (3) the catastrophe which finally defeats the hero but allows him or her a recognition of things as they are. Describe the action of *Phaedra* in terms of these common structural features of tragedy.

Answer Phaedra's initial motivation is her overwhelming passion for Hippolytus. But her desire for her stepson is stymied by the fact that their relationship gives it the odor of incest and, more seriously, by her fierce sense of honor. Even in the first scene, when her love is still a secret and before she has acted on it, Phaedra seems nearly mad with guilt. To her conscience, the desire is as disgraceful as the act. She feels entirely defiled by wishes that violate her fervor for "purity," a word she uses constantly and dies exclaiming. The conflict which ultimately destroys Phaedra is between love and honor, each taken to an extreme and implacably opposed to the other. This is the typical complication of tragedy.

The catastrophe which defeats Phaedra is the unexpected return of Theseus, although this blow is preceded and followed by two crucial events which also contribute weightily to her doom: her confession of love to Hippolytus and, later, Oenone's lying accusation of Hippolytus to Theseus. Accompanying this catastrophe is Phaedra's recognition that her momentary hopes of somehow happily attaining Hippolytus have been illusory. Thus, the conflict between love and honor is absolute and unresolvable. Here the reader encounters the most crucial element in what may be called the "logic" of tragedy: the fact that the tragic conflict is by nature insoluble.

2.3 The sheer extremity of Phaedra's suffering challenges the reader to make some sense of it. Does she suffer in proportion to her sins? Are the moral authorities that rule over the world of *Phaedra* just?

Answer   In her own estimation, Phaedra is so thoroughly guilty that for most of the play her only expectation is the scorn of those who know her shame, her only hope the eventual release of death.

But her judgment of herself seems extravagantly harsh. Is her love for Hippolytus really so reprehensible? It is not literally incestuous. And even though it does represent disloyalty to Theseus, the extraordinary fervor of her love seems admirable compared with Theseus's inconstancy and casual promiscuity. Hippolytus's primness, high-minded moralizing, and utter lack of sympathy for Phaedra make it much easier to sympathize with her than to appreciate the awkwardness of his position. The sheer power of Phaedra's passion seems to take it beyond the reach of simple moralizing condemnation. Her love in the face of such obstacles may make the reader feel that there is something great about it which is undiminished by the charge of sin or folly.

Even if the reader decides that Phaedra's love for Hippolytus must be condemned, the question of her degree of culpability remains. Why must she bear the responsibility for feelings which by their nature come unbidden? Her love for Hippolytus is beyond her control, and for that reason, one might argue, it should be forgiven. In any case, by struggling against this passion, she demonstrates that she is essentially innocent and wills only the good.

Her guilt is further mitigated by the interference of other forces—fate and accident—which are beyond her control. She seems fated by genealogy to a tormented sexuality: Her ancestors include her mother Pasiphae, a notorious copulant with Poseidon's bull, and Helios, who exposed Venus in Mars's embrace and whose descendants are cursed for his voyeurism. In addition, the mischance of bad timing (Theseus's unexpected return) and bad advice (Oenone's unfortunate counsels) lessens her responsibility for the final disasters.

The reader may be moved to agree with Racine in his "Preface": "In all truth, Phaedra is neither completely guilty nor completely innocent." However, we must recognize that Racine speaks here from outside the tragedy proper and in terms foreign to tragedy. According to the logic of tragedy, Phaedra's love and her honor are absolutes and are wholly at odds, with no midground between them. The tragic conflict is inherently insoluble and unnegotiable. If Phaedra could see herself as Racine sees her in the "Preface," she would not be the character she is. She might give herself a lecture, resolve to act sensibly, and take up a pastime to clear her mind of foolishness. Instead, of course, she must have Hippolytus, and yet she must abolish even the wish to have him. She lives on the tragic terms of all or nothing. In recognizing the way in which Phaedra spurns the more temperate view of things that Racine offers in his "Preface," the reader can define Phaedra's greatness as her courage in choosing to live the all or nothing life of tragedy.

The reader can take the measure of this courage by considering its consequence: her death. Is this justice? On Phaedra's severe terms, it is, yet from any more lenient estimation of her culpability, it is hard to feel that justice has been done. Her punishment seems to exceed her crime: misguided love. Not only does Phaedra's punishment outweigh her crime, the whole disastrous course of events has been so filled with madness, misunderstanding, accident, and fatality that it is impossible to ascribe the quality of justice to such a chaotic world. What rules in *Phaedra* is not the humane reason of justice but the humanly senseless logic of tragedy, the perfect incommensurability between things as they should be and things as they are.

The injustice that reigns, quite literally, over *Phaedra* is nowhere more apparent than in the play's figures of authority. Theseus seems more pirate than king, a lifelong plunderer of cities and women and the usurper of the Athenian throne. His latest exploit has been an invasion of the underworld to abet the rape of Persephone. When Oenone decides to accuse Hippolytus and expose him to Theseus's anger, arguing that "A father is still a father when he smites," she underestimates Theseus's vengeful intemperance, which transforms him from father to outraged homicidal rival.

Theseus's injustice in so easily believing in Hippolytus's guilt is matched by the injustice of the gods in executing his sentence. Even as Theseus recognizes his mistake and tries to revoke his command, Poseidon is murdering Hippolytus with a readiness that seems truly malicious. In the closing moments of the play, Theseus addresses the gods who have silently presided over this tragedy and then intervened on the side of disaster: "I pleased you. This is my reward: I killed my son. I killed him! Only a god spares his enemies and wants his servants' blood."* Justice and reason are mocked by a seeming malevolence in the very nature of things.

2.4   Phaedra's speeches as well as those of some of the other characters are highly figurative and contain a number of recurring images. Do these images function as symbols? That is to say, can they be interpreted, either singly or in groups, in a way that adds to the reader's understanding of the characters and themes of the play?

Answer   The key images in Phaedra's speeches are those of light and exposure (day, sun, fire, eyes, torches, nakedness) and those of darkness and concealment (night, blindness, caves, forests, veiling garments). In the first scene, Phaedra walks out to expose herself to the staring sun which blazes down on Troezen, asks the frantic Oenone to tear off the elaborate clothes in which she has just been dressed, and then suddenly changes her mind, pleading to be taken "to some sunless forest lair." Phaedra's hysterical vacillation parallels her ambivalence about the prospect of confession. She feels that she must keep her secret and subdue the desires which she wants to express, but she also feels the need to give in to these desires, to break through her solitude and reveal herself. Neither action offers any real hope, however, and the pattern of strict binary opposition which is used to organize these images—day against night, light against dark—repeats the pattern of insoluble conflict that characterizes her dilemma: confession against silence, love against honor. The parallel between the binary pattern of these images and the structure of Phaedra's conflict increases the reader's understanding of her character and gives the images the augmented meaning of symbols.

    Although this pattern of binary opposition organizes most of the important images in the play, there is a second cluster of images which seems to violate this scheme. These are the references to animals and monsters that swarm through the play. Hippolytus asks Aricia rhetorically, "Am I a bear, a bull, a boar?"; Hippolytus's enraged father calls him "reptilian"; Phaedra frequently

*Translated by Robert Lowell, *Phaedra and Figaro*, New York, Farrar, Straus and Company, 1961. All references to *Phaedra* in this chapter are to the Lowell translation.

refers to the Minotaur, half bull, half man, who is her half brother; and Hippolytus is finally murdered by a monster "half dragon, half bull."

These images differ from those in the first group in that they express not opposition but combination, most often the intermingling of human and animal. The product of these combinations—witness the grotesque Minotaur—is unnatural. In their violation of nature's law, they become the palpable symbol for the unnatural act of incest which haunts the play. These symbols are appropriate because according to myth, the progeny of incestuous unions are malformed and monstrous and because in their odd mixing up of things they duplicate the structure of incest.

Incest is a confusion of categories, a failure to distinguish properly between spouse and child, that ends with the illicit replacement of one by the other. This is precisely what happens in Phaedra's confession to Hippolytus, when in a remarkable passage she retells the story of Theseus's slaying of the Minotaur and places Hippolytus in Theseus's role and herself in Ariadne's. Some process of commingling has gone on in her mind so that, as she says, when she looks at Theseus she sees Hippolytus, and when she gazes at the beloved son the offended husband glares back at her. Combining son and husband in one, the incestuous imagination begets a sexual Minotaur, symbolizing the violation of taboos in the monstrous combination of distinct categories.

2.5 Phaedra displays two emotions toward the end of the play which may weaken the reader's sense of her nobility of spirit: her unjust rage at Oenone and her bitter jealousy on hearing of Hippolytus's love of Aricia. In both cases Phaedra seems petty, acting from anger and spite, and in both cases the consequences are murderous. On first impression, these incidents seem out of keeping with the inevitability of tragic action, mere fits of bad temper that could have been controlled. Is there some way to justify these incidents within the terms of tragedy?

Answer   We might begin trying to answer this difficult question by considering why Phaedra is attracted to Hippolytus. She is fascinated by Hippolytus's reputation for fanatical chastity and his complete invulnerability to the charms of women. He incarnates the purity she so much desires in herself, and at the same time, the passion with which he adheres to chastity is an appealing parallel to her own high pitch of emotion.

But the paradoxes fly thick and fast. The quality which makes Hippolytus so fatally attractive to Phaedra virtually guarantees that she can never have him; if she somehow does, his chastity will be instantly undone. It almost seems that the impossibility of the situation, the opportunity it gives for tragic conflict, is what attracts Phaedra. In choosing Hippolytus, Phaedra has chosen the all or nothing of the tragic life. She must have both purity and passion or be destroyed in the attempt.

When his capitulation to Aricia reveals that Hippolytus can love in the ordinary way, these tragic complexities vanish and he is no longer a fit object for Phaedra's high aspiration. He has entered the tepid world of ordinary love and desire.

Similarly, when Oenone provokes Phaedra's rage by means of her machinations, it is because Oenone has lured her into the petty realm of hopes and compromises. From the tragic point of view, Oenone's sin is that she draws Phaedra into a world which, from the first scene, Phaedra knows she must reject. Both Hippolytus and Oenone come to seem no more than intrusions of the paltry everyday world into the severe world of tragedy in which Phaedra must live and die. Thus, Phaedra's otherwise inexplicable reactions to these two figures are in fact the inevitable outcome of her tragic nature.

D.E.

SUGGESTED READINGS

Abraham, Claude, *Racine* (1977).

Aristotle, *Poetics*.

Auerbach, Erich, *Mimesis* (1974). See the chapter on Racine.

Barthes, Roland, *On Racine* (1963).

Brereton, Geoffrey, *Jean Racine* (1951).

Butler, Philip, *Racine: A Study* (1974).

Goldmann, Lucien, *The Hidden God* (1955).

Goldmann, Lucien, *Racine* (1972).

Knight, R. C. (ed.), *Racine* (1969).

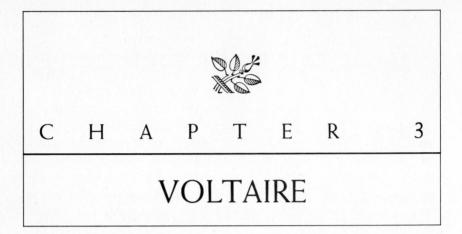

C H A P T E R 3

VOLTAIRE

Literary Reputation

Voltaire (1694–1778) was perhaps the preeminent literary artist of his day. A writer of drama, history, poetry, essays, and tales, he captured the attention of much of Europe and held it throughout his long career. *La Henriade* was greeted by his contemporaries as the national epic France had awaited, and his many successful plays were applauded as original and lasting contributions to the drama. Yet aside from a few philosophical tales such as *Candide*, Voltaire is little read today. Changes in literary taste are one reason for this decline in popularity, but equally important is the fact that so many of the ideas and attitudes with which Voltaire challenged his age have become accepted features of modern culture.

Along with Montesquieu, Rousseau, and Diderot, Voltaire was among the most important eighteenth-century formulators of the group of new, critical attitudes that has come to be called the Enlightenment. Although more politically conservative than some of the other *philosophes*, Voltaire shared their most characteristic attitudes: a passionate belief in freedom of thought and religion, faith in the sovereignty of reason over all other human faculties, and a critical and analytical attitude toward the institutions and received ideas of the past. The skeptical and rationalistic style of Enlightenment inquiry which Voltaire so daringly championed has become a defining element of modern intellectual culture. Thus, Voltaire may not be read in part because we have absorbed his lesson so well; our kinship with him obscures the originality of his ideas.

Early Years

Voltaire was born François Marie Arouet in the Paris of Louis XIV. His father was a notary, the son of prosperous Parisian tradespeople. His mother, who died when Voltaire was 7 years old, came from the lesser rural nobility. Voltaire sometimes liked to imply that he was the illegitimate son of an aristocratic friend of the family, although there was more pretension than truth in this claim.

At the age of 10, Voltaire was sent to the Collège Louis-le-Grand, a distinguished boarding school run by Jesuits. Clearly, the religious aspect of his education there had little positive effect on Voltaire, who was always outspokenly anticlerical and scornful of the rituals of the Roman Catholic Church. Nonetheless, his education gave Voltaire a solid grounding in the classics, and in later life he spoke not unfondly of his Jesuit instructors and their dedication to teaching and scholarship.

Even while he was at Louis-le-Grand, Voltaire's worldly education proceeded apace. His cosmopolitan godfather, the abbé de Châteauneuf, introduced the young boy to his freethinking and sybaritic Parisian friends. Voltaire's wit and precocious facility at versemaking made him a favorite of these sophisticates. His godfather's mistress, the famous courtesan Ninon de Lenclos, was so taken with the young Voltaire's literary promise that she left him 2000 francs in her will with which to buy books. These early associations no doubt helped form Voltaire's lifelong taste for the pleasures of aristocratic society.

By the time Voltaire left Louis-le-Grand at the age of 17, he was confirmed in his ambition to become a man of letters. His father, however, felt that law would be a more suitable and profitable profession. When Voltaire rebelled, his father sent him to Holland as amanuensis to the French ambassador. But Voltaire was quickly summoned back to Paris when his father discovered he was having an affair with a young Huguenot girl of unexceptional prospects.

On his return from Holland, Voltaire halfheartedly read law for a while to mollify his father. His main energies, however, were devoted to poetry. Most of his efforts were witty assaults in verse on the public figures of the day. Nobody, whether of church, court, or nobility, was safe from his barbs, and Voltaire in turn was not safe from revenge on the part of his powerful targets. On more than one occasion he had to absent himself from Paris while tempers cooled. When he directed a particularly scurrilous attack against the duke of Orleans, regent for the young heir to the throne, later Louis XV, Orleans banished Voltaire from the capital. Orleans lifted the ban after a few months, and Voltaire returned to Paris, but it was not long before he was again in difficulties. This time the trouble was not of Voltaire's making. He was accused of directing another libelous poem against the regent which he had not in fact written. In May 1717, Voltaire was sent to the Bastille.

Early Works

Showing the industriousness that typified his career, Voltaire put his confinement to good use. By the time of his release in April 1718, he had finished the drama *Oedipe* (a reworking of Sophocles's tragedy) and begun work on the *Henriade*. Also at this time, he adopted the name Arouet de Voltaire, later simply Voltaire. The origins of this famous name have been frequently if inconclusively disputed.

Voltaire's *Oedipe* opened in Paris at the Comédie Française in November 1718. To the classic Greek tragedy, Voltaire added a new love interest as well as contemporary references, such as oblique criticisms of the Church. This combination was well received by the Parisian public, and *Oedipe* brought the young playwright fame and a sizable profit.

Voltaire had more difficulty getting *La Henriade* before the public. In this verse epic modeled on Homer and Virgil, Voltaire celebrated the life and character of Henri IV (1553–1610), the king who saw France through the civil wars of Catholic against Protestant to a time of peace and prosperity. In his worldly wisdom and tolerance and his opposition to fanaticism and factionalism, Henry embodied qualities that Voltaire felt were among the greatest virtues. However, these same qualities made Henry seem rather a subversive figure to the authorities of Voltaire's day, and Voltaire was unable to secure permission to publish his epic. Undeterred, he had it printed secretly in Rouen in 1723. As copies arrived in Paris, Voltaire's celebration of Henry was acclaimed as a monument to the French national character and its author as a writer of national significance. The newly invested Louis XV granted Voltaire an annuity, the wealthy and titled wooed him, and he was showered with rewards—social, sexual, pecuniary—that were very much to his taste.

Voltaire's celebrity brought new opportunities to get into scrapes. In late 1725, he was insulted by the chevalier de Rohan, a minor noble; Voltaire replied with his usual asperity. Shortly afterward, he was waylaid by Rohan's men and beaten as Rohan looked on. Voltaire was incensed not only by the beating but by the fact that none of his aristocratic friends had defended him. When Voltaire challenged Rohan to a duel, the chevalier's family had him thrown into the Bastille. This confinement ended shortly when Voltaire was released on his promise to leave France for England.

English Journey

Voltaire's English sojourn lasted from 1726 to 1729 and was to be one of the most significant influences on his intellectual development. Voltaire's literary renown had preceded him, and on his arrival in England he was taken up by some of the most distinguished authors and public figures of the day, including William Congreve, Alexander Pope, and Queen Caroline. For Voltaire, England was preeminently and in contrast to France a land of liberty where freedom of thought and outspoken individuality were not only tolerated but encouraged.

Voltaire read widely in English literature and philosophy. The empiricist epistemology of John Locke and the scientific investigations of Isaac Newton made an especially strong impression on him. Voltaire's stay in England provided an excellent opportunity for him to exercise his talent for comparing one culture critically against another, an ability he later employed to advantage in his historiography and his philosophical tales. Voltaire's comparative critique of English and French society can be found in his *Lettres philosophiques* (*Philosophical Letters*), whose publication in 1734 once again caused him trouble with the French authorities.

Voltaire's English journey also brought him financial opportunities of which, as always, he took handsome advantage. He returned to Paris in 1729 with a purse swollen by several thousand pounds of earnings from the English edition of the *Henriade*, which he had cannily dedicated to the queen.

Paris and Cirey

During the next several years, Voltaire produced a series of tragedies for the Parisian stage—*Brutus* (1730), *Ériphile* (1732), and *Zaïre* (1732)—the last of which was a notable financial and critical success. He had trouble with his prose works, however. His history of Charles XII of Sweden ran into opposition from the censor and had to be printed surreptitiously. Worse trouble came with the publication of the *Lettres philosophiques* (*Philosophical Letters*), in which Voltaire used an account of his English travels as a vehicle to criticize everything he found lacking in French society. The book was formally condemned, copies were seized and burned, Voltaire's publisher was thrown into the Bastille, and a warrant was issued for Voltaire's arrest. Fortunately, he was able to escape imprisonment by fleeing with his mistress, Emilie du Châtelet, to her country estate, Cirey, in Champagne.

The next fifteen years, which Voltaire was to spend with his beloved Emilie, mostly at Cirey, was a period of unexampled stability and security in Voltaire's life. Together with Emilie, who also was a scholar, Voltaire embarked on an organized study of philosophy, religion, science, and history. In this enterprise, Voltaire can be seen as a member of what was perhaps the last generation of scholars who could think, not entirely unreasonably, that it was possible for an individual to master all that was known in the human and natural sciences.

During the Cirey period, Voltaire also wrote three of his most successful plays: *Alzire* (1736), *Mahoumet, ou le Fanatisme* (*Mohammed*, 1742), and *Mérope* (1743). He also wrote works in the other formats in which he had become equally adept, such as the prose history *The Age of Louis XIV* (1763), the poem *The Man of the World* (1736), and the philosophical tale *Zadig* (1747).

Although Voltaire's life at this time centered on the rural and domestic pleasures of Cirey, he continued to advance his career at Versailles and Paris. In 1745, he was appointed to the post of royal historian at a handsome stipend. Voltaire was an eager if not always politic courtier, and the enemies he made at court no doubt delayed a second honor he had long desired, election to the Académie Française. By 1746, however, this reward had also come.

Toward the end of the 1740s, Voltaire and Emilie, although always kindred spirits and devoted friends, began to turn their attentions elsewhere. Voltaire began an affair with his recently widowed niece, Mme Denis, and Emilie fell in love with a young army officer. Emilie became pregnant by her lover, and in 1749 she died in childbirth. With Emilie's death, Voltaire lost the intellectual and spiritual companion whom he called "a soul for which mine was made."

Frederick II of Prussia

Beginning in 1736, Voltaire was pursued by another "suitor," Prince Frederick, later king of Prussia, who desired to add the renowned French writer to his coterie of academicians. With the death of Emilie, there seemed little reason to resist Frederick's promises of position, money, and intellectual independence. By the summer of 1751, Voltaire was established at the court of Frederick in Potsdam. The relationship between the imperious monarch and the mercurial poet was doomed from the first. Voltaire overstepped all bounds of prudence in dealing with his royal patron and his fellow courtiers. He quarreled with the other scholars at court, meddled in matters of state, engaged in improper financial dealings, indulged his penchant for *ad hominem* satire in verse, and perhaps worst of all, ridiculed Frederick's own versifying. As one trespass followed another, the reconciliations between the king of Prussia and the monarch of letters became increasingly testy. With his *Diatribe du docteur Akakia* (*Diatribe of Doctor Akakia*, 1752), a scathing satire on the king and his retinue, Voltaire at last went too far. Although Frederick is reported to have been amused by a private reading of the poem, he explicitly prohibited its printing. Heedless as always, Voltaire published it. Frederick in turn arrested the wayward poet and burned every copy of *Akakia* he could find. It was thought best that Voltaire leave Prussia, which he did in March 1753.

Shortly after Voltaire's departure, Frederick discovered that he had taken with him several unpublished poems in which the king had cruelly satirized some of his fellow heads of state. Frederick had Voltaire detained in Frankfort, recovered the poems, and had Voltaire and his traveling companions placed under house arrest for a time. Thus, with a last farcical episode, ended the great public quarrel between two of the sovereign egotists of the day.

Geneva

The republic of Geneva seemed to offer an attractive refuge from the tyranny of monarchs, and so Voltaire took up residence outside that city in a country home he christened Les Délices. During his Geneva years, Voltaire wrote his *Poème sur le désastre de Lisbonne* (*Poem on the Lisbon Earthquake*, 1755) as well as *Candide* (1759). Voltaire's residence in Geneva was also the occasion for his correspondence with another famous Genevan, Jean Jacques Rousseau. Although there was early mutual admiration between the two *philosophes*, they quickly experienced a personal and intellectual falling out.

While Geneva's political liberalism was congenial to Voltaire, its puritanical culture was not. He soon found himself in conflict with the government's prohibition on theatrical performances and began to search for a new home. In 1758, he moved a short distance to a grand country estate at Ferney, on French soil.

The Sage of Ferney

At Ferney, Voltaire lived the life of a country squire and local patriarch. With his usual business sense, he quickly increased his holdings; he built roads, planted vineyards, encouraged local industry, and turned a sleepy village into a bustling and prosperous town. He also served as host to many of the leading lights of the day, who came to pay their respects to the aging sage who was still, as described in their memoirs, an engaging host and a sparkling wit.

Voltaire wrote more prolifically than ever. He published *The Age of Louis XV* (1763), the *Philosophical Dictionary* (1764), philosophical tales such as *L'Ingénu* (1767), and numerous pamphlets, articles, and poems. In these last years, Vol-

taire also took an active role in a number of social causes. The most famous of
these was the Calas affair, in which Voltaire campaigned vigorously and successfully to clear the name of a Protestant falsely accused by religious bigots of
murdering his own son. The Calas affair was the catalyst for Voltaire's *Traité
sur la tolérance* (*Treatise on Tolerance*, 1763), in which he summarized his lifelong
opposition to religious fanaticism.

Return to Paris

Ever since his residence with Frederick, Voltaire had been under an unspoken
banishment from Paris, largely because of the enmity of Louis XV. When Louis
died in 1776, Voltaire felt that this interdiction might be lifted. In February
1778, he dared a return to the capital, in which he had not set foot for twenty-
eight years. Voltaire's homecoming was a triumph. He was greeted with general
acclaim as a champion of justice and enlightenment. He attended a performance
of his new tragedy *Irène* during which an actor descended from the stage and
placed a crown of laurel on Voltaire's head while the audience applauded wildly.
He was visited daily by old friends, admirers, and notables.

These exciting days were to be Voltaire's last. He died in Paris on May 30,
1778, after a brief illness. Shortly before his death, Voltaire had signed a simple
confession of loyalty to the Roman Catholic church in order to ensure the
decent burial he felt his clerical enemies would want to deny him. His fears
were justified. Seizing on the fact that he had not been given the last rites, the
Church refused him burial in consecrated ground. Undeterred, Voltaire's nephew
had the body smuggled to an abbey in Champagne, where it was properly laid
to rest. In July 1791, however, Voltaire's body was returned to Paris by the
leaders of the French revolution and interred in the Pantheon, the state mau-
soleum, as a national hero and herald of the revolution. When the political
climate changed during the Terror, Voltaire's remains were once more dis-
interred, this time to be buried in a potter's field.

Drama and Poetry

Throughout his life, Voltaire wrote for the stage, producing nearly sixty verse
dramas. Despite his talent for comedy, nearly all Voltaire's plays are tragedies.
The most notable are perhaps *Zaïre* (1732) and *Mérope* (1743). To the elevated
diction and regular form of neoclassical drama, Voltaire added contemporary
references, exotic settings, and an emphasis on ideas that often verged on the

propagandistic. His tragedies, particularly those with love themes, frequently succeeded in reducing Parisian audiences to tears, although their sentimentality makes them seem dated today. Although Voltaire was esteemed in his day as the equal of Racine as a tragedian, his plays now seem burdened with all the artificiality of neoclassical tragedy without any of the energy and psychological acuity which give Racinian tragedy its power.

Voltaire's poetic practice also followed neoclassical tenets. In his *Temple du goût* (*Temple of Taste*, 1733), he summarized his entirely conventional poetic values: simplicity, fidelity to nature, and regularity of form rather than originality. His poetry, like his drama, has few modern partisans and is valuable chiefly as a guide to Voltaire's thinking and a window on his age.

The *Henriade* was without question Voltaire's chief poetic achievement in the eyes of his contemporaries. In it, Voltaire managed a faithful if unimaginative marriage between native French materials and the classical epic tradition of Homer and Virgil. As a long homily on the virtues of religious toleration, it is a forceful statement of one of its author's abiding concerns.

Voltaire's thinking on religion is perhaps best summarized in the verse *Epistle to Urania* (1722), in which he declared his opposition to Christian dogma but affirmed his belief in a just and loving God. Voltaire's faith may be described as *deism*, which was the Enlightenment's contribution to theology. Deism rejected formal worship and supernatural religion in favor of a nondogmatic faith in a God who manifested himself not in church but in nature and whose existence was demonstrated by the harmony of natural laws. Although Voltaire was often labeled an atheist by the Roman Catholic church he so frequently pilloried, it appears that he was nourished throughout his life by a sincere but nondoctrinal faith.

In *The Man of the World* (1736) and *Discourse in Verse on Man* (1738), Voltaire developed his philosophy of the good life. People are placed on earth to seek pleasure but to seek it wisely, with moderation and without doing harm to others. It is the urbane pleasures of the civilized life—art, society, and conversation—which are most conducive to happiness. Voltaire rejects religious doctrines which stress humanity's essential sinfulness and concomitant need for expiation. He believes that our modest understanding does not permit such ultimate judgments on human nature. He counsels instead a simple faith that God's Creation, while not designed solely for humankind, is an estate not unsuited to our abilities and understanding. This optimistic sense of the ultimate harmony between people and their circumstances was decisively abandoned in the *Poem on the Lisbon Earthquake* and *Candide*.

Voltaire as Philosopher

Voltaire was less an original thinker than a skilled advocate and popularizer of a group of critical attitudes. The constant object of his criticism was what he called *l'infame* ("the infamous thing"): the abuses of superstition, privilege, and authority. His essential tenet was a skepticism that presumed nothing and questioned everything. Voltaire's thinking was scientific in spirit and was influenced greatly by English empiricists such as Locke, Bacon, and Newton. His goal was always practical. Voltaire believed passionately in the possibility and necessity of progress, and nearly all his writings were meant to pave the way for such change. His most characteristic work in this respect is perhaps the *Philosophical Dictionary* (1764). The *Dictionary* is not a book of theoretical inquiry but an armory of critical ideas meant to be launched against the authority of church and state. The *Dictionary* can help modern readers recognize Voltaire as one of the originators of the now familiar posture of the intellectual as subversive vis-à-vis the establishment. Well before Shelley had coined the phrase, Voltaire self-consciously adopted the role of the poet as "unacknowledged legislator of the human race."

Voltaire as Historian

Voltaire has often been described as the first modern historian. In prose histories such as *Charles XII* (1731), *The Age of Louis XIV* (1751), and *The Age of Louis XV* (1769), Voltaire abandoned such traditional explanatory devices as the hand of God and national destiny in favor of a new emphasis on natural and human forces. His reluctance to accept the judgments of earlier writers led him to engage in original research to a degree unprecedented in historiography. Most importantly, Voltaire widened the scope of historical writing beyond its usual concentration on court, church, and battlefield to include what has come to be called social history: the culture and manners of people.

Voltaire's most significant historical work is undoubtedly the *Essai sur les moeurs* (*Essay on Customs*, 1756). Traveling from China to Europe, America, and Africa and across hundreds of years, the *Essay* is at once universal history, philosophy of history, polemic, and comparative cultural anthropology. The thread which runs throughout is the battle, which Voltaire finds repeated in all times and nations, between the forces of reason and tolerance and the forces of superstition and fanaticism. While this moralistic "plot" and Voltaire's ultimate faith in progress now seem naive, the *Essay*'s emphasis on social institutions has provided a legacy to modern historians.

Philosophical Tales: *Candide, or Optimism*

Although his philosophical tales were very much the work of Voltaire's spare time, they are today perhaps his most appealing writings. In tales such as *Zadig* (1747), *Micromégas* (1752), *Candide* (1759), and *The Story of Johnny* (1775), Voltaire developed a unique combination of fantasy, satire, and philosophical speculation. Although these tales deal with the great philosophical questions— freedom and fate, our place in the universe—Voltaire's lively style and wit make them amusing reading.

Candide is Voltaire's masterpiece in this form. Like the Book of Job, *Candide* is a theodicy, an inquiry into the vexing question of God's justice: How can a good and omnipotent God allow evil to exist and humanity to suffer?

Two classic answers to this question are optimistic in that they affirm the belief that good ultimately triumphs over evil. The first is the traditional Christian attitude expressed, for example, in Milton's *Paradise Lost*: Evil is necessary in the world, although people are able to choose good, for only the possibility of choosing between good and evil allows people to be truly free. Though this choice is painful, such suffering contributes to the saving of a person's soul. Voltaire makes no attempt to refute this form of optimism in *Candide*.

The second form of optimism, which is represented in *Candide* by Pangloss's philosophy, Voltaire associated, somewhat unfairly and inaccurately, with the German philosopher Gottfried Wilhelm Leibniz (1646–1716). This kind of optimism, which was popularized by Alexander Pope's *Essay on Man* (1733), holds that people's perception of evil is really a misperception caused by the limited nature of human understanding. If people could see the whole scope of God's providential design, they would know that it is good. Pope writes: "All Nature is but art, unknown to thee;/All chance, direction, which thou canst not see;/All discord, harmony not understood,/All partial evil, universal good." The *Essay* ends with the famous affirmation "Whatever IS, is RIGHT." *Candide*, like his *Poem on the Lisbon Earthquake*, states Voltaire's objections to what he felt to be the optimists' too-facile acceptance of human suffering.

ESSAY QUESTIONS WITH ANSWERS

Candide, or Optimism

3.1 Does Voltaire object to the philosophy of optimism primarily on intellectual grounds? Does he argue against its merits as an idea, or does he present his objections in another fashion?

Answer Voltaire does not try to refute optimism by arguing in the abstract against its lack of consistency or sophistication as a concept. Instead, his strategy is to confront the philosophy of optimism with the experience it purports to explain. Since optimism claims that suffering is reconcilable with both the beneficence of God and the reasonableness of God's plan, Voltaire challenges optimism to see how much suffering it can actually reconcile. Accordingly, *Candide* reads like an encyclopedia of human calamities and natural disasters, presenting a catalog of murder, rape, torture, war, earthquakes, shipwreck, and flood—all interwoven with a hundred less spectacular consequences of human cruelty, vanity, and greed.

The philosophy of optimism rises to Voltaire's challenge; it is entirely unfazed by this catalog of misery. No matter how high the bodies are heaped, Pangloss, the ultimate exponent of optimism, is undeterred. Even amid the carnage of the Lisbon earthquake, he continues blandly expounding the principles of sufficient reason and absolute necessity. At such moments, optimism is impugned not because it breaks down intellectually but because it remains undisturbed in the face of such suffering. The complacency of Pangloss is both ridiculous and morally offensive. His failure to respond to disaster with compassion, outrage, or even surprise reveals his philosophy as a kind of moral idiocy. Thus, Voltaire impeaches optimism largely on moral rather than purely intellectual grounds.

3.2 The optimist claims that because individual natural phenomena are amenable to rational explanation through such laws as cause and effect, creation as a whole can be assumed to follow rationally comprehensible laws. The optimist then draws the conclusion that a creation which obeys such laws must be rational in overall design and must tend toward humanly reasonable ends, such as justice. How does Voltaire use the action and plot of *Candide* to impugn this conclusion?

Answer   The action of *Candide* is governed by two different but related principles which together create the impression that irrationality, not reason, lies at the heart of things. The first is a principle of additivity that is embodied in the episodic structure of the tale. The sheer rapidity and relentlessness with which one calamity follows another creates a mounting sense of absurdity. As each new disaster is piled on the one before, the order and proportion proclaimed by the optimists is overborne by chaos and excess. The hyperbolic zeal with which Voltaire presents each successive thrashing of his hapless characters imbues the tale with a grim lunacy which is poles apart from the optimists' calm rationalism.

Although each episode may be explicable in some sense—just as the earthquake at Lisbon may be due to rationally comprehensible principles of geophysics—their human impact is incomprehensible. The sight of 30,000 dead and a city in ruins confounds explanation according to such human terms as justice. If we follow the optimists' advice and take the long view of the ultimate justice of God's plan for us, all *Candide* presents is a madcap succession of equally crushing disasters. The additive, episodic structure of *Candide* resembles the despairing historian's definition of history as just one damn thing after another.

The second principle of action in *Candide* is one of exaggerated design that is actually mock design. Seen from the perspective of its conclusion, the plot of *Candide* does reveal an overall plan. The tale begins by introducing the residents of the idyllic Westphalian estate of the Baron Thunder-ten-Tronckh; it then scatters them literally all over the globe; and it finally brings them all together again for the story's conclusion at the farm in Constantinople.

In general outline, this story follows the pattern of the most fabled of God's designs: a fall from a state of grace, a period of travail, and a final return to grace. In its details, however, the plot of *Candide* is marked by absurd coincidences and wild improbabilities which travesty the notion of divine teleology. Throughout the tale, the characters disappear, reappear, die, and come back to life with a fine and funny disregard for plausibility. For example, Cunégonde's brother, the Baron, is presumed murdered by the Bulgars in Westphalia, turns up as a Jesuit in Paraguay in time to be murdered again by Candide, and pops up yet again, along with Pangloss, as a galley slave off Constantinople. As the characters are reunited in half a dozen countries on two continents, they greet one another with elaborate accounts of the improbable adventures which have happily brought them back together. Candide and Cunégonde decide that had it not been for this precise sequence of war, rape, murder, torture, and abduction, they would not be thus miraculously reunited.

However, the extravagances of the plot make it clear that no miracles are involved. Voltaire's characters are reunited not through any divine plan but only by means of the usual coincidences—exaggerated by Voltaire to the point of absurdity—common to romantic fiction. And the result of their reunion is not a return to grace. Candide regains his Cunégonde only when he no longer wants her; she has lost her beauty, and he has lost his innocence. Thus, the artificial contrivances and deflating conclusion of *Candide*'s fantastic plot parody the notion of a divine plan which tends mysteriously but inevitably toward some just and beneficent end.

3.3 How does the style of *Candide* serve Voltaire's critique of optimism? Does the style itself embody an attitude toward life different from the optimist's?

Answer   The style of *Candide* is simple, witty, and brisk. The typical sentence describes an action as plainly as possible, without resort to adjectives or adverbs. This economical style hurries the characters from one calamity to the next, assaulting the abstract system of optimism with the hard facts of experience. The propulsive energy of Voltaire's prose adds to the impression that the first principle of the cosmos is not design and order but pure force, which often explodes in anarchy and destruction.

The simplicity of Voltaire's style also allows him to score points against his intellectual adversaries with seeming effortlessness. Instead of railing against the optimists' complacence, he need only show Pangloss unperturbedly prattling on amid the carnage. With similar economy of effort, Voltaire can ridicule optimism by simply parroting its precepts and jargon. In the first chapter, he puts the optimists' favorite cause-and-effect terminology to ironic use in describing the household of Baron Thunder-ten-Trockh: "The Baron was one of the most mighty lords of Westphalia, *for* his castle had a door and windows," "The Baroness, who weighed in the neighborhood of three hundred and fifty pounds, was greatly respected *for that reason*," and Pangloss was "the greatest philosopher in the province and *consequently* in the entire world"* (emphases added). This deadpan application of the rationalist language of cause and effect to vanity and aristocratic pretension elegantly demonstrates the yawning gap between a mis-

---

*Translated by John Butt, Harmondsworth, England, Penguin, 1975. All references to *Candide* in this chapter are to the Butt translation.

applied rationalism and the irrational motives which really make the world go round.

The vivacity of Voltaire's prose and the Olympian ease with which he uses it to pillory his adversaries give *Candide* an undeniable charm. Voltaire's wit offers a sparkling relief to the plodding rationalizations of the optimists, and his ironic and knowing air presents the worldliness of the cosmopolitan as an appealing antidote to the airy moralizing of Panglossian cosmologists.

3.4   Does Voltaire endorse any philosophical alternative to optimism? Does he, for example, agree with the pessimistic Martin that people are basically evil?

Answer   Voltaire demonstrates that Martin's pessimism is, at least in some respects, simply wrong. For example, Martin believes that Candide's manservant Cacambo will run off with the jewels and money with which Candide has entrusted him, but Cacambo remains loyal. The tale is dotted with other examples of human goodness, such as the bravery and generosity of the Dutch Anabaptist who succors Candide and the loyalty of the old woman who accompanies Cunégonde. Martin himself is a kind and devoted companion. However, Voltaire takes no special notice of these instances of human goodness and offers no explanation of them. They seem as unmotivated and inexplicable as the malevolence of the sailor who hurls the good Anabaptist into the sea.

Voltaire appears to find no fundamental principle, either good or evil, which determines what people do. Indeed, the course of events seems to mock our efforts to understand human nature in such black-and-white terms, as when Candide comically complains:

> Alas, dear God! . . . I have killed my old master, my friend, my brother in law; I am the best man in the world, and here are three men I've killed already, and two of the three were priests. (Chapter 15)

Human behavior in *Candide* appears as phenomenal and inexplicable as an act of nature; the Seven Years War is no more susceptible to understanding than the Lisbon earthquake. Voltaire's attitude in *Candide* is essentially unphilosophical, since he seems unwilling or unable to press toward a fundamental understanding of human nature. His attitude suggests a skepticism about the philosophical enterprise of formulating such first-order explanations. In *Candide*, Voltaire is philosophical only in the everyday sense of someone who has resignedly accepted the fact of humanity's curiously mixed condition.

3.5   In Chaps. 11 and 12, Voltaire interrupts the adventures of Candide and Cunégonde with the old woman's account of her adventures. What values does the old woman stand for?

Answer   The old woman's story is a compendium of pain. She seems to have suffered every possible humiliation, disappointment, and loss, including, as Voltaire continually reminds us, the loss of one buttock. Yet she is somehow able to say, "I am still in love with life." Her resilience is like that of the Baron and Pangloss, who miraculously spring back to life each time they are killed.

Miserable as it is, life still gets the old woman's vote. Among all the unhappy people she has met, she tells Candide, only a few have committed suicide. Even at the close of *Candide*, it is the old woman who fears that a quiet life of work will be boring: "I should like to know which is the worst, to be ravished a hundred times by negro pirates, to have one buttock cut off, to run the gauntlet of a Bulgar regiment, to be whipped and hanged at an auto-da-fé, to be dissected, to row in the galleys—in fact, to experience all the miseries through which we have passed—or just to stay here with nothing to do?"

The old woman concludes her tale with a boast to which her adventures have entitled her: "I am a woman of experience: I know the world." The old woman affirms the value of life in the world. Experience, no matter how torn and tattered it has left her, allows her the pride of having survived it and the privilege of turning it into a story. These are pleasures philosophy cannot offer, especially a philosophy like Pangloss's, which denies the hard realities of life in the world.

3.6   Through most of *Candide*, Voltaire paints a horrifying picture of humanity helplessly adrift in a sea of suffering. In two episodes, however, he imagines the possibility of a happier accommodation between people and their circumstances: the Eldorado episode in Chaps. 17 and 18 and the last chapter, in which the characters retire to the farm at Constantinople. What do these episodes suggest about the possibility of human happiness and the circumstances suited to it?

Answer   Eldorado is a utopia which sets right all that is wrong with the world beyond its borders. It is a peaceful land where all are free, equal, untroubled by want, and naturally pious. In contrast to the cruel and fanatical religiosity Candide has everywhere met in his travels, the religion of Eldorado is non-dogmatic and humane. It is a religion without church or doctrine, where every person is a priest. Its daily prayers are prayers of gratitude, not supplication.

Candide is delighted to hear that the Eldoradans "have no monks, teaching and disputing, governing and intriguing, and having people burned if they don't subscribe to their opinions." Unlike the tyrannical and lawless civil authorities that have bullied Candide, the government of Eldorado, though monarchical in form, is perfectly democratic in spirit. King and citizen meet each other as equals and embrace with casual good fellowship. Ruled by custom rather than law, the inhabitants of Eldorado are naturally peace-loving. Candide finds the Palace of Science in place of law courts and prisons.

Paradoxically, Eldorado seems too perfect for Candide and Cacambo. Candide complains that even with all his riches he is no different from anybody else in Eldorado, since all are equally wealthy. Just when Candide is finally free of the inequities that have victimized him throughout his travels, he longs to return to them, especially since his Eldoradan wealth would give him the highest place in that world. Some ineradicable dissatisfaction compounded of restlessness, vanity, and greed propels Candide and Cacambo from the paradise of Eldorado back into the unhappy world.

The Eldorado episode suggests that people can imagine far better worlds than they are capable of establishing. When presented with an ideal world, Candide and Cacambo are incapable of being satisfied with it.

The farm to which Candide and his friends retire at the close of the tale is a much more modest utopia than Eldorado. Its key principle is prescribed by the Turkish farmer who tells Candide that it is only "work which banishes those three great evils, boredom, vice, and poverty." Indeed, work on the farm is redemptive. Carpentry turns the vile Brother Giroflée into an honest man, Pâquette leaves prostitution for embroidery, and Cunégonde, though she has lost all her charms, can at least make excellent pastry.

The farm at Constantinople represents a number of compromises: Candide can have Cunégonde, but only when she is a repulsive hag; a small community can live at peace, but only by withdrawing from the world; work can save them, but only by distracting them from their troubles, not because of any intrinsic value. The happiest possibility the farm seems to offer is a bearable life. It is a utopia of reduced expectations. People, this last episode seems to tell the reader, can live most happily by wanting little and seeking in themselves what they cannot find in the world.

However, it is difficult to believe that Voltaire is wholeheartedly endorsing this strategy of solitary self-cultivation. By having his hero retire to a life of seclusion, Voltaire seems to be depreciating the single value he has affirmed throughout Candide: the kind of active experience that allows the old woman to say, "I know the world." Yet the tension between the contradictory postures of withdrawal and worldliness may be precisely the point. Neither way of life can assure happiness if, as Martin says, "man was born to suffer from the restlessness of anxiety or from the lethargy of boredom."

Taken together, the episodes of Eldorado and the farm at Constantinople suggest that people suffer not because they are evil or because creation is malevolent but because of their small though perhaps ineradicable imperfections: their restlessness and changeability, their endless desire for something better. The modest scale of this explanation is very different from the cosmological theorizing of the optimists, with their concern for such ultimates as good, evil, and divine justice. Most significant, though, is its exclusively human scope: People are unhappy simply because of their human limitations. Ultimately, then, Voltaire does not solve or even truly confront the problem of evil in God's world. Rather, he evades it by seeing suffering as largely a consequence of humankind's shortcomings and, true humanist that he is, by eliminating God from the equation.

D.E.

SUGGESTED READINGS

Adams, Robert M., *Candide, or Optimism: A Critical Edition* (1966).
Aldridge, Alfred, *Voltaire and the Century of Light* (1975).
Besterman, Theodore, *Voltaire* (1969).
Lanson, Gustave, *Voltaire* (1966).
Richter, Peyton, and Ilona Ricardo, *Voltaire* (1980).
Wade, Ira O., *The Intellectual Development of Voltaire* (1969).
Wade, Ira O., *Voltaire and "Candide"* (1959).

Part Two

ROMANTIC AND REALIST

INTRODUCTION

The literature produced in Europe during the late eighteenth and nineteenth centuries was brilliant, varied, and hard to characterize. There were swings and counterswings, sometimes from generation to generation and sometimes within a single lifetime. The young "romantic" Goethe of Part I of *Faust,* for example, grew into the older, more "classical" author of Part II; the young "romantic" Flaubert later became a scrupulous "realist." Terms such as "romantic" and "realist" are inevitably simplistic and thus misleading. However, they also suggest waves of influence and affinity that did, in fact, sweep Europe and stimulate literary innovation.

The most important movement in European literature in the second half of the eighteenth century was a reaction against neoclassicism—the belief that reason, discipline, dignity in style and subject, and the imitation of Greek and Latin models offered the surest path to literary greatness. From Rousseau onward, each generation of writers insisted instead on redefining its relation to literary conventions. Stimulating this desire for redefinition were political, social, and scientific developments which provided added reasons for making a break with the past.

Rousseau's concept of the "noble savage," free, virtuous, and happy in his natural state, was the earliest manifestation of this break. Society, Rousseau insisted from 1750 on, was a source of corruption, inequality, and unhappiness. Only by returning to nature, by contemplating natural beauty in isolation from society, could one regain some of this original innocence. Where the neoclassicists had most highly valued their cultural inheritance and their disciplined intelligence, Rousseau embraced spontaneity, emotionalism, and individualism. His social and literary influence was immense. Goethe's romantic hero Werther, cultivating his own stormy emotions and contemplating blades of grass, is no "noble savage," but, like Rousseau, he rejects the artificiality and suffocating conventionality of society, preferring simple folk and a simple life in the country. Tolstoy's admiration for children and the poor owes a similar debt to Rousseau. So, too, does the 19th century tendency toward self-absorption; Rousseau was fascinated by his own emotions and uniqueness and wrote his *Confessions* in order to explain himself to the world. Goethe, too, wrote a lengthy autobiography. Literature came to be viewed, as it had not been previously, as primarily self-expressive—the artist's attempt to define himself in relation to a disconcertingly chaotic universe.

What made the universe chaotic for nineteenth-century thinkers was a widespread sense of social change. Increasing industrialization had led to the growth of cities and an increasingly numerous urban middle class. Political upheaval resulted as this newly important bourgeoisie struggled for power. A series of revolutions—in 1789 and 1830 in France and in 1848 in France, Germany, and Austria—reinforced this sense of instability and disorder. In such a world, literary precedents and conventions seemed confining and dated.

In the wake of the French Revolution and the subsequent upheavals in France, it seemed evident also that certain Enlightenment beliefs about human nature were simply wrong. It no longer seemed likely that people could or would improve their condition by acting rationally and objectively. The violence and brutality of the revolution, the transformation of republican France into a Napoleonic empire, and the decade of war into which Europe was plunged all suggested that there was one human quality whose importance the Enlightenment philosophers had underestimated: irrationality. Romanticism was in part an attempt to recognize and express this irrationality.

Romanticism as a literary school did not actually peak in France until the first quarter of the nineteenth century. Led by Victor Hugo, the romantics advocated a wider range of subjects for literature, viewing the grotesque and the lowly as being as significant and valid as the beautiful and the aristocratic. They also exhibited a disregard for what they considered outmoded rules for versification and playwriting. In Germany, romanticism brought a renewal of interest in the Middle Ages, gothic art and architecture, folk tales, and the folk themselves—the common people who reflected the nation's characteristic traits and temperament. In Germany and in Russia, a strain of intense nationalism mingled with other aspects of romanticism. Tolstoy's Russian peasants, like Goethe's fictional Gretchen, possess a simple goodness inseparable from their attachment to the land. As such, they are quintessentially romantic creations.

Around the middle of the nineteenth century, social, political, and scientific events contributed to a deepening pessimism about human potential and a disillusionment with romantic tenets. Urban poverty, crass materialism, and political cynicism all seemed on the upswing, and the revolutions failed to produce any noticeable improvements. This changing mood found varied expression in literature. Baudelaire describes the sordid side of Paris life in *Les Fleurs du mal*; Flaubert's Homais in *Madame Bovary* epitomizes the triumph of mediocrity in modern civilization. The abolition of serfdom in Russia in 1861 was no more successful than the revolutions in the west in terms of producing a genuine improvement in social conditions; Chekhov chronicles the social upheaval that resulted.

Karl Marx made sense of the upheaval by explaining it in terms of class conflict. The first volume of his *Capital*, which appeared in 1867, predicted inevitable conflict between the working class, or the proletariat, and the capitalists, who controlled the means of production and hence the workers' livelihoods. While Marx's view was essentially optimistic, since he believed that class struggle would lead eventually to the triumph of the proletariat, his theories produced consternation. The specter of revolution and Marx's hard-nosed view of man as the product of economic, rather than cultural, intellectual, or spiritual factors disturbed many.

The theory of evolution, also popularized at mid-century, seemed to place a similar emphasis on the purely physical side of human life. While Darwin did not argue that man was directly descended from ape, his theory implied that the same forces shaped the development of man and animal, and that these forces were random and natural, not purposeful and divinely ordained. The concept of natural selection, described in Darwin's 1859 *Origin of Species*, was felt by some (though not by him) to have removed God from the universe.

The idea that people were the products of their economic circumstances and physical inheritance had implications for fictional characterization. Perhaps inspired in part by Balzac's massive *Human Comedy* (1842–8), which depicted ordinary people and their environment, writers began to describe what they actually saw around them: the streets of Paris, the middle-class drawing rooms of Russia and Norway. Characters' social circumstances and environment were described in minute detail, drawn presumably from the artist's meticulous observation. Literary depiction took on a scientific aura. The assumption was that the ordinary could offer a profundity of its own if only it was observed scrupulously enough.

Though these writers, who came to be known as realists, felt themselves in revolt against romanticism, they were also deeply indebted to it. The romantics' interest in wide-ranging subjects, rejection of convention, and emphasis on individuality all underlay the realistic movement in literature. By emphasizing the uniqueness of the artist's emotional life, they laid the groundwork for a growing sense of alienation between the artist and society. Nineteenth-century realists were often viewed as social critics, and even those who rejected the label seemed, by virtue of their mercilessly accurate descriptions of a mediocre or corrupt society, to indirectly advocate social change. Flaubert, Baudelaire, Rimbaud, and Ibsen despised above all the bourgeois world into which they had been born. All cultivated a kind of artistic heroism which pitted their individual visions and commitment to art against the materialism and philistinism of the middle class.

Realism was closely related to romanticism in another respect: while emphasizing the influence on people of physical circumstances, many realists took note also of human irrationality. They aimed at *psychological* realism: the accurate depiction of a person's inner life. This is the realism embraced by Dostoevsky, by Ibsen, and by Chekhov. It may seem less "realistic," or even "romantic," in its use of symbol and suggestion to portray the intangible surges of emotion characteristic of ordinary human beings. It may even seem to merge, at times, with romanticism. The two movements are not, finally, that far apart, and many major figures have characteristics of both. Tolstoy the realist created a huge panorama of society in *War and Peace*; Tolstoy the romantic sought a simple religious faith and idealized the life of the peasant. Chekhov tempered his depictions of social change with a wit and sympathy that suggested transcendent beauty lay just beneath the surface. And, in their glorification of the artist suffering for his insights, laboring to forge the perfect work of art out of mundane materials, Baudelaire, Rimbaud, Flaubert, and Ibsen suggested both the exalted, isolated, suffering heroes of romanticism—Rousseau himself in the *Confessions*, Goethe's Werther and Faust—and the self-conscious aestheticism of modernism.

C H A P T E R 4

ROUSSEAU

Rousseau and His Times

Jean-Jacques Rousseau was one of the most colorful figures of the eighteenth century. His quirky, unstable personality helped shape his distinctive beliefs in the innocence of childhood, nature, and primitive society and the primacy of emotional sensitivity. His writings helped shape almost all the tenets of romanticism and have exerted an incalculable influence over the last two centuries. Rousseau always considered himself an outsider and never tried to conform to his times and surroundings, yet he also represents a century in transition.

He was born in 1712, soon after Isaac Newton's discovery of the mathematical laws of motion seemed to promise similarly decisive advances both in science and in morals. The brilliant discoveries of Newton and others made possible a generally optimistic intellectual atmosphere. But by the time Rousseau died in 1778, that atmosphere had dissipated, and Europe was on the verge of upheaval. Four years before, the American Revolution had begun, and eleven years later, the much more dramatic and radical French Revolution would take place. More than any other person, Rousseau expressed and helped shape the change of consciousness that took place between Newton and Napoleon.

Early Life

Rousseau was born in Geneva, Switzerland, the son of a watchmaker. His mother died in childbirth, and his father seems not to have been very interested in the boy's upbringing. At age 11, Jean-Jacques was sent to study with a clergyman, and soon after, he was apprenticed to an engraver. At age 16, he ran away from Geneva and, after a few days, met a wealthy woman in her late twenties, Mme de Warens, a recent convert to Roman Catholicism. She was to be the major figure in Rousseau's life for the next fifteen years. She took Rousseau under her wing, sending him to Turin, Italy, where he received instruction in Catholicism and converted to that faith.

However, Rousseau soon left the company of his religious teachers to become a footman and then a secretary in Turin and then he abandoned his prospects of advancement to take a walking tour back to Mme de Warens's house in the Savoy. She again took him in and found him a position, first as a surveyor and later as a music copyist.

In his early twenties, Rousseau took up residence with Mme de Warens, whom he always called "Mamma," becoming for a time her lover and the supervisor of her affairs and properties. He never stayed in one place long but was often on the road to Lyons, Geneva, or Paris seeing to Mme de Warens's affairs. In his *Confessions*, Rousseau says that he felt happiest and freest when in the middle of a walking trip with no concerns other than the road and his surroundings. He never owned a house and never really had a permanent place of residence. In his later years, Rousseau was never able to settle long in any one place because of repeated harassment by church authorities, government officials, or the general public; however, his own dissatisfactions, quarrels, and fears caused many of these moves.

After a few years of relative contentment, Rousseau found himself supplanted in Mme de Warens's affections by a younger man. He moved to Paris, where he made just enough to live on by copying music. Soon after his arrival, he became involved with a Parisian maid named Thérèse le Vasseur; although they were never formally married, she remained his companion for most of the rest of his life. They had five children, all of whom were placed in a foundling hospital, or orphanage. Of all the blots on Rousseau's character, this persistent denial of responsibility for the lives he had brought into being must rank as the least defensible. In the *Confessions*, Rousseau barely tries to excuse his course of action; he has regretted it many times, he says, but he does not declare or defend the reasons which led to it.

Literary Emergence

In addition to establishing his relations with Thérèse, Rousseau began at this time to make friends among the leading lights of the literary and intellectual circles in Paris. He had always been a passionate reader and had begun to educate himself systematically during his last years with Mme de Warens. On the basis of these continuing efforts and his native talents, he was accepted in the salon of Mme d'Epinay and became an intimate friend of Denis Diderot, the editor and principal author of the voluminous *Encyclopedia*, which trumpeted Enlightenment ideas, and Friedrich Grimm, another prominent member of French literary circles.

Until he was 38, Rousseau seems never to have thought of becoming a writer. One day, however, while walking down the road, he came across a notice that the academy of the city of Dijon was offering a prize for the best essay on the question of whether the arts and sciences had done more to improve morals than to corrupt them. Consideration of this question threw him into a state of delirium in which everything he had read, thought, and experienced in his erratic life came together into a series of insights and arguments that were to shape his writing for the next fifteen years. Sitting under a tree, he had a vision from which he woke with his shirtfront wet with tears. There he began the essay, his *Discours sur les sciences et les arts* (*Discourse on the Arts and Sciences*), which was to win the academy's prize and bring him fame, tribulations, and even persecution. Here, Rousseau argues with originality and force that the arts and sciences have corrupted rather than advanced morals.

As the prizewinner, Rousseau made a name for himself but not much money. He continued to copy music for a living. In 1752, the success of an opera of Rousseau's performed before the king and the court opened up the possibility of a royal pension, but he refused to visit the king and thus forfeited the pension, in part because of embarrassment, in part because he believed that acceptance of a pension would compromise his freedom to speak and write his own thoughts. Having turned his back on royal favor, Rousseau entered another twenty-year period of wanderings and difficulties.

Middle Years

After this incident, Rousseau returned to Geneva and to the Calvinist religion into which he had been born. In 1755, he published his *Discours sur l'origine et les fondements de l'inégalité parmi les hommes* (*Discourse on the Origin of Inequality*). His native city showed no gratitude for his praise of their spirit of liberty in this work, so Rousseau moved back to France, to a cottage lent to him by his patroness of the time, Mme d'Epinay, where he wrote the novel *La Nouvelle Héloïse* (*Julie, or, the New Eloise*). However, in 1757, after a long series of bitter disagreements, Rousseau broke entirely with Mme d'Epinay and her friend Diderot. For the remaining twenty years of his life, he continued to believe that he was the victim of elaborate plots and schemes engineered by these former friends and their agents.

Having removed to yet another cottage owned by yet another protectress, in the next few years Rousseau completed his most accomplished works: *Emile, or Education* (1762) and *The Social Contract*. The latter book, containing Rousseau's political ideas, begins with the famous sentence "Man is born free, but is everywhere in chains." Since its publication in 1762, it has been Rousseau's most famous work and has exercised an incalculable influence on political thought. It is a short work but a unique, challenging, and in its own time subversive one. When both books were condemned by the religious and political authorities in Paris, Rousseau accepted a generous offer of asylum from the Scottish philosopher David Hume.

While staying with Hume in England, Rousseau worked on an account of his life that was intended to serve as a counterweight to the slanders of his old enemies and former friends. *The Confessions* was not published until after Rousseau's death (it appeared in two parts, in 1781 and 1788). Once again, in England Rousseau spurned the offer of a royal pension. He also soon split with Hume and returned to Paris, where he again scraped by as a music copyist. Under one last patron, he moved to Ermenonville, where he took up botany, wrote his *Reveries*, and continued to suffer from fantasies of persecution. In 1794, sixteen years after his death, his body was moved to a place of honor in the Pantheon in Paris.

The Influence of Rousseau

In his vagabondage, his liaison with Thérèse, his tendency to paranoia, and his repeated cycle of reliance on the great and rebellion against them, Rousseau lived his life outside the usual pattern of the times. Perhaps as a consequence, he formulated a great many thoughts and feelings that shook Europe in the eighteenth century and continue to shape the way people see things today. In fact, many of his most startling positions have become so commonplace that people take them for granted now.

Rousseau argued passionately that civilization corrupted the natural human being. In his view, people are naturally truthful, industrious, fair-minded, and generous, but social institutions introduce inequalities, and with them jealousy, ambition, greed, deceit, and self-interest. Rousseau's critique of existing social forms accounts for the two main streams of his influence. First, his influence has been political. His insistence on the natural rights of all people helped spark the French Revolution and through that event has indirectly inspired many revolts against systems of unequal privilege in the last 200 years. Second, by calling for a return to natural feelings and means of expression, he influenced the shape of literature in the west over the same time period. More than any other person, he laid the groundwork for the romantic movement in the arts, whose power can still be felt in the idea that originality, individuality, spontaneity, intensity, and the honest expression of the artist's feelings are the hallmarks of a great work of art.

Although he was the exception and the outsider in his own day, Rousseau's influence has outreached that of any other writer of the eighteenth century. As his *Confessions* make clear, he has passed on a heritage of perverse strengths and profound weaknesses. His extreme emotional sensitivity anticipates both the disciplined explorations of psychoanalysis and the reflexive glorification of feeling over thought. His concept of the noble savage led to an increased appreciation of cultural differences as well as to the projection of European ideals onto the very different and often harsh realities of non-European peoples. Finally, his reverence for the innocence of nature helped foster both a genuine respect for natural forces and resources and a sentimental, aesthetic vision of nature that can be used as a screen for its massive exploitation.

ESSAY QUESTIONS WITH ANSWERS

The Confessions

4.1 Rousseau is the only source for many of the incidents recounted in the *Confessions*. How fully can we accept his versions of these incidents? How much of what he says can be verified, and how much seems inaccurate?

Answer Where it is possible to check on what he says, one finds that Rousseau commits more than a few slips of memory in his narrative, some of them significant. For example, the amount of time he spent in the Roman Catholic seminary in Turin seems to have been greater than what is reported in the *Confessions*. Similarly, in regard to a matter much closer to the heart of the book, Rousseau says that he spent about a year alone with Mme de Warens at her country house, les Charmettes. But from other sources it seems clear that Mme de Warens did not move to les Charmettes until after Jean-Jacques had been replaced in her affections. Rousseau may have spent time with her there, but only in the company of her newest young man and only on the threshold of his permanent departure from her before heading for Paris.

Rousseau's memory, then, is fallible; he makes mistakes of chronology and detail. But in a curious and important sense, such inaccuracies do not matter in this case. Rousseau is not trying to chronicle his movements and activities for all the years of his life. The *Confessions* do not pretend to be a historical account whose dates and events have been carefully and objectively researched. It has an entirely different organizing principle. "I may omit or transpose facts, or make mistakes in dates," Rousseau admits, "but I cannot go wrong about what I have felt. . . . The true object of my confessions is to reveal my inner thoughts exactly in all the situations of my life" (Book VII, p. 262).* External facts and the progression of events are only props against which the real drama of Rousseau's story is played out.

*Translated by J. M. Cohen, New York, Penguin, 1953. All references to the *Confessions* in this chapter are to the Cohen translations.

Thus, the truth of Rousseau's account is subjective rather than objective. In remembering the happiness he felt with his "Mamma" in his middle twenties, he may expand one summer into two or telescope two into one, but he makes no mistake about the emotion: "I got up at sunrise, and was happy; I walked, and was happy; I saw mamma, and was happy; I left her and was happy; I roamed the forests and hills; . . . and happiness followed me everywhere" (VI, 215).

The question remains whether Rousseau is experiencing this emotion more in memory than he did in experience, but there is no easy answer. In a sense, all depends on the success of Rousseau's writing, on whether his descriptions are vivid and lifelike enough to persuade the readers that it could have happened that way or even that it must have happened that way. The reader cannot contradict Rousseau on the matter of his own life but can fail to be persuaded.

At this point, one begins to see why the *Confessions* were so original and influential. The very few autobiographies that preceded Rousseau's had been cast in spiritual terms. Saint Augustine's *Confessions*, for example, are addressed to God in thanks and praise and secondarily to Augustine's fellow human beings in the hope of converting them to Christianity as he had been converted. Augustine seeks to convince his readers that they are like him: no matter how seriously they have sinned, they can be saved. In recounting his story, Augustine meditates on the meaning of each event and detail as it expresses God's will, and he finds that his life fits into a meaningful pattern which regulates all human affairs. For Augustine, meaning and value derive from God alone.

Rousseau's work breaks the mold of spiritual autobiography. It is directed solely to his fellow human beings, mostly those of future generations, and not even rhetorically to God. Rousseau accentuates the differences between himself and others; by portraying his strengths and weaknesses in the sharpest light, he challenges others to be as honest and revealing as he has been. He writes the story of his life solely in terms of his worldly experience. His personal philosophy has only the most tenuous connection with the doctrines of established religion. Unlike Augustine, who wrote to justify God's works through his own discovery of faith, Rousseau writes of himself in purely secular and personal terms.

Thus, Rousseau's project does not depend for its success on the literal accuracy of individual statements. It depends, rather, on convincing readers that even considering all of Rousseau's peculiarities and faults, this was a good and decent man.

4.2   In the *Confessions*, Rousseau often weeps; at other times, he appears to be restless or dissatisfied with little reason. But he goes into raptures when taking a long walk in the hills or recalling a long-dead friend. Rousseau emerges in the story as an emotional and unpredictable character. How would this emotionalism have struck readers in the eighteenth century?

Answer The eighteenth century has come to be known as an age of enlightenment or reason. In some ways the label is well founded, especially with reference to the first half of the century. Thus, among Rousseau's older contemporaries, many might have been expected to disapprove of his passionate fits, rantings, and emotional inconstancy.

But from the 1750s on, a countercurrent had begun to build in most European countries. In reaction to the tendency toward rationality, stiffness, and artificiality of the preceding decades, various forms of sentimentality became fashionable. The melancholy contemplation of graveyards by increasing numbers of poets exemplifies this trend; so does the increasing number of characters in fiction who suffer fainting fits on hearing good news or bad. In both the theater and in life, the individual of sensibility, with a delicate sensitivity to the suffering and pathos of others, began to replace the severe rationalist of the earlier years of the century.

It is hard to say how much Rousseau was responding to and how much he was contributing to this development. It is probable, however, that many of his first readers accepted his emotional highs and lows as signs of a sensitive nature.

To modern readers, Rousseau in his melancholy moods sounds sentimental; when he is exclaiming, he sounds affected. Part of the problem is that the language of his time has not aged well, and even the most romantic writers today use a more restrained style to describe their emotions. But one should recognize that this is the case partly because Rousseau was so successful in his *Confessions*, and had so many imitators.

One should also recognize that Rousseau's language reflects his character. "I have a passionate temperament and lively and headstrong emotions," he says. When he is in the grip of his feelings, nothing else exists for him; he is fearless, impetuous, shameless. At the other extreme, when no passion holds him, he becomes timid and incapable of action: "a fly, buzzing past, alarms me; a word which I have to say, a gesture which I have to make, terrifies my idleness; fear and shame overpower me to such an extent that I would gladly hide myself from the sight of my fellow-creatures" (III, 113). The heated quality of the writing gives the reader a vivid idea of the person. One other detail that Rousseau provides about himself confirms this impression. He was psychologically nearsighted, capable of focusing only on things or feelings near at hand and temperamentally incapable of making long-range plans or commitments. Rousseau's peculiarly intense focus on the feelings and sensations of the moment accounts in part for the highly wrought tone of his narrative.

4.3   Throughout the *Confessions* and especially in the account of his early years, Rousseau goes out of his way to emphasize his weaknesses and embarrassments. Why does he dwell on this aspect of his character in such detail? Is he merely trying to tell the truth, or is he exaggerating in order to strike a pose?

Answer   In the course of his story, Rousseau confesses to a sizable number of weaknesses and even vices. For example, in explaining why he has never been tempted to steal money, he admits that he has a habit of stealing unimportant items when they attract his eye. He calls it "pilfering" and implies that even as a middle-aged man he has not stopped the practice. The thought does not seem to cause him any pangs of conscience. About his short-lived career as an exhibitionist, he only chuckles good-naturedly and thanks heaven that a good fright made him stop.

Many of these revelations naturally have to do with sex. For example, one discovers early in the book that Rousseau's desires run in what would now be called a masochistic pattern. A strong strain in his character revels in being embarrassed or threatened with punishmnent: "To lie at the feet of an imperious mistress, to obey her commands, to ask her forgiveness—this was for me a sweet enjoyment" (I, 28). There is no reason to doubt the truth of Rousseau's self-portrait here. Nor is there any reason to doubt him when he goes on to say that this taste turned out to be largely self-correcting; that is, because he tended to be passive and timid, he never had much success in initiating adventures. Pleasures which might have brutalized Rousseau remained for the most part in his imagination, where they did no harm.

It is possible that some of the scandalous revelations in the book gave Rousseau a shiver of masochistic pleasure as he made them, that the psychological motivations for these confessions are tangled and deep. Perhaps no episode better illustrates these complications than the affair of the pink ribbon at the end of Book 2.

After Rousseau had worked in Turin for a few months as a valet to an old woman, his employer died. Her household was to be broken up, and Rousseau stole a pink ribbon from her room. When he was accused of the theft, he blamed it on a young servant named Marion. Even when placed in her presence, Rousseau maintained that she had given him the ribbon. Nothing could be proved either way, and both he and Marion were dismissed with suspicion. Rousseau explains that he had accused the girl of giving him the ribbon because he had in fact intended to give it to her; that is why her name was on the tip of his tongue when he was found out.

As psychologically intriguing as the reversal may be, it is not this aspect of the case to which Rousseau pays the most attention in his account thirty years later. What bothers him the most, he says, is the thought of what might have happened to the innocent but discredited girl. Without a recommendation, she could hardly have expected to find a job. Would she be led to crime, theft, or even prostitution in order to support herself? It is clear that Rousseau feels genuine remorse for what he did, but the shudder of shame he feels may not be entirely unpleasant as he imagines how the innocent and pretty Marion may have been forced to make a living because of his own thievery and dishonesty. Like a Dostoevskian character, Rousseau confesses his baseness but seems to delight in his shame.

The other episodes that cast Rousseau in a bad light do not rest on such complicated motivations. They paint him as a fairly unattractive character. One betrayal in particular stands out. When M. le Maitre falls into an epileptic fit in the middle of a street in Lyons (in Book III), Rousseau abandons the man who was his teacher, friend, traveling companion, and fellow countryman, leaving him friendless and jobless in a strange city at a time of urgent need. To this should be added Rousseau's commitment of his children to an orphanage. Rousseau does not seem to feel any tingle of pleasure about either of these betrayals; instead he seems genuinely and simply saddened by his behavior.

However, a number of Rousseau's confessions may be embarrassing without providing evidence of wickedness of character. For example, when Rousseau wants to illustrate his remark that he is much more fluent in writing than in speaking, he quotes a few of his gaffes in conversation that must have been mortifying. Here Rousseau portrays idiosyncrasies of his character without any attempt at apology. His inability to remain in any occupation and his constant wandering may strike the reader as evidence not only of independence of character but of unsteadiness and even ingratitude toward his patrons and friends. But after the first few reports of sudden changes in residence and habits, he attempts neither to excuse nor to explain this trait in his character. He describes his actions or his feelings, observes himself with a smile or a shrug, and then passes on.

On the first page of the *Confessions*, Rousseau imagines himself on the day of judgment presenting this book in his own defense and saying,

> Here is what I have done. . . . I have displayed myself as I was, as vile
> and despicable when my behavior was such, as good, generous, and noble

when I was so. I have bared my secret soul as Thou thyself hast seen it, Eternal Being! So . . . let my fellow-men groan at my depravities, and blush for my misdeeds. But let each one of them reveal his heart at the foot of Thy throne with equal sincerity, and may any man who dares, say "I was a better man than he."

Rousseau's project was to write about himself with all the candor and truthfulness he could muster. He knows that, being human, he cannot be entirely accurate or absolutely honest. But by setting the highest priority on sincerity in the expression of his thoughts and feelings, he sets a challenge as well as an appeal before the rest of the world: Let his critics bare their own souls before they attack him.

Still, the reader should not infer that one must write autobiography in order to be credited with sincerity and candor. Many poets and essayists before Rousseau conveyed a vivid picture of their own personalities in their writings without adopting the autobiographical mode. In fact, the memorable pose Rousseau strikes when he imagines himself presenting his *Confessions* before the judgment seat should alert the reader to the strong possibility that the very act of writing one's confessions for public examination inevitably constitutes a pose. Rousseau's strategy of self-revelation, then, may be considered a rather ingenious literary tactic that refines the art of posing in such a way as to make it appear perfectly natural.

The passion for self-analysis and self-absorption that Rousseau displayed came to characterize the entire romantic movement in art. Literature took on an autobiographical tone in which memories of youthful experiences were seen as crucial. Thus, in a sense Rousseau was a precursor of Freud. Being the first to make an absolute virtue of sincerity (even if he could not always meet his own standard), having decisively helped turn the focus of literature onto the psychology of the self, Rousseau has a good claim to being considered the first distinctively modern author.

4.4 After being considered an irresponsible and scandalous figure during his life, Rousseau achieved the status of a respectable thinker after death, exerting a strong influence on such staid personalities as Kant and Goethe and on such moralists as Tolstoy and Sartre, all of whom took inspiration from the *Confessions*. Why? What positive contributions did Rousseau make to ideas of morality through his writings?

Answer Rousseau set out his ideas on moral and political questions most systematically in *Emile*, *Julie*, and *The Social Contract*. In the *Confessions*, his ideas emerge more randomly through association or explanation. All in all, they possess a striking freshness, as if Rousseau were merely the first to put into words many obvious truths that had been widely felt but never before expressed.

For example, looking back on his apprenticeship, Rousseau remembers that he was so often beaten unjustly for shirking and stealing that he decided to behave so as to deserve the punishment and enjoy the satisfactions of the criminal, since he would be treated as one in any case. He depicts convincingly how an overly suspicious authority often creates a criminal instead of reforming one.

Many of Rousseau's observations possess such a critical edge. Speaking of the emptiness of most social conversations, he reflects that it would be less mindless to play with a cup and ball than to take part in the false wit and gossip produced by the pressure to say something in order to avoid appearing dull. This "morality of the cup and ball" (V, 195) reflects not only on the society but on Rousseau, who plays the role of an idealistic but whimsical nonconformist. Even more paradoxical and suggestive is his assertion that "believers in general create God in their own image" (V, 218). This formulation combines shrewd psychological observation with a challenge to conventional religion in a sentence that echoes and reverses one of the most famous verses in the Bible.

Rousseau's lasting influence as a moral figure, however, does not proceed from any of these fragmentary observations but rather from a principled stand that Rousseau first took soon after he won the prize for the *Discourse on the Arts and Sciences*. He resolved to be his own person, to speak his own thoughts, and to live and write without depending on the powerful and the rich. He felt that this was the only way to preserve his credibility as a critic of existing institutions and morals.

Because of this resolve, he declined the offer of a royal pension from both the French and British kings. Rousseau's stance may seem unduly theatrical now, because many undistinguished and self-important posers have tried to imitate him. But the reader should remember that his writings were seen as threatening the most powerful forces in Europe, and that he lived his last years in relative poverty and obscurity, when he could have been rich and publicly honored. Many later artists, thinkers, and reformers, however distasteful they may have found other sides of Rousseau's character, have admired and imitated this deep strain of stubborn independence.

4.5 Rousseau remarks that the descriptions he had read and heard of Paris were so exceedingly beautiful that the city itself could not help but disappoint him because of its dirtiness, noise, and poverty. Although Rousseau lived in

Paris for more than fifteen years, he says that he spent most of his time there trying to figure out ways to escape into the country. Why didn't Rousseau simply move to the country? What were his ideas about nature?

Answer   Rousseau spent his last few years in a remote spot outside Paris, in a relatively rural setting. Like many modern people, he expresses conflicting feelings about nature and cities. When he is out walking, the wilder the landscape the better. He is not satisfied by plains; he needs "torrents, rocks, firs, dark woods, mountains, steep roads to climb or descend, abysses beside to make [him] afraid" (IV, 167). The ever-changing or menacing prospect thrills him, and he goes into the mountains and woods in order to feel a shiver of contact with the power of nature.

However, Rousseau never proposes actually living next to abysses and torrents. When he talks about moving to the country, the scene he paints is hardly exciting; instead, it is full of rural and domestic details such as cows, fences, orchards, flowers, and vineyards. In other words, on his excursions he wants to see and touch nature at her wildest, but for day-to-day living he prefers nature tamed. The cottages in the forests where he did much of his writing were picturesque, not awe-inspiring.

Although these two ways of regarding nature are not quite consistent, both became strong currents in romantic thought and feeling. Romantic literature in general expresses both views: the first, that the good life is the more natural and less complicated life of the villager or the peasant who lives closer to the earth, and the other, that nature is an aesthetic experience which can be enjoyed as a relief from the corrupting and suffocating life of the city.

Perhaps one should not criticize Rousseau too harshly for his inconsistency. Most people today follow Rousseau's lead either by trying to return to the land, to nature, and to innocence, or by escaping the confinements of a city through weekend contact with streams, lakes, trees, mountains, and stirring vistas. It is a sign of Rousseau's importance that his ideas are as alive, if unrecognized, in the attitudes of millions as they are in the studies of scholars.

SUGGESTED READINGS

Babbitt, Irving, *Rousseau and Romanticism* (1919).

Blanchard, W., *Rousseau and the Spirit of Revolt* (1968).

Cassirer, Ernst, *Rousseau, Kant, Goethe* (1945).

Crocker, L. G., *Jean-Jacques Rousseau: A New Interpretative Analysis of His Works* (1973).

Einaudi, Michel, *The Early Rousseau* (1968).

Green, F. C., *Jean-Jacques Rousseau: A Critical Study of His Life and Writings* (1955).

Höffding, Hans, *Rousseau and His Philosophy* (1930).

McManners, J., *The Social Contract and Rousseau's Revolt against Society* (1968).

Yale French Studies, No. 28 (1962).

C H A P T E R 5

GOETHE

Background and Youth

Johann Wolfgang von Goethe was born August 28, 1749, in the west German city of Frankfurt-am-Main. Although Goethe was one of eight children, only he and his sister Cornelia survived childhood. His family was fairly well-off; his father was a lawyer, and his mother was connected to some of the town's leading citizens. Until the age of 16, Goethe was educated by his father and by tutors at home, where he learned a wide range of subjects with astonishing ease.

Germany at that time was a conglomeration of states, principalities, duchies, and self-governing cities under the rule of the Holy Roman Empire, which was then so weak and decentralized that it was, as Voltaire pointed out, neither holy, Roman, nor an empire. As a result, a wide range of foreign cultural influences were available to Goethe, but little in the way of a native German tradition.

In 1765, Goethe left Frankfurt for Leipzig, where he studied law at the university. He immersed himself in French drama, architecture, and literature and began to write poems and plays. After a few years, however, he became seriously ill and returned to Frankfurt to recover in his parents' home. During his year-long illness, he became interested in religious mysticism, astrology, and alchemy, performing experiments in his private laboratory.

After his recovery, Goethe returned to studying law, but in a vastly different cultural milieu. He went this time to the university at Strasbourg, a French city dominated by German art and architecture. The city is known for its soaring gothic cathedral, and for Goethe its beauty was a revelation. Gothic art, with its roots in the Middle Ages, had been looked down upon by the eighteenth-century thinkers whose philosophy had shaped Goethe. These thinkers, proud of current intellectual and cultural advances, called their era the Enlightenment and rejected gothic art as barbarous and ignorant. The standard Enlightenment view was that only the classical tradition of ancient Greece and Rome, as adopted by Renaissance scholars, offered a valid model for art and literature. Only the rational pursuit of knowledge, through painstaking study and intellectual effort, could provide access to truths about the universe. The Strasbourg Cathedral, on the other hand, grew out of medieval northern European culture, not classicism, and as such was held to exemplify religious devotion rather than learning. In admiring the cathedral and embracing gothic architecture in general, which he felt to be characteristically Germanic, Goethe was turning away from Enlightenment assumptions.

Sturm und Drang

Goethe moved further from Enlightenment thinking through his association with Johann Gottfried Herder, a controversial literary figure who resided at Strasbourg during the winter of 1770–1771. Herder was leading an attack on the prevalent literary theory that great works could be achieved only through imitation of classical models. Pointing out the beauties of nonclassical art—art produced, in Herder's view, from the heart, by the ordinary people (not only by the learned)—he argued that feeling, not imitation, should be the source of art.

Some of Herder's many followers formed a movement that became known as the *Sturm und Drang* (storm and stress), the title of a play by Friedrich Maximilian von Klinger. The name suggests how interested they were in the expression of emotional turmoil. The storm and stress writers admired the Bible, Homer, gothic architecture, folk songs and tales, and the works of "Ossian," the Celtic bard whose third-century epics were in fact written by the eighteenth-century poet James MacPherson (who insisted he had merely "found," not written them). They also worshipped Shakespeare, whose wide-ranging moods, varied characters, and freely mixed structures seemed to offer a passionate antidote to the carefully structured, emotionally contained French drama. They admired the expression of deeply felt emotion in these works; their closeness to the "folk," or the ordinary people; and their use of nature as an inspiration. All offered a stark contrast to what was regarded as the stultifying rigidity of neoclassicism, the empty elaboration of rococo, and the Enlightenment belief that rationality alone held the key to truth.

This major shift in cultural values did not, of course, happen overnight, nor does it fully explain Goethe's work. It was part of a gradual movement away from Enlightenment views toward the romanticism that would dominate late eighteenth-century and early nineteenth-century thought. In the forefront of this movement were the storm and stress writers, whose influence on Goethe's early work was profound.

Early Works

Under Herder's influence, Goethe began in 1771 to write *Götz von Berlichingen* (published in 1773), a play with many folk characters that was modeled after Shakespeare's historical dramas. His poems from this time reflect a peculiarly intense relation to nature and to his own emotions. In poems such as "Maysong" and "Welcome and Farewell," he expresses his passionate love for Frederike Brion, one of the many women whom he was to love and leave. Natural phenomena are described in these poems as almost eerily animate: "The evening was already cradling the earth, and night hung on the mountains," he writes in "Welcome and Farewell"; "The oak, a towering giant, already stood in its cloak of mist where darkness peered out of the bushes with a hundred black eyes." In poems such as "Prometheus," he exalts the power of the individual heart to defy the gods, a quintessentially romantic theme related to that of *Faust*.

In 1771, Goethe returned to Frankfurt as a lawyer. He soon moved to Wetzlar, where he could gain valuable legal experience at the site of the supreme court of appeals of the Holy Roman Empire. The stay at Wetzlar provided much of the raw material for *Die Leiden des jungen Werthers* (*The Sorrows of Young Werther*), the epistolary novel whose publication in 1774 made Goethe and his anguished hero famous. Goethe's attraction to a friend's fiancée and the suicide of an acquaintance came together in the character of Werther, who so immerses himself in his own emotional turmoil and in his obsessive love for someone else's fiancée that suicide becomes his only escape. Werther's passion for nature, for Homer, and for Ossian links him to the storm and stress movement, of which he has remained perhaps the most characteristic exemplar. Many decades later, Goethe was still best known to the general public as the creator of Werther.

Years at Court

In Wetzlar, Goethe also wrote several plays and operettas and was briefly engaged to be married. The engagement ended when he moved again, this time to the court at Weimar. Although Goethe continued to travel, Weimar remained his home from 1775 until his death. Already well-known as a writer, Goethe was invited to the court by Duke Karl August, and he quickly became an indispensable government functionary, administering everything from military recruiting to mining. He also worked during this time on numerous plays—early versions of *Faust*, *Egmont* (1787), *Iphigenie auf Tauris* (1787), and *Torquato Tasso* (1790)—and a novel, *Wilhelm Meisters Lehrjahre* (*Wilhelm Meister's Apprenticeship*, 1796), which he had no time to finish. In 1786, he left for Italy, where he took a lengthy vacation visiting ancient ruins and rethinking his theories about art.

Later Life

On his return to Weimar in 1788, Goethe began living with Christiane Vulpius, whom he married in 1806 and who bore him a son. He rewrote and completed much of the work he had begun before his departure, and he continued to write new plays and lyrics. The influence of the storm and stress movement faded, replaced by a new classicism—the result of his visit to Italy. The *Roman Elegies* (1795), written during this time, reflect his new attachment to Italy and to Christiane Vulpius. All the works begun before the Italian journey and finished afterward reflect this change in attitude.

During the 1790s, Goethe became a friend and voluminous correspondent of Johann Christoph Friedrich von Schiller (1759–1805), the poet and dramatist. Schiller formulated in theoretical terms much of what Goethe did instinctively in his poems, plays, and novels, encouraging in particular Goethe's return to and rethinking of poetry and *Faust*. Their close friendship lasted until Schiller's death in 1805. During this time, Goethe also directed the duke's theater at Weimar and pursued his scientific interests, publishing works on plant morphology and on optics. Throughout his life, Goethe studied geology, botany, and anatomy; of his massive collected works, fourteen volumes deal with scientific subjects.

In 1808, Goethe wrote *Die Wahlverwandtschaften* (Elective Affinities), a strange novel in which two couples waver between adulterous passion and deliberate self-mastery. The conflict between the demands of self-expression and those of self-control (necessary for one's own sake and for the sake of others) was of deep concern to Goethe and surfaces often in his work, particularly in *Faust*. Toward the end of his life, his outlook and interests continually evolving, Goethe came under the influence of oriental motifs, as reflected in his book of poetry *Der Westöstliche Divan* (*West-Easterly Divan*, 1819). He also wrote an autobiography, *Dichtung und Wahrheit* (*Poetry and Truth*, 1811–1833). Goethe died in 1832.

Faust

Regarded by most critics as Goethe's greatest achievement, *Faust* fascinated the poet throughout his life. He seems to have begun writing the play in 1773, borrowing the subject from a sixteenth-century German story about a magician who sells his soul to the devil. Apparently there was a historical Faust, Georgius Sabellicus Faustius, sixteenth-century teacher, magician, and astrologer of bad character. The earliest account of his life is known as the first *Faust-book*, published in 1587 in Frankfurt-am-Main. There Faust is said to have traded his soul to the devil for twenty-four years of pleasure. A later version, translated into English, became the basis for Christopher Marlowe's *The Tragicall History of Dr. Faustus* (1604). In eighteenth-century Germany, a much-abridged, far-cicalized version of the drama was frequently performed in puppet theaters. All these earlier *Fausts* end with the hero's damnation.

Goethe's version went through many transformations. Gradually, the early emphasis on Faust's emotional life, typical of storm and stress, gave way (in what became Part II of the play) to an exploration of Faust's actions in the world. The earliest version of Goethe's *Faust* was written in 1773 and became known as the *Urfaust* when it was finally published in 1887. In 1790, Goethe published *Faust: A Fragment*, which was longer than the earlier version, and in 1808 came *Faust, Part I*, which was longer yet. Twenty-three years later, Part II was finished and in 1832, after Goethe's death, it was finally published.

Because it was written over so long a period of time, *Faust* has a fragmented quality. Its various episodes reflect different verse styles, moods, and even literary doctrines. Goethe, always a bundle of contradictions, was fond of referring to himself as a chameleon. More than any of his other works, *Faust* reveals his variability, his shifting views of the same problems.

One major change in Goethe's attitude is said to have occurred during his trip to Italy, where he visited ancient ruins and absorbed the artistic and architectural achievements of ancient Rome. Certainly, as he grew older Goethe became less interested in gothic art and more interested in classicism. The shift is clearly visible in *Faust*. The "gothic" depictions in Part I of the scholar's study (a narrow room with a soaring, vaulted ceiling), of alchemy, and of witches are succeeded by the classical characters, meters, and symbolism of Part II. Instead of focusing on a stormy Promethean figure scorning compromise, Part II depicts an entire world.

In Part II, Faust magically conjures up for the German emperor a pageant of classical figures. Among them is Helen of Troy, with whom he falls in love. The pageant explodes, but in Act III Faust is present at the fall of Troy and rescues Helen. They marry, and in their son, Euphorion, said to mingle the passion of romanticism with the order of classicism, is achieved a perfect if momentary balance between classical and gothic elements. Euphorion dies, however, as does Helen, and in Act IV and Act V Faust is back in Germany, seeking satisfaction in social engineering. With the help of magic, he drains and cultivates land formerly under water and then has an elderly couple killed so that their land will be available for his plans. Finally he renounces magic, goes blind, and dies, mistaking the workers who dig his grave for the industrious builders of a new society. To Mephistopheles's chagrin, however, Faust is apparently not damned; cherubs carry him up to heaven.

Part II of *Faust* is rarely performed; its shifts between dream and reality and between Greece and Germany make it hard to produce or even read. The contrast it provides to Part I, though, is important and is characteristic of all of Goethe's work, where classical and romantic elements are never wholly separated. Even the intensely sentimental *Sorrows of Young Werther* contains an antiromantic element, for Werther is seen not only through his own self-indulgent eyes but through the eyes of his editor as well, whose dry objectivity makes Werther seem inevitably a bit silly. As a result, the reader feels torn, half caught up in the hero's turbulent emotions and half detached and skeptical. Goethe seems to have felt both ways at once, and he believed that each half needed the other. Personal passion, he felt, must be balanced by a sense of social responsibility and self-control; otherwise, it will destroy either the impassioned soul itself, as in Werther's case, or another soul, as in Faust's destruction of Gretchen. The struggle to achieve this balance is depicted again and again in Goethe's work.

R.H.

ESSAY QUESTIONS WITH ANSWERS

Faust, Part I

5.1   The "Prologue in Heaven" depicts the Lord and Mephistopheles conversing about the state of humanity. The Lord calls Faust his servant and evidence that his hope for humankind is justified. But Mephistopheles finds Faust a perfect example of humankind's pitiable, misguided state. How could the same man suggest such opposing views of the human condition?

Answer   Both the Lord and Mephistopheles agree that Faust epitomizes the scholar wholly dedicated to the pursuit of knowledge through reason, a powerful gift granted to humankind by heaven. But they differ radically in their views of humankind's use of reason. The power of reason includes the power to make mistakes. Reason allows human beings to judge, to aspire, and to err. It also cuts them off from the rest of nature so that they cannot be simply and un-self-consciously content. The result, according to Mephistopheles, is that people use reason "not the least/except to be more beastly than any beast."* The human error and self-torment born of the abuse of reason are for Mephistopheles a cause for ridicule and even pity and lead finally to damnation.

To the Lord, on the other hand, the unquiet caused by a person's ability to reason is inseparable from that person's aspiration to greatness. True, the intellectual human being has a greater ability to do evil than a plant, but that is no reason for a person to be cut off from the natural world. People are in fact bound to nature by reason, which fuels a person's restlessness, forcing the person to change and grow. This process of change and growth is the same natural force that turns acorns to trees: "The gardener knows when the sapling first turns green/That flowers and fruit will make the future bright," the Lord tells Mephistopheles. Faust's striving is as integral a part of natural life as the bud which unfolds into a flower.

*Translated by Louis Macneice, New York, Oxford University Press, 1957. All references to *Faust* in this chapter are to the Macneice translation.

Faust's study suggests this two-sided view of his pursuits. It is a claustro-phobically small room with vaulted ceilings. Oppressively stuffed with manu-scripts and instruments, it nonetheless symbolizes Faust's soaring aspirations. The discontent that makes Faust a candidate for salvation makes him also a willing accomplice of Mephistopheles. Yet it allows Faust to escape damnation. To win Faust over, Mephistopheles fans the restlessness that he will then futilely seek to satisfy with trivial pleasures. Ultimately it is self-satisfaction, not emo-tional turmoil, that Mephistopheles needs to induce in Faust in order to prove his point. Faust's restless aspirations are inseparable from his profound frustration and from the havoc he wreaks on Gretchen's life and family, but they are also inseparable from his human and natural essence, which is to grow and change.

Faust's peculiar yet exemplary position as the archetypal human soul being struggled over by heaven and hell can be clarified if he is compared with Gretchen. Unlike Faust, she is not restless and dissatisfied, yet she is clearly saved and heaven-bound at the end of Part I. Certainly, she seems closer to God throughout her pious life than is the skeptical Faust. From the start, Gretchen is a lost cause as far as Mephistopheles is concerned. "Over that girl I have no power," he says after he sees her leaving church. Gretchen's simple faith is a straighter and less dangerous road to salvation than the one taken by Faust. Even after she has accidentally killed her mother, borne an illegitimate child, and drowned it, she can be saved because she acknowledges her guilt and welcomes the judgment and punishment that follow. When Faust urges her to flee, she cannot, despite her fear of death, for in accepting the execution she accepts the authority of God and her need for absolution. Ironically, when Faust enters her cell, she mistakes him for her executioner. His recklessness has killed her body just as his "rescue" of her from death would kill her soul.

Had the Lord said to Mephistopheles, "Look at Gretchen, my servant," he would have won that particular point instantly. But he would also, by impli-cation, have left all the restless souls, like Faust, to the devil. In choosing the apparently unlikely Faust as his example, the Lord startles Mephistopheles and encourages a false confidence that will blind him to the hopelessness of his wager. Of course, when God ultimately wins, he wins more decisively for the unlikeliness of his standard-bearer.

5.2 Faust's soul does go up to heaven at the end of Part II, as Gretchen's does at the end of Part I. But in the meantime Faust's aspirations have caused many people around him to suffer abominably. Given the fact that Goethe subtitled Faust "A Tragedy," can the last-minute salvation of Faust and Gretchen be read as a happy ending?

Answer   Certainly the bulk of the play seems tragic. Unlike earlier versions of the story, Goethe's *Faust* is not really about a battle for a soul, and so the Lord's final victory has far less impact than the series of defeats Faust undergoes during his life. Faust's striving may be a source of affirmation, but it results in loss as well as growth, in self-deception as well as self-education. At the end of Part I, Gretchen and her family have been demolished. At the end of Part II, Faust mistakes workers digging his grave for the builders of a new society. As it has been realized on earth, which to him is all that counts, Faust's life has been unhappy and misguided.

Yet Goethe himself said, "I'm not born to be a tragic poet, since my nature is conciliatory."* *Faust* is not a wholly pessimistic play. The last-minute salvation represents a conciliation of sorts, and Goethe's universe finally embraces both tragedy and comedy. Change and loss also imply animation and continuity. As the "Prologue in Heaven" makes clear, the cosmos must include negative as well as positive forces. Raphael, Gabriel, and Michael present increasingly violent descriptions of the cosmos, which contains not just the sun but also "dread night" and "blight of lightning." Yet all are contained within a divine order. The universe is meant to include both sun and storm, order and chaos, good and evil. The Lord chats casually with Mephistopheles because Mephistopheles too belongs to the universe and plays a role in the overall scheme of things, provoking error and thus movement. For people must be active if they are to enjoy "the living wealth of beauty./The changing Essence which ever works and lives. . . ."

This "changing Essence" contains a logical contradiction that is essential to Goethe's view of the cosmos. For the essence is by definition *un*changing, a divine element in humanity and the world that remains perfectly constant, keeping, as the Archangels say, the "high state of their first day." But *change* also is evident in "the gentle movement of Thy day." Paradoxically, this essence can be experienced only in change as it manifests itself in life, "which floats in flickering appearance."

This inclusive view of the universe, then, embraces both tragic and comic aspects. Faust's immersion in what he calls "eventfulness" results in the ruin of Gretchen and in his own self-deception. But it also aligns him with the ceaseless movement of all things in nature.

In such a world, Mephistopheles's purely negative efforts are doomed. Goethe's universe teems with movement and creativity, with deaths and new births.

---

*Quoted in Henry Hatfield, *Goethe*, New Directions, New York, 1963, p. 36.

Mephistopheles is like a person who steps on an ant hill in the hope of killing all the ants; a few ants may be killed, but many scurrying insects will survive, will reproduce, and will defeat that person's hopeless effort to de-create a world bent on endless self-renewal. Faust's destructive nature is even part of that process, though he cannot recognize this. "Always new blood, fresh blood, circulates again," he complains. "So it goes on, it's enough to drive one crazy."

If Goethe's vision of the cosmos precludes the triumph of Mephistopheles's negativism, it does not preclude individual tragedy. If people are aligned with the divine essence, they are also a vulnerable, fleeting manifestation of it. In Part I, Faust identifies himself alternately with God and with a worm crushed "by some casual heel," and in a sense he is both.

5.3　Why does Faust reject the scholarship through which he had hoped to learn the secret of the universe? What tempting alternative does Mephistopheles offer?

Answer　Faust is above all fed up with his inability to affect life outside his tiny study. The medicines he made with his father did not really cure anyone during the plague. The magical visions he conjures up cannot be grasped or imitated. He cannot use what he learns and sees in order to act, yet only action now appeals to him.

The two visions Faust conjures up before the arrival of Mephistopheles suggest his frustration with mere knowledge. The sign of the Macrocosm provides a vision of nature in its entirety, but it is merely a vision of a process. Only if he discovers the source of that process can he not merely see but also act: "Infinite Nature," he asks, "where can I tap thy veins?"

Faust's rejection of scholarship is symbolized by his disgust with words. His cell-like room is heaped high with books he now calls "skeletons." He wants to end his "traffic in words" and find instead "what it is that girds the world together in its inmost being." He refuses to translate the start of the Gospel of John with the standard "In the beginning was the Word," insisting instead that "In the beginning was the Deed." Faust seeks the secret of the universe at the opposite extreme from words, of which he has had enough.

The Earth Spirit seems to offer power and action but scoffs at the inexperienced scholar as ill suited to action. It is then that suicide seems to be the only action available to him. But Mephistopheles's arrival provides an unexpected alternative: adventure in the world with supernatural aid. In following Mephistopheles into the world, then, Faust is following the Earth Spirit, rejecting mere words for deeds, scholarship for experience. Desperate for action, he can, with Mephistopheles's aid, become youthful, sophisticated, well dressed, and most of all, mobile, thus gaining the experience he has sadly missed.

Mephistopheles's offer of pleasure and complacent sensual enjoyment is not what lures Faust, who believes that satisfaction of any kind will always fade into restless striving. Faust's bargain, then, is a safe one for him. If ever Mephistopheles presents him with an experience so pleasurable that Faust wants it to endure, "Then let *that* day be my last," he says, certain that such a day will never occur. When he does say the crucial words at the end of Part II, he is deceived—mistaking gravediggers for builders—and he is dying, suggesting that that experience alone is truly satisfying.

In the meantime, Faust gains experience. "It is restless action makes the man," he tells Mephistopheles, and restless action is what he gets.

5.4   As a young man, Goethe aligned himself with the storm and stress revolt against Enlightenment values. Is Faust's insistence to Gretchen that "feeling is all" an endorsement of individualistic passion and a rejection of the Enlightenment belief in rationality?

Answer   Ultimately, the opposition of feeling and rationality must be seen as a false dichotomy. Intellect and emotion were never directly opposed for Goethe, as is suggested by his lifelong interest in scientific investigation as well as lyric poetry. In the context of *Faust*, the question is important but essentially unanswerable. As in *The Sorrows of Young Werther*, Goethe seems at once to be depicting and critiquing the storm and stress figure of the restless seeker who, guided by nature and the heart rather than by rules of conduct, is potentially dangerous to himself and others.

In contrast to the single-minded, passionless Wagner and the narrow-minded small-town gossipers around Gretchen, feeling is certainly an appealing alternative. Such feeling is not mere self-indulgence, for as Faust tells Mephistopheles of Gretchen, "Even when I catch fire upon her breast/Do I not always sense her woe?"

But as long as actions have consequences, feeling is not all. A world exists outside one's own desires, and in that world, as Gretchen discovers, what seemed beautiful can become as sordid as illegitimate pregnancy and infanticide. Feeling can become the tool of willful self-deception, as when Faust insists to Mephistopheles that his avowal of eternal love to Gretchen will not be false. Individual self-fulfillment demands the exploration and expression of emotion, while social responsibility requires its control. The reader's wavering between endorsement and condemnation of Faust's emotional intensity is an inevitable response to this paradox.

5.5 There is a good deal of apparently Christian symbolism in *Faust*. Faust is prevented from drinking poison by a burst of Easter music. It is Easter when Mephistopheles first visits him. Gretchen, of course, is deeply religious, and we learn of her grief and self-condemnation through her prayer to the Virgin Mary and her fainting at a hymn. The Lord appears in the "Prologue in Heaven," and heavenly voices intervene to announce Gretchen's salvation. At the end of Part II, cherubs carry Faust's soul to heaven. Is *Faust*, then, a Christian play with a Christian message?

Answer Not really. The Easter song that rescues Faust from his bottle of poison does so not by bringing him faith but by bringing back childhood memories which bind him to earthly existence. Easter itself, besides signifying the resurrection of Christ, suggests the world's natural rebirth as spring follows winter. Easter's significance for Faust, then, is essentially secular, a reminder of childhood pleasures and a symbol of his entry into the world from his tomblike study. Its significance for the townspeople is similarly secular; they take advantage of the holiday by singing suggestive songs and chatting of women and politics as they stroll outside the city gates.

For those with faith, Christ offers a vision of spiritual unity and an opportunity for purposeful action that might well appeal to Faust if he had faith and could accept a vision gained through another. But as Faust is constituted, skeptical and rebellious, Christianity provides no answers for him.

The final salvation of Gretchen and of Faust serves more as closure to their earthly lives than as entry into an afterlife. Goethe's play is not really concerned with what will happen to Faust's soul; it is not a theological speculation on whether particular actions lead to damnation. It is an exploration of how to live on earth, how to reconcile incompatible needs, how to be at once an individual and a harmonious part of a larger world. The ascension of Faust's soul to heaven is an affirmation not of Christianity but of life.

5.6 Many readers of *Faust* have felt that the play is fragmented, a collection of episodes more than a coherent whole. There is even confusion about what actually happens. How many times do Faust and Gretchen see each other? Does the murder of Valentin follow the initial seduction by several days or by a year?

When does Gretchen kill her mother? What reason could Goethe have for dramatizing his story in so confusing and piecemeal a way?

Answer   Goethe said of *Faust* that while it has a beginning and an end, it does not form a whole—as life does not. The fragmentation of *Faust* does give it a feeling of inclusiveness that resembles life. The play seems open-ended, as if anything could happen, and it seems to leave nothing out. A wide range of verse styles appear, from the typically German four-beat rhyming lines borrowed from the sixteenth-century poet Hans Sachs, to the witches' doggerel, to Gretchen's ballads, to Faust's meditative blank verse, suggesting again that nothing has been left out.

This inclusiveness allows contradictory points of view to appear equally valid at different moments: Faust's rejection of scholarship is convincing, even though we know from Mephistopheles that it is playing into his hands; Gretchen's revulsion from Mephistopheles has impact, even as we feel the devil's charm. As Faust accepts the bargain, his denigration of all life has to offer seems true, as does his contradictory yearning for experience. As in life, many questions are left unanswered. The openness and uncertainty allow Goethe to portray life in extraordinarily broad terms so that it can embrace the contradictory elements of light and dark, good and evil, chaos and order—all integral parts of the cosmos, according to the Archangels.

The fragmentation also results from the requirements of the play's action. If Faust is to retain the reader's sympathy and interest, his seduction of Gretchen must take place to a certain extent out of earshot, lest he appear too vile and she too gullible. Thus the intimacy proceeds during those times when we do not see the couple; each time they return to our view, they seem closer. In contrast to the utterly corrupt tone of Martha's conversation with Mephistopheles, their growing intimacy seems innocent, almost inevitable.

The reader's confusion about precisely what happens to Gretchen results in part from her isolation from the community. She has no one to whom she can explain herself or her actions, nor—as revealed by the spinning-wheel song—does she fully understand them herself. Her emotions can be inferred from her sympathy with the pregnant, unmarried Barbara and her fainting in church, but she never tells anyone what has happened to her. On the reader's part, the result is an intense sharing of Gretchen's confusion. Without a community with which to share her experience, Gretchen is desperately alienated. The fragmented presentation of her story forces the reader to share that alienation.

Gretchen's only form of self-expression is through "folk songs" (actually written by Goethe), those simple, apparently anonymous ballads expressing communal experience. Her song about the king of Thule suggests her idealistic notion of love; her song at the monotonously revolving spinning wheel suggests her hypnotic imprisonment by love and the futile restlessness it causes; and in prison, she sings a gruesome tale of murder and resurrection. Similarly, the church hymn expresses her self-condemnation. Gretchen has no private voice in which to express her dreams and disappointments. She is the very opposite of Faustian individualism, for her only outlet is through the communal language of folk songs and hymns. When that language judges and condemns her, she has no escape.

If the story of Gretchen's seduction seems at times hackneyed and at times obscure, it is because the reader can understand it only where it coincides with common knowledge and can be expressed in communal terms. This limitation is also its strength. The reader's ignorance is the result of, and an equivalent to, Gretchen's dumb suffering.

R.H.

SUGGESTED READINGS

Atkins, Stuart, *Goethe's Faust: A Literary Analysis* (1969).
Fairley, Barker, *A Study of Goethe* (1947).
Gillies, Alexander, *Goethe's Faust: An Interpretation* (1957).
Hatfield, Henry, *Goethe* (1963).
Lange, Victor (ed.), *Goethe: A Collection of Critical Essays* (1968).

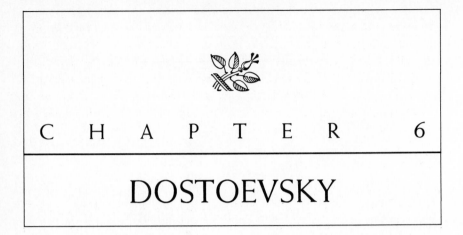

C H A P T E R 6

DOSTOEVSKY

Social and Historical Background

"Worst of all is that my nature is base and too passionate: everywhere and in everything I go to the ultimate limit, all my life I have crossed beyond the frontier," Dostoevsky wrote in a letter, sounding much like one of his characters. The shameful act—in this case, having again gambled away all his money— and the self-contempt are familiar features of Dostoevsky's novels. Most suggestive, however, is the metaphor of extremity, of limits transgressed. The heroic figures of the nineteenth-century Russian novel, characters and authors alike, carry immensities within them. Their introspections discover no meager "I" but whole landscapes of thought and feeling where crises of private life grow into struggles with the ultimate, where the limits of human possibility are tested, human nature defined, and the future of Russia decided. In the hands of a Dostoevsky or a Tolstoy, novels widen into epics.

One might ascribe the amplitude and intensity of the Russian novel to the Russian soul, but the historical situation of Russia in the nineteenth century offers a better explanation. In many ways, Russian writers felt themselves involved in occasions of national and human destiny, for in the last part of the century Russian society underwent an epochal transformation. The constellation of processes that is often called modernization—the development of a market economy, the shift in domination from the landed gentry to the monied classes, urbanization, secularization, democratization, an increase in the social mobility of all classes—had changed the nature of life in western Europe dramatically in the years between the French Revolution (1789) and the Great Exhibition in

London (1851). Russia, which in this period felt only the incipiency of these developments, faced the modernized west apprehensively. Russians had always felt uncertain about their country's status in the community of western nations and painfully aware of its political backwardness and economic underdevelopment; this customary anxiety over the nation's cultural identity moved toward crisis as the century progressed. It is against this background of events and the variety of Russian reactions to them that we can begin to develop a sense of Dostoevsky's career as a writer and intellectual.

Early Life and Work

Fyodor Dostoevsky was born in Moscow in 1821. The most striking event of his early life was the murder of his father, a small landowner, by the serfs he customarily mistreated. Freud's essay "Dostoevsky and Parricide" (1928) speculates on the significance of this calamity in relation to Dostoevsky's lifelong epilepsy, bouts of compulsive gambling, and treatment of parricide in *The Brothers Karamazov.*

Dostoevsky's schooling prepared him for a career as a military engineer. However, he left government service after only a short time, and with the publication of *Poor Folk* in 1845, he began his writing career. In this short novel, Dostoevsky treats the subject that Nikolai Gogol had recently brought to the nation's attention: the miserable lives of the poorest class of clerks and civil servants. However, where Gogol describes the comic failure of small men like Akaky Akakyevich in "The Overcoat," Dostoevsky sees worthy souls degraded by social injustice. In *Poor Folk,* he wrote a novel exactly suited to the new humanism and increased concern with social questions so characteristic of Russian intellectual circles in the 1840s, and the book was an immediate success. Dostoevsky was quickly and flatteringly brought into the highest circle of literary society, which included Belinsky, Turgenev, and Nekrasov. However, as a result of his involvement in literary quarrels and jealousies and, perhaps, his clumsiness in society, he quickly found himself an outsider again.

Dostoevsky's second book, *The Double* (1846), while dealing with the same strata of society as *Poor Folk,* struck out in a new direction. Its depiction of the disordered consciousness of Golyadkin, a man haunted by his double, anticipates the psychological dramas of Dostoevsky's later novels.

Political Involvements

Dostoevsky's social sympathies led in 1846 to his joining the gatherings of the Petrashevsky Circle, a group of intellectuals who met regularly to discuss political philosophy and their hopes for reform. The Petrashevists were not a highly radical group; their sympathies lay with the ideas of utopian, nonrevolutionary socialists such as Cabet and Fourier. Dostoevsky's initial enthusiasm was for a Christian socialism which would combine piety, self-sacrifice, and cooperation to the end of creating a universal brotherhood of peoples on earth. However, there is evidence that he moved during these early years toward an atheistic and materialistic socialism of the kind he opposed vigorously in his later career, joining a second political circle that was more inclined toward revolutionary action. In 1849, Dostoevsky and a number of other Petrashevists were arrested and charged as conspirators. After several months of imprisonment and a lengthy trial, Dostoevsky and some of the others were sentenced to death. On the day of execution, the condemned were brought to the parade ground to be shot. The whole grim ceremony of preparation was performed, but at the last moment their reprieve was announced. The mock execution had been contrived by Nicholas I as a prelude to their official punishment. Dostoevsky was sent to Siberia, where he spent four years in penal servitude and four more years as a soldier.

Dostoevsky somehow derived from these painful years in exile what he felt to be a kind of personal resurrection. His prison experiences put an end to his optimistic socialist humanism. They brought him into contact with people at the extreme limits of human behavior who contributed much to the figures in the later novels: convicts who admitted their crimes with a pride and contempt that took them beyond morality to the region where, as Raskolnikov of *Crime and Punishment* and Ivan Karamazov propose, "all things are permitted"; men of immense, violent energy without any positive object, like Stavrogin of *The Possessed*; and many more in whom, despite their debasement, Dostoevsky saw something to be valued. The understanding that Dostoevsky brought away from his exile was also a kind of humanism, but one from which any facile belief in natural human rationality and goodness had been expunged, replaced by a humbling conviction of people's present sinfulness, a faith in their possible redemption, and an insistence that people be allowed the freedom which alone could allow genuine regeneration.

Slavophilic Theories

On his return to Saint Petersburg in 1859, Dostoevsky, now married, resumed his writing with high purpose. In his journalism of the 1860s and 1870s, he developed a vision of Russian culture that combined religion, politics, philosophy of history, and prophecy. He proposed a return to the soil from which, he felt, the rationalist intellectuals and reformers of the day had become damagingly estranged. For Dostoevsky, it was the Russian peasants, with their mystical faith and natural relation to the land, who embodied the distinctive national identity of Russia. Furthermore, Russia, entrusted with this population of the truly human, was destined in time to work the salvation of a west sunk in soulless materialism.

This extreme Slavophilism, which Dostoevsky developed over the last twenty years of his life, was an implausible solution to the problems of social change and dislocation it was designed to remedy. Dostoevsky's own works illustrate both the problems themselves and the weaknesses of his proposed solution. The heroes of these novels are indeed cut off from any positive tradition; their energies and passions, though considerable, too often achieve no end but self-destruction. Their malady is in part social; they suffer from the historical processes which had put an end to the old Russia without yet bringing a new world into existence. To this generation of "superfluous men," as they were called, Dostoevsky proposed a return to the old world, to the traditional values represented by Orthodox religion and the czar. The poverty of this hopeful but backward-looking proposal is manifest in Dostoevsky's novels, in which he could nowhere bring into existence the "positive hero" who would embody the values of this tradition.

Notes from the Underground and Crime and Punishment

Dostoevsky's life in the year 1864 gives a good sense of the hellish conditions under which he did much of his best work. In this year, Notes from the Underground was written in the shadow of his wife's painful illness and death and the imminent bankruptcy of the journal Dostoevsky and his brother edited; it was written, furthermore, under the pressures of serial publication, which required that he submit early parts for publication before later parts were written or even planned. By year's end, Dostoevsky had also lost his brother, fallen disastrously into debt, signed a cruelly disadvantageous contract which made him the virtual chattel of an unscrupulous publisher, and, finally, fled to Germany to escape his creditors.

Dostoevsky's five-year stay in western Europe was no less hectically eventful, dominated by his uncontrollable gambling, an unhappy affair with Apollinariya Suslova, a second marriage, and the continued pressure of working with the printer's copy boy at his elbow. The first novel he published under these circumstances was Crime and Punishment (1866). The protagonist, Raskolnikov, who murders an old pawnbroker in the name of humanitarianism and reason, is a significant figure in Dostoevsky's long argument with the rationalist intellectuals of his day. Raskolnikov is one of Dostoevsky's "strong personalities" who is willing, for the sake of an idea and the love of humanity in the abstract, to place himself beyond morality. Reasoning that this greedy old woman is no more than a parasite, he resolves to kill her in the name of the greater good. Dostoevsky demonstrates that this is the necessary outcome of any philosophy that places the practical good of the individual, that is, material interest, above morality. The long process of Raskolnikov's expiation and spiritual regeneration represents Dostoevsky's antithesis to the rationalist thesis.

Later Works

The three other great novels of Dostoevsky's maturity are *The Idiot* (1869), in which Prince Myshkin stands as his first, highly ambiguous, attempt to create the "positively good man"; *The Possessed* (1871), Dostoevsky's attack on what he felt to be the low amoralism that posed as political daring, in which he again treated the appalling freedom of intellect unrooted in faith or morality; and *The Brothers Karamazov* (1879).

"The Legend of the Grand Inquisitor," which Ivan tells to Alyosha in *The Brothers Karamazov*, is the culminating exposition of Dostoevsky's philosophy of humanity. In this parable, Christ returns to earth at the time of the Inquisition. He is recognized by all and walks among the people, heals the sick, and raises the dead. On the orders of the ancient and powerful Grand Inquisitor, he is imprisoned. The tale that Ivan tells is the Grand Inquisitor's monolog as he stands alone at night with his holy prisoner. The Inquisitor accuses Christ of burdening humankind with the excruciating responsibility of its own freedom. He, the Inquisitor, has served humanity better by replacing the freedom that people dread with the authority of the Church and giving people instead benefits more in keeping with their real capacities. Christ, the Inquisitor insists, has overestimated people, who are in truth "weak and vile," willing to trade their freedom for any rule which will promise "earthly bread" and a light yoke. Like Raskolnikov, the Grand Inquisitor is one of Dostoevsky's humanitarians who, in the act of putting material well-being above all, have lost touch with any higher vision and thereby degraded humankind. As Ivan admits, his Grand Inquisitor is an atheist. With the loss of faith in God, people know no limit in the pursuit of their lower needs. The Inquisitor's humanitarianism, which Dostoevsky meant to stand for the spiritual poverty of Roman Catholicism and socialism, begins by eliminating God and ends by subjugating a people much diminished in humanity.

As "The Legend of the Grand Inquisitor" suggests, Dostoevsky's later novels became parables and metaphysical melodramas that linked dramas of personal conflict, rendered with great psychological acuity, to issues of political and spiritual significance. In these novels and in his Slavophile journalism, many of Dostoevsky's Russian readers saw an alternative to the materialist philosophy which seemed to go hand in hand with political liberalism. In the last great event of Dostoevsky's life, his 1880 speech at the unveiling of the Pushkin Monument in Moscow, he was acclaimed by an adulatory crowd as the prophet and avatar of a spiritualized Russian nationalism. Dostoevsky died half a year later, in January 1881.

ESSAY QUESTIONS WITH ANSWERS

Notes from the Underground

6.1 In what sense can these "notes" be said to issue from underground? Is the underground a physical location, or is it some other kind of place?

Answer Although the underground man speaks to us from what he calls "my corner," a dingy room on the outskirts of Saint Petersburg, the "underground" (a more literal translation would be "the space beneath the floorboards") refers to no physical place but instead to the underground man's sense of himself as an outsider, alienated from the common territory of ordinary feelings and everyday life. He has no friends and no work; his past is featureless, and he anticipates no future. The underground is in one respect, then, a location in society, the shadowy region where solitary and unhappy lives run their course.

However, the underground takes on another aspect when one considers the underground man's attitude toward his own alienation. His first words, "I am a sick man," suggest that he is an unfortunate, deserving of pity. But his next words, spoken after a significant pause—"I am a spiteful man"—decline any pity and suggest that he is not so much an outcast as a willing and unrepentant exile.* Although his marginal situation in life seems to deprive him of dignity and pleasure, the underground man writes as if he had freely chosen this degradation. He boasts of his most shameful feelings: envy, spitefulness, self-pity. He wears his failure and misery as badges of honor. The underground man may in some sense be sick, but he refuses any cure. As he tells the reader, he takes pleasure in his pain.

The underground life is thus more than just a fate dealt out by society; it is also a posture, a way of situating himself in relation to the world at large that the underground man has willfully and perversely adopted. It is also a posture

---

*Translated by Constance Garnett, with revisions by Avraham Yarmolinsky, *Three Short Novels of Dostoevsky*, Garden City, New York, Doubleday and Company, 1960. All references to *Notes from the Underground* in this chapter are from the Garnett translation.

of opposition. The underground man's willing descent into self-abasement challenges the reader's confidence in what the underground man sarcastically calls "the true normal interests of man"—interests such as success, dignity, self-respect, and happiness. From the perspective of the underground man's behavior, any view of humanity which focuses only on these "normal interests" and assumes that people will rationally pursue them is damagingly incomplete, excluding the irrationalities, the quirks of will and emotion, and the sheer malignity which the underground man displays. Any such optimistic view of human nature is reproached by the underground man himself with his mad outbursts and self-lacerations, which issue from the underground that represents the irrational in people.

6.2 Who tells the story of the underground man? In what way is this method of narration well suited to the subject and themes of *Notes from the Underground?*

Answer The underground man tells the reader his story in the form of a diary or memoir. The events of the story, which consist entirely of his own experiences, are conveyed to the reader as the underground man understands and represents them. It is the underground man's understanding of his experiences rather than these events in themselves which occupies the story's foreground. The true subject of *Notes from the Underground* is thus the idiosyncratic consciousness of the underground man himself, or more accurately, his self-consciousness. The underground man's constant and inescapable subject is himself: his grievances, shame, frustration, and anger. These feelings are described with the same distinctive colorations and distortions he brings to everything he tries to grasp.

The underground man's most distinctive habit of mind is his ambivalence, his inability to let any judgment or course of action stand without reversing it. He courts acceptance and then rejects it; he plans endlessly but never acts; he suspects every motive of concealing its opposite. If he confesses to being spiteful, he later claims that he was lying—from spite. Because the underground man can view himself only from the standpoint of his ambivalence, his sense of identity is hopelessly unstable and insecure. His remorseless self-examination leads only from one provisional and exaggerated self-conception to the next: Am I a coward? A hero? An insect? A man?

The first-person narration allows the reader to experience this giddy process as it is enacted by the underground man in his attempts to make himself understood both to himself and to his readers. This allows Dostoevsky to dramatize with great vividness the agitation and endless ambivalence characteristic of obsessional self-regard. The underground man stares, transfixed by his changing expression in the mirror that is his memoir. He makes faces. He scowls and sets himself laughing; he jeers and frightens himself.

The underground man's memoir is thus not merely a description of his distressed consciousness but an enactment of it, and this lends the story an immediacy and animation which edge it from narrative toward performance. In fact, the underground man often addresses his readers as if we were an audience assembled before him. Sometimes he addresses us as "gentlemen" in tones which range from wheedling to sarcastic. He yells and shouts recriminations at us. At times, his tone places him far above us; at other times, he softens and conde-scends to address us as "we."

The immediacy and direct address of the first-person voice allow the un-derground man to buttonhole the reader like an insistent stranger on a city street. We may want to ignore him and walk away, but we are forced to stop and listen and—at least for the moment—consider, Who is he to me? Thus, the first-person narrative not only serves to vivify the distinctive consciousness and self-consciousness of the underground man but is an ideal method by which Dostoevsky can insist that we examine the consequentiality to ourselves of this inconsequential hole and corner stranger.

6.3   Can the underground man's eccentricity be understood in psychological terms? At the dinner for Zverkov, what emotions does the underground man experience?

Answer   The incident of the dinner for Zverkov shows the underground man at his most typical. During a rare visit to an acquaintance, the underground man encounters some school fellows he has not seen in years, who are planning a dinner for one of their number, Zverkov, who has been appointed to an army post. Despite his long-standing contempt for these men, whom he sees as petty and smug—shallow, dull-witted boys, he tells us, who have become shallow, dull-witted men—and despite his special contempt for Zverkov, he offers to join them.

He spends the day of the dinner in anxious anticipation, fussing over the threadbare clothes he fears may embarrass him and imagining a triumph: "I dreamed of getting the upper hand. They would abandon Zverkov, he would sit on one side, silent and ashamed, while I should crush him. Then, perhaps, we would be reconciled and drink to our everlasting friendship. . . ." (Part II, Chapter 3). But even while envisioning this extravagant success, he is smitten with despair. He is certain they will despise him and thus is almost too frightened to go. Finally, as if to round out his vacillation, he tells us, "I did not care a straw really."

Of course, at the dinner he immediately destroys whatever goodwill the company may have felt toward him. He mimics Zverkov, he bridles at imagined insults; he withdraws into himself; he insults Zverkov, he harangues the table; he abjectly pleads for their friendship. When they leave, he dashes after them, uncertain whether to issue a challenge or beg their pardon.

It is easy enough to recognize the underground man's difficulty: a painfully exaggerated version of the hopes and anxieties all people feel in their relations with others. It seems reasonable to assume that the underground man's eccentricity has grown, at least in part, out of the wreck of these relations, which have foundered on the unpleasant but ordinary obstacles of a thwarted need for love, self-contempt, and anger. But the extraordinary magnitude of his distress is created by the underground man's sense of himself as utterly deprived. He feels that everybody else, including Zverkov and his friends, has what he lacks. He scorns them all for their undeserved success, but he also envies what they have and who they are, and he feels himself infinitely inferior to them. The underground man's endless vacillation between grandiosity and abjection represents the alternative pulsing of his envious rage at others and his terror at the emptiness within himself.

6.4 In a footnote at the beginning of the story, Dostoevsky directs our attention to the underground man's social and historical significance: "the writer of these notes not only may, but positively must, exist in our society, when we consider the circumstances in the midst of which our society is formed." What are the social circumstances surrounding the underground man? Do these circumstances suggest in what way the underground man may be, as Dostoevsky intimates, representative of his age?

Answer   The story takes place in Saint Petersburg, the cosmopolitan capital of a country in the middle of the long transition from a feudal and autocratic state into a more modern and egalitarian society. The chief agitators for this change were the intellectuals who demanded that Russia's political and social institutions be democratized and rationalized in accordance with the principle of "enlightened self-interest," the watchword of the utilitarian political economists who already dominated social thought in the west. These intellectuals were largely of the same class that predominates in Notes from the Underground, the educated people of the day who, given the nature of contemporary Russian society and the absence of a satisfactory outlet for their energies and ambitions, often had little choice but to join the nation's immense, stagnant bureaucracy. The underground man, who takes pains to remind us of his education, is a member of this unhappy legion of clerks who populate so much of nineteenth-century Russian literature.

It is impossible to imagine the underground man in any other setting than the city, and it is fitting that Dostoevsky has placed him in Saint Petersburg, which represented to his Russian readership the essence of modern, urban experience. The underground man is the prototypical stranger in the urban crowd, the anonymous passerby who conceals a life and a history which we never expect to hear. But in this case we do hear it, and we find out in addition how the crowded street we share, "that cheap bustle, that bare prose," looks to him. The underground man's obsessed plot to revenge himself on the officer who never makes way for him on Nevsky Prospekt is a classic dark comedy of city life, where a walk is "not a stroll so much as a series of innumerable miseries, humiliations, and resentments." The underground man's isolation is beyond remedy as long as he suffers from the belief that afflicts all people for whom society is no more than a crowd. As he says, "I am unique and they are all alike."

In addition to what it reveals about the milieu of the modern city, the underground man's conflict with the officer contains the germ of virtually all the story's social themes. The underground man acts to defend his dignity, which he feels the officer has offended. His implicit assumption is that he has a natural and indisputable right to the officer's respect not because of his character—the officer does not know him at all—but simply as a man and a citizen. Despite the fact that I am shameless, cowardly, and undignified, the underground man seems to say, it is my right to be treated honorably like any other person. His attitude assumes a society that is democratic in spirit if not yet in law or practice.

The underground man calls himself "a man affected by progress and European civilization" and "a man of the age." The political significance of these phrases can be understood in the context of events in France near the start of the century: the revolution and the career of Napoleon. The first, with its Declaration of the Rights of Man and Citizen, enacted democracy as theory, as force, and as national destiny, while the second demonstrated what democracy, the opportunity for any person to reach the highest ranks, could mean for the career of the individual. However, with the spread of liberal democratic sentiment during the nineteenth century came a growing awareness of the abiding contradictions of democratic life: the discrepancy between the abstract universal right to dignity and the free development of one's potential and the hard fact that the real exercise of this right was still largely limited to the privileged and propertied. The Napoleonic promise of "the career open to talents"—recall that the underground man models one of his daydream triumphs on Napoleon's victory at Austerlitz—was often foreclosed by economic and social realities.

The underground man suffers, albeit in an exaggerated way that he is not above lampooning, from this discrepancy between heroic aspirations and meager opportunities. He longs for some "vista of suitable activity . . . beneficent, good and, above all"—and here he sarcastically twists the knife in his own wound—"*ready made* (what sort of activity I had no idea, but the great thing was that it should be all ready for me) . . . I should come out into the light of day, almost riding a white horse and crowned with laurel. Anything but the foremost place I could not conceive for myself, and for that reason I quite contentedly occupied the lowest in reality. Either to be a hero or to grovel in the mud—there was nothing between."

As these mocking lines suggest, Dostoevsky was critical of what he thought of as liberal democratic politics and its conception of the individual in society. Dostoevsky endows his unhappy protagonist with ample quantities of that unbecoming emotion Tocqueville identified as most characteristic of democratic society: envy.

Yet when the underground man speaks of "the hell of unsatisfied desires turned inward," we can sense Dostoevsky's sympathy with his hero's aspirations. And when Dostoevsky claims that the underground man "positively must exist in our society," we are being asked to take his existence very seriously indeed. The underground man's grandiose ambitions, morbid sensitivity to insult, resentments, and paradoxical pride, which even insists on defending his inalienable right to act shamefully, dramatize the tragicomedy of democratic expectations encountering the more limited possibilities of an imperfectly democratic world.

6.5 "Which is better—cheap happiness or exalted sufferings?" the underground man asks. In Part I of *Notes from the Underground*, in a rambling diatribe, the underground man makes his case against "cheap happiness." What does he offer as an alternative? On what grounds does this alternative way of life make a claim on the reader?

Answer Amid the sarcasms and caprices the underground man launches in Part I, it is possible to discern an argument directed against the so-called utilitarian political economists, the predominant school of progressive social thinkers of the day. These were theorists who, attempting to formulate a science of society as successful as the rapidly developing sciences of nature, seized upon what they perceived as the individual's pursuit of pleasure and avoidance of pain as the natural law that would be the foundation for such a science. By recognizing self-interest, defined as the maximization of pleasure and the minimization of pain, as the single universal human motivation, we would have access to a "calculus of utility," which, it was argued, would allow society to rationally arrive at decisions to ensure "the greatest good for the greatest number."

It is this elegant formula for rationalizing society which the underground man derides as a formula for "cheap happiness." If the Crystal Palace—the showpiece of the 1851 Great Exhibition in London and the preeminent symbol of the nineteenth century's faith in material progress—is no more than an overelaborate manifestation of people's need to keep out of the rain, he asks, what makes it any better than a hen house? By reducing people to physical needs and their behavior to a mechanical subjection to these needs, the utilitarians reduce the individual to an animal or a machine, without true consciousness and free will. Society becomes "the ant heap." For the underground man, the utilitarians' claim to derive the "whole register of human advantages from the averages of statistical figures and political-economic formulas" cheapens the individual by replacing free decision with calculation, making the individual "not a human being but an organ stop" and reducing all human aspiration to the pursuit of material advantage and animal comfort.

Furthermore, the utilitarians are wrong to assume that a person need only be apprised of his or her best interest in order to pursue it. Do we, the underground man asks, always follow the rule of reason and act in our own best interest? What of the perversities, the appetite for pain, and the unmotivated malevolence that make up our personal and collective histories? Turning to Henry Thomas Buckle and his optimistic History of Civilization in England (1857–1861) which viewed universal history as the necessary progress of reason, the underground man asks how history, from Attila to the farcical Louis Napoleon and the recent invasion of Schleswig-Holstein, can be judged to have become more rational or less bloody.

If the individual is in one sense higher than the utilitarians claim, with their reduction of people to their needs, the individual is in another sense baser and less capable of rationally pursuing "his true normal interests" than the utilitarians realize. True to the underground man's nature as a "paradoxalist," it is precisely in people's unending perversity and irrationality that he places his faith for the individual's attainment of his or her "most advantageous advantage"—freedom. For it is the perverse unpredictability of the individual which shatters every system that tries to confine human possibility to the rule of elementary laws. Only freedom can allow people continued possession of what the underground man feels is "most precious and most important—that is our personality, our individuality." Against a narrow notion of humanity and its promise of "cheap happiness," the underground man urges the necessity that we be fully human and truly ourselves—in a word, authentic. In a world where the "normal and positive" has as its highest ambition the "snug berth" and where the complacent Zverkov is the standard of heroism and health, authenticity may be forced to show itself in negative forms—suffering, doubt, irrationality, sickness, coward-ice, self-abasement—all the traits of the anti-hero. To the degree that the underground man's highest claim is made in the name of authentic life itself, and against the "cheap happiness" that offers prudence in place of full humanity, his ultimate claim on the reader may not be so much psychological and historical as existential.

6.6   The underground man's claim on us is extreme. He argues that for the sake of our own authenticity it may be necessary not only to neglect but actually to oppose our own "normal and positive" advantage. Our full humanity, our "most advantageous advantage," may be won, he claims, only through a will-ingness to suffer. How does the underground man attempt to persuade the reader that authenticity is worth this price? What rhetorical ploys does he use to engage the reader in his argument?

Answer   The underground man enacts the painful heroism of authenticity with which he challenges us; he proves his argument on himself. He demonstrates the bravery of confessing his cowardice, and the honesty of admitting his in-sincerity. However, it is important to note that the antithetical elements in his behavior do not, as these paradoxical descriptions might suggest, cancel each other out, leaving him simply brave or simply honest. There are always further cowardices and insincerities. The underground man's real heroism lies in his inability, in fact his refusal, to come to rest in honesty or dishonesty or in any other fixed point in his hectic encounter with himself and the world. His courage lies in his submission to the endless processes of this encounter. The underground man's painful ambivalence is thus, from another perspective, a courageous open-ness, especially when compared with the closed-mindedness and complacency of Zverkov and his kind.

The underground man is a hero of uncertainty. He embodies the commitment to authentic life which he recommends to us: "perhaps the only goal on earth to which mankind is striving lies in this incessant process of attaining, in other words, in life itself, and not the thing to be attained, which must always be expressed as a formula, as positive as twice two makes four, and such positiveness is not life, gentlemen, but is the beginning of death." The final victory of the underground man's negative heroism is this creation of a way of attaining which may lead to the possibility of the fully human life.

Thus, the underground man's case for real life at any cost receives its most persuasive endorsement from his own willingness to pay the price. However, he also tries to persuade his audience by anticipating our responses to him and manipulating them to his own advantage. He recognizes the likelihood of our desire to separate ourselves from him, to dissociate ourselves from his repellent excesses and retreat behind our notion of normality. But he cuts off our escape by anticipating our objections. In Chap. 11 of Part I, he in effect speaks our lines for us: " 'Isn't that shameful, isn't that humiliating?' you will say, perhaps wagging your heads contemptuously." And he goes on, directing a ventriloquized tirade of outraged propriety against himself, only to conclude coolly, "Of course I have myself made up all the things you say." Among the myriad viewpoints the underground man can adopt is our own, and this destroys any confidence we may have in our ability to view him from some privileged remove. He knows us. When he addresses us as "gentlemen," it is impossible to miss the hint of mockery. He classes us among the few "gentlemen" of his story—Zverkov, the implacable officer on Nevsky Prospekt—philistines to whom, we must admit, we prefer the underground man.

The underground man's willingness to confess motives and feelings we all have but rarely have the courage to admit gives him a moral authority that allows him to speak for everyone. At the end of his narrative, the underground man asserts this authority to the fullest. "We," he writes, "are all divorced from life, we are all cripples, every one of us, more or less." If we in turn try to withdraw, denying our unhappy kinship, we only bring the final judgment against ourselves:

> Speak for yourself, you will say, and for your miseries in your underground holes, and don't dare to say "all of us"—excuse me, gentlemen, I am not justifying myself with that "all of us." As for what concerns me in particular I have only in my life carried to an extreme what you have not dared to carry half-way, and what's more, you have taken your cowardice for good sense, and have found comfort in deceiving your-selves. So that perhaps, after all, there is more life in me than in you. Look into it more carefully! (Part II, Chapter 10)

The underground man has thoroughly turned the tables on us. He, the scorned and deprived, has more of real life than we, with our families and homes and jobs. The underground man's performance has become a rhetoric of implication which challenges us to measure ourselves against this madman and suggests that our sanity and self-restraint may be the index of our inferiority to him.

6.7 What attitude toward literature is displayed by Dostoevsky in *Notes from the Underground*? How does that attitude relate to the theme of "authentic life" discussed by the underground man?

Answer The underground man is well-read, and he lets us know it. He mentions Shakespeare, Rousseau, Byron, and Heine as well as the Russian masters of the age: Pushkin, Gogol, Goncharov, and Lermontov. His own writing is at times consciously literary; he begins Part II of the "notes" with an epigraph from the poet Nekrasov and gives it the belletristic title "Apropos of the Wet Snow." Even his daydreams smell of literature; they are stagy and melodramatic. In a passage awash with clichés, he imagines dealing Zverkov a crushing public insult and the tragic consequences to himself:

> I shall be arrested, I shall be tried, I shall be dismissed from the service, thrown in prison, sent to Siberia. Never mind: In fifteen years when they let me out of prison I will trudge off to him, a beggar, in rags. I shall find him in some provincial town. He will be married and happy. He will have a grown-up daughter. . . . I shall say to him: "Look, monster, at my hollow cheeks and my rags! I've lost everything—my career, my happiness, art, science, *the woman I loved*, and all through you. Here are pistols. I have come to discharge my pistol and . . . and I . . . forgive you." Then I shall fire into the air and he shall hear nothing more of me. . . . (Part II, Chapter 5)

The underground man himself admits, embarrassed, that these are bits of Pushkin and Lermontov. Even the prostitute Liza knows enough to be able to say, "You speak somehow like a book."

At this point, Dostoevsky seems close to identifying literature itself with its capacity to embody our fantasies, as a variety of inauthenticity. In his closing peroration, the underground man explicitly associates our love for books with our "loathing for real life"; we have literature, he says, instead of life. Yet if we take this claim at face value, we cannot help but extend it to Dostoevsky's writing. Is there any way to save *Notes from the Underground* from the charge of inauthenticity?

It may be that Dostoevsky is not condemning literature as such but only a certain kind of literature and art. In Chap. 6 of Part I, the underground man tells us that among the many "careers" he has contemplated but never actually pursued is that of a "sluggard and glutton":

> I should have been a sluggard and a glutton, not a simple one, but, for instance, one with sympathies for everything good and beautiful. . . . I should have found for myself a form of activity in keeping with it, to be precise, drinking to the health of everything "good and beautiful." I should have snatched at every opportunity to drop a tear into my glass and then to drain it to all that is "good and beautiful." . . . An artist, for instance, paints a picture worthy of Gué. At once I drink to the health of the artist . . ., because I love all that is "good and beautiful."

This gourmandizing aestheticism is another form of "cheap happiness." It leaves the underground man, in this imagined vignette, with the full flesh, "good round belly," "triple chin," and "ruby nose" of a prosperous burgher. Art devoted only to the "good and beautiful," that is, art whose only ambition is to please, can never be adequately responsive to the full range of human experience. It refuses to stoop to the region of extreme and unpleasant feeling that the underground man inhabits. Unlike the underground man, the artist of the good and beautiful can never be truly honest, because he or she is too eager for the reader's good opinion. Instead of giving us ourselves and our world, such art endlessly copies itself. We get not even a picture *by* Gué but a derivative cliché "worthy of Gué."

The art of the good and beautiful, which gives us nothing but countless versions of the great-souled duelist who forgives all and fires nobly into the air, has much in common with the liberal rationalism that offends the underground man. Both replace the real individual, seen in ignoble particularity, with, as the underground man says, "some sort of impossible generalized man . . . born somehow from an idea." Both forsake reality for abstractions. Most damagingly, an art which is blind to people as they really are, unregenerate though that may be, also forfeits any hope of recognizing and welcoming the better person whom an individual may someday become. The underground man's vivid image of the utilitarians' "laws" is the "stone wall" which imprisons possibility. The art of the good and beautiful traps us in the same way as that stone wall.

Dostoevsky's concern with the need for a more candid and tough-minded literature is evident in the way he has written his story. *Notes from the Underground* is anything but the art of the good and beautiful. Its hero is defiantly repellent. In his few opportunities for modest heroism, far from undergoing a sudden ascent to nobility, he acts as badly as possible. As he admits, "I have never been a coward at heart, though I have always been a coward in action." Of course, it is precisely this discrepancy between the underground man's grand literature-nourished daydreams and his shameful actions which convicts the art of the good and beautiful of shallowness and unreality.

Dostoevsky's insistence that our understanding of the individual come not from literary abstractions but from real people casts some light on his decision to construct the story as he has. Part I is devoted to ideas; it is a philosophical monolog on the great themes: the nature of humanity, the structure of society, and the life worth living. However, the underground man's ideas on these themes draw their authority not primarily from their merit as ideas but from the authority of the underground man himself, the authenticity of his experience and the tangibility of his presence. When he argues for the ineradicable irrationality of humankind, his perverse behavior is the warrant for his claim.

Part II takes what one might call Dostoevsky's need to incarnate his ideas one step further. It consists of three stories: the conflict with the officer on Nevsky Prospekt, the dinner for Zverkov, and the encounter with Liza, the prostitute. These stories give the reader a further chance to consider the ideas presented in Part I, but now, significantly, not only as the underground man represents them but as they are embodied in experience—the play of thought, speech, and action between the underground man and other people. Part II represents the encounter of ideas with "real life." It is only in real life, and perhaps in a literature scrupulously faithful to real life, that we can test the underground man's most pressing claims: that "our most advantageous advantage" is our freedom to be fully, authentically ourselves and that only this freedom, though it allows us to degrade ourselves, can allow the possibility of a better future.

6.8 The conclusion of *Notes from the Underground*, which takes place far from the good and beautiful—amid the insulted and injured—seems intended to test the belief that some good may rise miraculously from what is negative and degraded in life. What conclusion on this issue is reached in the story? Can we find in the story's resolution some hope for the underground man's redemption?

Answer When Zverkov and his friends leave for a brothel, the underground man follows them. He does not find them there but, sensing another opportunity for shame, takes a young prostitute to bed. This, the underground man's first intimate encounter with another person, is what the story has been building to. For the first time, we no longer have only to listen to the underground man; we can watch him and draw our own conclusions.

The encounter begins with his feeling Liza's eyes on him: "Suddenly I saw beside me two wide open eyes scrutinizing me curiously and persistently. The look in those eyes was cooly detached, sullen, as it were, utterly remote." His confused and contradictory description of Liza's regard embodies his ambivalence about this opportunity for intimacy, and this will be the keynote of the episode. He asks her a few clumsy questions. He draws her into a halting conversation, and suddenly he realizes, "So she, too, was capable of certain thoughts." Modest as this insight is, it is a significant realization for the underground man, for it represents the first time he has recognized his kinship with another person. For a moment he can no longer say, "I am unique and they are all alike."

However, the underground man retreats from Liza, denying this momentary sense of connection to her by construing his feelings and motives in the most damning way: "It was the exercise of my power that attracted me most." He wavers ("I swear she did interest me") and then convicts himself: "And cunning so easily goes hand-in-hand with feeling."

These vicissitudes of approach and avoidance continue as the underground man goes on "speaking stiffly, artificially, even bookishly." He lectures Liza on the wages of sin but finds to his surprise that his shopworn tale has reduced Liza to despair. She has mistaken his recitation for true concern—or does he really care? By this point, he has lost track of what is true and false in his feelings.

In Liza's vulnerability and the underground man's tentative trust and concern, small epiphanies of genuine feeling struggle into being. This element of possibility, the gift of true feeling and perception, haunts the last pages of *Notes from the Underground*. It springs up in Liza's sudden sympathy when, in the middle of the underground man's most savage and insulting tirade, she recognizes his pain, and again in the underground man's moment of release and confession: "They won't let me . . . I can't be good!" Even at the close, when the underground man has contrived to insult her beyond all forgiveness and defeat for both of them any higher hope, Liza's parting gesture—throwing his money at him—yields her an unexpected moment of dignity which the underground man recognizes with a degree of admiration and empathy that is unprecedented for him. If in these last pages the reader gets an intimation of what the underground man knows only as "something different, quite different, for which I am thirsting, but which I cannot find," this is neither entirely affirmed nor entirely negated but cast forward as a possibility.

D.E.

SUGGESTED READINGS

Berdyaev, Nicholas, *Dostoevsky* (1957).

Blackmur, R. P., *Eleven Essays in the European Novel* (1964). See the essays on Dostoevsky.

Fanger, Donald, *Dostoevsky and Romantic Realism: A Study of Dostoevsky in Relation to Balzac, Dickens, and Gogol* (1967).

Freud, Sigmund, "Dostoevsky and Parricide" (1928).

Magarshack, David, *Dostoevsky* (1963).

Mochulsky, Konstantin, *Dostoevsky: His Life and Work* (1947).

Wellek, Rene (ed.), *Dostoevsky: A Collection of Critical Essays* (1962).

C H A P T E R 7

FLAUBERT

Early Years

Gustave Flaubert was born December 12, 1821, in Rouen, Normandy. His father was an eminent surgeon and the director of the municipal hospital in which Gustave was born. This hospital, in which the Flauberts had their living quarters, was the scene of much of Gustave's childhood play. He grew up surrounded by the grisly scenes of the operating room and the mortuary, and these early experiences may have contributed to what has been described as the clinical quality of his later realism.

From an early age, Flaubert was absorbed in literature both as reader and writer. He and his young friends wrote and performed bloodcurdling melodramas with titles like "Matteo Falcone, or Two Coffins for One Outlaw" and "The Iron Hand." In these early years, Flaubert was entirely in tune with the taste of the nation, which was being swept with a romantic passion for everything sentimental, exotic, and violent. Inspired in part by the recent appearance of Shakespeare on the French stage, a new generation of writers, including Alexandre Dumas, Victor Hugo, Théophile Gautier, and George Sand, was creating a literature that would burst the confines of classicism. Much more than just a literary event, this new wave of romanticism expressed aspirations that could find no other outlet in the conservative political and social climate of the 1830s. The age of Louis Philippe, the "shopkeeper king," the 1830s marked the ascendancy in France of the bourgeoisie and their commercial ethos. The romantic movement may be seen in part as a reaction to this climate.

Between literature and commerce Flaubert felt there was really no choice.

From the first, he wanted to be a writer. However, his father had plans for him to become a lawyer. In 1840, Flaubert spent a year at home studying for admission to law school. However, finding law uncongenial, he took refuge in literary pursuits, producing a 100-page confessional novel entitled *Novembre*. This work, like all his early literary productions, he enthusiastically shared with his closest friend and literary confidant, Alfred le Poittevin, who pronounced it excellent. Heartened by Poittevin's praise, Flaubert embarked on a second project with the working title *L'Education sentimentale*.

In accordance with his father's plan, Flaubert went to Paris and enrolled in law school, but his legal studies languished, and at the end of the year he failed his examinations. Flaubert seemed trapped between his literary ambitions and the need to retake examinations for a profession he detested, but an unusual providence intervened to save him. During the Christmas vacation of 1843, he was suddenly stricken by an epilepsylike seizure that left him first unconscious and then for weeks afterward depressed and debilitated. There was nothing to do but give up his legal studies and remain in the family home at Rouen.

As these attacks recurred from time to time, Flaubert became ensconced in the comfortable life of an invalid, with free time to write and the specter of a legal career growing more and more remote. Thus, whatever its cause, the effects of the malady were not entirely unpleasing to Flaubert.

The last threat of a legal career was soon removed with the death of Dr. Flaubert. This was followed in a few months by the death of Gustave's beloved sister, Caroline, who left behind her, as ward to her mother and brother, the little daughter she had recently borne. Now the head of the household, Flaubert, with his much-reduced family, retired to their country house at Croisset, where he was to remain for the rest of his life with few intermissions.

Youthful Attachments and Early Work

Soon after this, Flaubert began an intermittent romance with Louise Colet, a minor poet who was the mistress of Victor Cousin, the French philosopher and educator. In this affair, Colet was the pursuer and Flaubert the pursued. On the whole, Flaubert preferred to keep this a romance by mail, and his letters contain some of his most significant pronouncements on literature.

The only other intrusion into Flaubert's life as a provincial recluse was the companionship of his friends Louis Bouilhet and Maxime Du Camp and his occasional travels to Brittany, Paris, and later, memorably, Egypt, in the company of Du Camp.

From 1848 to 1849, Flaubert engaged in the first serious writing project of his adulthood, his *Temptation of St. Anthony*. The result was a literary oddity of the first order, a goulash of ancient history, confession, and philosophical fantasy. On reading it to Bouilhet and Du Camp, Flaubert was shocked to find that they thought it a complete failure. Bouilhet's criticism was especially biting; he accused Flaubert of giving in to his penchant for romantic ravings and stylistic excesses and counseled him to study Balzac, a writer whom Flaubert had dismissed as too bourgeois to be worth serious consideration. Nonetheless, he was chastened by Bouilhet's criticism and began a revision of his early romantic aesthetics.

On the completion of the *Temptation*, Flaubert and Du Camp embarked on their long-meditated trip to Egypt. Flaubert glutted himself with exotic, sensual experiences, visiting Alexandria and the pyramids, traveling up the Nile, and stopping at brothels everywhere. This trip was a final indulgence and purgation of Flaubert's romantic tastes, and he felt that it left him free to write in a new fashion.

Madame Bovary

On his return, Bouilhet had waiting for him the subject for the realistic novel he hoped Flaubert would write: the story of a local medical official, a distant acquaintance of theirs named Eugene Delamare, who had recently committed suicide after discovering that his wife, herself a recent suicide, had betrayed him regularly during their life together. This was the story which Flaubert was to transform into *Madame Bovary*. Of his efforts to put aside his romantic tendencies and write this book about inglorious provincial life, Flaubert wrote to Louise Colet:

> There exist within me, speaking from a literary point of view, two distinct persons: one in love with eloquence, with lyricism, with the soaring of eagles, with all the sonorities of phrase and mountain-peaks of idea; another seeking and probing the truth as much as he can, liking to state the small fact as forcefully as the large, wanting to make you feel almost tactilely the things he describes; the latter loves to laugh, and takes pleasure in man's animalities.

Madame Bovary was to be the willed triumph of this second self.

Flaubert labored at *Madame Bovary* for six years. It finally appeared in serial form in Du Camp's literary journal, the *Revue de Paris*, in 1857. The book was a great success from the start, and Flaubert was suddenly a literary celebrity. However, the government of Louis Napoleon, which was out to suppress the

Revue de Paris, brought suit against the journal and Flaubert, charging that *Madame Bovary* was immoral. For once, Flaubert bestirred himself in matters practical. He hired a noted barrister and succeeded in winning acquittal for himself and the book. After this legal triumph, the reputation of both book and author grew even faster.

Later Works

Flaubert's next book, *Salammbô* (1862), was set in the exotic locale of Carthage and marked his return to matters antiquarian and romantic. In 1869, Flaubert published a greatly revised version of the *Education sentimentale* that he had begun many years earlier while in law school. This novel, set during the French revolution of 1848, features Frederic Moreau, a character some have seen as a male version of Emma Bovary. It is even more pessimistic than *Madame Bovary*, since it takes place at the heart of nineteenth-century European culture—in Paris, during a period of widespread political turmoil—yet represents this time and place as being as issueless and empty as the provincial world of *Madame Bovary*.

Flaubert's last novel, unfinished at his death, was *Bouvard and Pecuchet*, a lampoon of bourgeois learning and culture centered on the intellectual misadventures of its clerkly heroes. Flaubert died at his beloved Croisset on May 8, 1880.

Place in Literature and Art

Flaubert stands at a culminating and pivotal point in the history not only of literature but of the arts as a whole. To generalize broadly, in modernist art and literature, the realist's representational ambition—the goal of getting at the truth by depicting the look and feel of everyday life—is subordinated to an absorption with style and form. The foremost example of this tendency is so-called abstract painting, where line, form, and color have become the artist's subject; in other words, style *is* the subject. Representational and formalist modes are always simultaneously present and interrelated in the development of any art form; it merely seems that at certain moments one becomes the louder voice in the continuing dialog. Flaubert's career is a privileged place in which to consider this dialog, which is conducted in his texts in a particularly animated way.

Flaubert was the realist *par excellence*, rendering with consummate care the details of the daily lives of ordinary people—the "small facts" he speaks of in his letter to Louise Colet—but he was also a stylist of fanatic intensity. If we read further in Flaubert's correspondence, we discover that every word of *Madame Bovary* was chosen with painstaking attention to rhythm, tone, and the structure of the novel as a whole. For his modernist successors, Flaubert the stylist has had the more significant influence. At times in his perfectly crafted texts we can, with the advantage of hindsight, seemingly see the formalist aesthetic of modernism in the process of coming to predominate over the representational values of the realist novel.

Flaubert's writings can also tell contemporary readers something about the historical circumstances of the modernist turn toward formalism. In novels such as *Madame Bovary* and *Sentimental Education*, Flaubert both reflected and helped shape the attitudes of an age in which the word "bourgeois" had become a term of contempt. The members of the commercial and professional classes depicted by Flaubert display what were widely felt to be their characteristic deficiencies. They are grasping in matters of business, shallow in matters of intellect, and vulgar in matters of taste. However, Flaubert's antipathy extended beyond any one class to embrace the entire dominant culture of the age, which he felt was debased by its popular literature and mass press and the banalities they retailed to a mindless public. Flaubert satirized the insipidity and prejudices of the day in his *Dictionnaire des idées reçues* (*Dictionary of Accepted Ideas*), an anthology of clichés. Among the entries are the following:

ART. Shortest path to the poorhouse. What use is it since machinery
     can make things better and quicker?
PRINCIPLES. Always "eternal." Nobody can tell their nature or number;
     no matter, they are sacred all the same.*

The paradox of Flaubert as a realist is that he depicted this philistine society with an almost religious concern for accuracy at the same time that he was unremittingly disdainful of it and felt it to be entirely inhospitable to his values and beliefs. Given this alienation between Flaubert and his circumstances, it is not surprising that he should increasingly devote his attention to matters of style and form. No matter how debased the subject, the task of shaping it into art always remains a challenge. The processes of art become a way for the artist to practice virtues—discipline, critical intelligence, and craftsmanship—that have been devalued by a society that has little use for them. Style becomes a world unto itself, a repository of value that has been banished by a vulgar society.

*From the translation by Jacques Barzun, New York, New Directions, 1968.

Thus, realism may be viewed as a victim of its own success. The achievement of realism in so vividly depicting an uncongenial world was a catalyst to the development of the modernist novel, in which the real subject is no longer the everyday world but the artist's struggle to achieve aesthetic goals which transcend that quotidian realm.

ESSAY QUESTIONS WITH ANSWERS

Madame Bovary

7.1 *Madame Bovary* begins with the entrance of an awkward new boy—Charles Bovary—into a rowdy classroom. Who describes this opening scene? Who narrates *Madame Bovary*?

Answer The novel begins: "We were in class when the headmaster came in, followed by a new boy. . . ."* Apparently, Charles Bovary's unhappy first day of school is being described by one of his classmates. However, we hear little more from this classmate narrator, who never even becomes an "I" differentiated from the "we" he uses to refer to the class as a whole. Instead, this narrator disappears from the novel after a few pages. His final words are a disclaimer of any further knowledge about Charles: "It would now be impossible for any of us to remember anything about him." Since the story that follows tells the intimate history of Charles's life, it must be told by someone other than the classmate who describes the novel's first scene.

Aside from the first few pages, *Madame Bovary* is narrated from a third-person omniscient point of view that allows Flaubert to shift his attention between the internal thoughts and feelings of his characters and their external circumstances. Clearly, such narrative flexibility is essential to the thorough treatment of the subject: the romantic aspirations of Emma Bovary and the prosaic circumstances that defeat them. But why does Flaubert not begin the novel with this point of view instead of introducing and then abruptly dropping the narrator of the first few pages?

We can suggest an answer to this question by imagining what the novel might be like if it were narrated entirely by the classmate of the first few pages. As a classmate of Charles's, this person would eventually have to be given some relation to him. For example, in the first scene he would have to join in the

---

*Translated by Paul de Man, New York, W. W. Norton, 1965. All references to *Madame Bovary* in this chapter are to the de Man translation.

teasing of Charles or perhaps become his ally against the other boys. In other words, as a real character sharing the setting in which Charles exists, the narrator would have to act in relation to Charles, and these actions would necessarily indicate some feeling toward Charles or some judgment about him.

Here we begin to see the difference between the novel's two narrators. The third-person narrator who dominates the work is not a real person but an abstraction and does not, as a character would, inhabit the same sphere of action as Charles. The third-person narrator need not act in relation to Charles or adopt any attitude toward him. He is free to watch, describe, and analyze without ever having to judge.

This suggests the most striking aspect of Flaubert's narrative method: its objectivity and impartiality. Flaubert never tells the reader what to think of Charles or any of the other characters. He never obtrudes his judgments or interpretations into the action of the novel. Instead, his narration maintains an almost imperial aloofness and calm.

This is not to say that as readers we do not make judgments about Flaubert's characters, but we feel that we reach these conclusions on our own, not as a result of any direct prompting by Flaubert. This objectivity is subtly emphasized by the brief presence of an alternative narrative possibility, the first-person classmate narrator who recounts the first scene. By introducing and then dropping this narrative viewpoint from within Charles's world, Flaubert demonstrably ascends, so to speak, to the viewpoint of the third-person narrator who observes the world "from above," with cool impartiality.

7.2   *Madame Bovary* begins with Charles Bovary rather than with Emma, the character who is clearly at the heart of the novel. Why does the novel begin at this distance from Emma?

Answer   In its original edition the subtitle of *Madame Bovary* was "Provincial Manners," thus highlighting the fact that the novel is not only a study of character but an anatomy of a segment of French society. While Emma may be the heart of the novel, she can be understood only in relation to the world in which she lives, the world that eventually defeats her ambitions. For Emma, Charles is consubstantial with that obdurate world. Charles's ordinariness, mediocrity of thought and feeling, and lack of distinction frustrate Emma, and these are exactly the qualities apparent in him from the novel's first scene. Thus, the novel begins with Charles and the provincial banality that is his element in order to show us, before the fact, the circumstances to which Emma's romantic dreams will be opposed and which will finally defeat them.

In addition, Charles is a character of considerable importance. In some ways, he is the novel's most tragic figure, since he leads his entire life under the stunning misapprehension that Emma is a devoted wife. At the end, after Emma is dead, Charles again takes center stage. The ultimate gloom of Flaubert's vision in *Madame Bovary* is brought home nowhere more clearly than in those last few pages where Charles, finally disillusioned, realizes that he has lived his life in a trance.

7.3   The first readers of *Madame Bovary* coined the term *Bovarysme* to describe, as if it were an illness, the peculiar unhappiness that afflicts Emma Bovary. What is *Bovarysme?*

Answer   Emma suffers an aching discontent with everything that is ordinary and prosaic. Given the narrow provincial circumstances in which she finds herself, this amounts to a disgust with her world as it is, especially with Charles, the very incarnation of ordinariness. In her imagination, Emma constructs a counterworld of romance and excitement, a world of dashing aristocrats, strong-limbed lovers, and exotic adventures in foreign lands. She draws the details for these flights of imagination from romantic literature, such as the works of Walter Scott, Alfred de Musset, and a thousand less famous writers of historical romances and gothic melodramas, the escapist fantasies common to the popular literature of every age.

Bovarysme is thus a disease of the imagination. More particularly, it is a disease of the literary imagination. Its most marked symptom is Emma's propensity to mistake the extravagances of romantic literature for genuine possibilities. In a sense, Emma suffers because she is a bad reader, unable to recognize fiction as fiction. In this confusion, she has a famous forebear, Don Quixote, who mistook the fantasies of chivalric adventure for reality. Like *Don Quixote*, the story of *Madame Bovary* is a contest between romantic illusions and the ordinary world which finally defeats them.

Emma's romanticism, however, is much more than a literary taste or a habit of imagination; it is an entire method of construing—or misconstruing—the world. By viewing the world entirely through the lens of her own dreams and desires, Emma comes to operate according to a principle of egotism by which everything is understood only in terms of how closely it matches her wishes. For Emma, a thing is true only if it strikes a romantic spark from her and is a nullity if it does not. Accordingly, most of reality—especially the reality of other people, with their own thoughts, feelings, and wishes—is as nothing to Emma. Her superheated imagination is really a failure of imagination which keeps her from perceiving anything beyond herself. As the narrator tells us, Emma is "incapable of understanding what she did not experience or of believing anything that did not take on a conventional form." Thus Emma is unable to understand that Charles truly loves her simply because his love is not expressed with the grand and ardent gestures that suit her preconception of love. When love comes to her dressed in these trappings, as it does with Rodolphe, Emma is entirely unable to perceive the absence of true feeling.

One brief, almost trivial scene captures the poverty of Emma's understanding. Early in the novel, Emma, feeling bored and trapped by her unpromising circumstances, has gone for a walk with Djali, her greyhound. She falls into a reverie and imagines a gay life, entirely the opposite of her dull lot. She glances at Djali and imagines that the dog is exempt from the misery that troubles her: "Come, kiss your mistress, you are free of cares." But then she imagines that Djali's expression is melancholy and assumes that the dog is bored and weary just like herself.

The point is that Emma can imagine only that the dog feels just as she does or that he feels the way she would like to feel. She is incapable of imagining that Djali has a reality of his own, independent of her wishes and moods. Emma's imagination is imperial. It subsumes everything to its own egocentric categories of understanding. Ultimately, Emma's disease is much more than a sin against good literature; it is a sin against the world, which it views with an almost immoral lack of true imagination.

7.4   At a few precious moments, Emma's experience accords with her elevated sense of how things ought to be. At these moments, what Flaubert calls "the tantalizing phantasmagoria of sentimental realities" becomes real and present. One such moment occurs during the ball at Vaubyessard. What characterizes this romantic experience?

Answer   Generally, Emma's consciousness is characterized by fantasies of distant times and places, some happier future or some far-off magic land. At Vaubyessard, however, Emma is able for one evening to live entirely in the present. The ball is presented as a rich montage of luxury, suave sexuality, and refinement, and Emma swirls through it ecstatically merged with her surroundings. She becomes so deliriously absorbed in her experience that she literally loses herself in it; then she undergoes an experience of dissociation in which she appears to be watching herself from outside. "When she opened [her eyes] again, in the middle of the drawing room three waltzers were kneeling before a lady sitting on a stool. She chose the Viscount, and the violin struck up once more." Lost in a dream come true, Emma manifests the odd double consciousness of the dreamer who both dreams the dream and acts in it. Put another way, she is like an actress who both plays a role and lives it. This romantic apotheosis blurs the boundary between literary imagination and reality as Emma becomes the heroine of an enchanting tableau vivant that miraculously embodies her extravagant book-fed fantasies.

7.5 To call a novel "realist" is to suggest something about both its subject and its method. In what sense are the subject of *Madame Bovary* and Flaubert's treatment of that subject characteristic of a realist novel?

Answer Flaubert has chosen to write about adultery, the most familiar and timeworn subject in storytelling. As a subject for literature, adultery is the height of banality, since it is the one drama indigenous to the humdrum world of middle-class domesticity. Boredom masquerading as adventurousness, adultery is the perfectly predictable melodrama that is not beyond the imagination of the most unimaginative person.

The characters in *Madame Bovary* are as ordinary as the drama they play out: a hysterical housewife, her plodding husband, a cardboard lady's man (Rodolphe), and a dozen other unexceptional characters who could be found in any small town. This is perhaps what is most ordinary and unelevated about *Madame Bovary*: its setting in a provincial society entirely devoid of vigor or imagination. Emma is forced to live in a narrow world that might well drive a less demanding soul mad with ennui. Thus, the subject of *Madame Bovary* is the perennial subject of realist literature—the ordinary everyday world—only more so. This world is ordinary with a vengeance.

The key to Flaubert's realism is his description of the physical world. Flaubert describes the material world of *Madame Bovary* with infinite patience and exactitude. The reader gets an initial bravura example of Flaubert's ability in his description of Charles's hat. The grotesquerie of this fantastic headgear is described with an intentness that seems to say, "In this novel, things, even such unpromising things as this, will signify." And it does signify; as Flaubert says of it, the hat is "one of those poor things whose dumb ugliness has depths of expression, like an imbecile's face." What it expresses is precisely the imbecility that infects every act and aspiration in the novel.

The objects of *Madame Bovary* are not described merely for the purpose of rendering their appearance but to express the wider significance they bear in the world of the novel. The whiteness of the sugar in a bowl at the Vaubyessard ball signifies for Emma a whole realm of nobility and refinement. Emma's wedding bouquet, which she comes upon in a moment of despair, symbolizes for her all the arid unhappiness of her marriage to Charles. The whiteness of Emma's fingernails, which is the first thing Charles notices about her, bespeaks a new, unexpected sensuality in his life. The rotting fetuses that swim in the jars displayed in Homais's window exemplify the corrupted pseudoscientific materialism that is his "philosophy" of life.

Thus, the psychological and moral situation of the characters in *Madame Bovary* is expressed in their tangible surroundings. Erich Auerbach in *Mimesis*, a history of realism in western literature, has described how the physical description of Emma at dinner in Part I, Chap. 9, expresses her psychology and mood. Her unappetizing milieu—the smoking stove, the damp walls, the plain boiled beef on her plate—is seen through the filter of Emma's despair so that this physical tableau becomes much more than a cheerless dining room; it becomes the tangible embodiment of her disenchantment with life.

But as Auerbach points out, although we see the dining room from Emma's emotional viewpoint, it is not presented as she would describe it. Her impressions would be confused and diffuse. Only the careful, deliberate ordering of the scene by Flaubert can convey the psychological state that Emma suffers but would be unable to express. Flaubert's language thus reaches a degree of analytical intelligence that is otherwise absent from the world it describes. If Emma could understand herself the way Flaubert understands her, she would be able to free herself from her romantic delusions. However, she cannot, and Flaubert's language remains the only true intelligence in a world trapped by its own stupidity and illusions.

7.6 Sartre accused Flaubert of practising a "spiteful" realism, and the purposeful banality of Flaubert's subject, the vapidity of the society he portrays, and his contempt for his characters all suggest the basis for Sartre's remark. Why has Flaubert taken as his subject such a debased and vulgar world?

Answer One could suggest a number of reasons why Flaubert chose to apply his talent to such an unappealing subject. First, Flaubert subscribed strongly to the ideology of the realist, which holds that truth is available in ordinary things if only they are observed and described ruthlessly enough. A not entirely logical corollary is the idea that the more ordinary, even vulgar, the object of observation is, the higher the degree of truth. Thus, in preparing to write *Madame Bovary*, Flaubert immersed himself in sentimental literature of the kind Emma reads and in medical texts of the kind Charles studied before performing his disastrous clubfoot operation in order to better know his subject.

Flaubert's researches suggest a second rationale for his choice of subject: his penchant for the asceticism of the craftsman. As Flaubert's letters reveal, he felt that writing *Madame Bovary* required an almost monastic discipline. Only such discipline could enable him to put aside his taste for romantic bombast and pursue the exactitude that makes the novel a marvel of stylistic purity.

Third, the mundane characters and themes of *Madame Bovary* presented Flaubert with the considerable challenge of making such lowly materials into the stuff of art. In *Madame Bovary*, Flaubert set out to make art from clichés: the hackneyed theme of adultery and Emma's own cliché-ridden consciousness. It is perhaps most of all Flaubert's prose, bringing intelligence and a fine ear to bear on every sentence, which allows him to turn the dross of his subject into gold. Consider the moment when Emma and Léon are on an adulterous day trip to a harbor island. Seen through the prism of Emma's romantic consciousness, an oil slick is transformed into precious metal, illuminating Emma's habit of mind and at the same time contributing a beautiful and striking image to the novel: "Tar smoke rose up between the trees and large oily patches floated on the water, undulating evenly in the purple sunlight like surfaces of Florentine Bronze." This gleaming transformation, achieved through the perfect rhythm of Flaubert's sentence, of the industrial waste of a harbor city recapitulates in small Flaubert's achievement of turning a purposely banal subject into a vehicle for high art.

7.7   While writing *Madame Bovary*, Flaubert said in a letter to Louise Colet that he would like some day to write a book about nothing. Is *Madame Bovary* in some sense a book about nothing?

Answer   When Flaubert spoke of a book about nothing, he meant a book with a subject so insignificant that it would exist as art purely by virtue of its perfection of style. In a sense, *Madame Bovary* approaches the condition of such a book. Its subject is trite, its action is negligible, and it holds no surprises. Much more than the tale, it is the manner of Flaubert's telling that makes the book what it is.

Here we reach a paradox of sorts. *Madame Bovary* is a realist novel, that is, a novel minutely concerned with the everyday world, "about" that world. Yet to call it a book about nothing in Flaubert's sense is to suggest that its real concern is not with the world at all but with its own style, its method of transmuting the world into language and form. Seen this way, *Madame Bovary* is really a novel about itself; its true subject becomes Flaubert's efforts to reach the artistic goals he has set for himself.

In *Madame Bovary*, we can see a bit of literary history unfolding. The classic realist novel concerned with the everyday world is transformed into the modernist novel, centrally concerned with form and language. *Madame Bovary* illustrates the fact that in this transformation the realist novel was the victim of its own success, for Flaubert's vivid depiction of the real world was accomplished by means of a perfection of style which then supplanted the everyday world as the novelist's prime object of interest.

7.8 Sainte-Beuve, a French critic and a contemporary of Flaubert, complained that there is no representative of virtue in *Madame Bovary*. Is this true? Is *Madame Bovary* a novel without a hero?

Answer Generally, the people in *Madame Bovary* are stupid (like Charles), deluded (like Emma), corrupt (like Rodolphe), or merely contemptible (like Homais). There are one or two exceptions. Justin, Homais's apprentice, is too young and innocent to be corrupt, and the old woman who wins an award at the Yonville fair is too humble to be anything but good. However, the most interesting island of virtue in the novel is Doctor Larivière, who presides at the death of Emma. Larivière's virtue is a kind of skepticism. He is too worldly-wise, has seen too many births and deaths, to be fooled by a false idea or sentiment. Flaubert describes him as "practising virtue without believing it." It is easy to see why he appeals to Flaubert. Both are craftsmen and skeptics; both see clearly without sentiment, faith, or belief.

Flaubert's admiration for Larivière is really a comment on his own work. It suggests that in the novel virtue and intelligence ultimately lie in Flaubert's craft, which, like Larivière's surgery, is an ascetic discipline practiced rigorously, almost cruelly. In a sense, then, Flaubert himself is the hero of *Madame Bovary*. Actually, this conclusion follows from the suggestion that the true focus of concern in the novel is not the characters or ostensible subject but the style and form. Here again, *Madame Bovary* serves as a signpost in literary history, pointing ahead to the modernist novel in which a characteristic subject is the artist and the artist's struggle with his or her medium.

D.E.

SUGGESTED READINGS

Auerbach, Erich, *Mimesis*. (1974).

Culler, Jonathan, *Flaubert: The Uses of Uncertainty* (1974).

de Man, Paul (ed.), *Madame Bovary: Background and Sources: Essays in Criticism* (1965).

Giraud, Raymond (ed.), *Flaubert: A Collection of Critical Essays* (1964).

Levin, Harry, *The Gates of Horn: A Study of Five French Realists* (1963).

Steegmuller, Francis, *Flaubert and Madame Bovary* (1967).

Steegmuller, Francis, *Flaubert in Egypt: A Sensibility on Tour* (1972).

C H A P T E R 8

BAUDELAIRE

Early Years

The poet, Charles Baudelaire writes, is blessed by God but cursed by humankind. Inevitably, the poet must suffer terribly in everyday life. This suffering, though, is worthwhile, for it signifies the poet's special calling, replaces earthly with spiritual concerns, and purifies the poetry. Baudelaire's life was miserably unhappy—he was poor, frequently ill, and vastly underrated by his contemporaries—yet he found in suffering a path to spiritual beauty, to a salvation inseparable from his art.

Baudelaire was born in Paris in 1821, the son of Caroline Dufäys and her much older husband, François, who died when Baudelaire was 6. A year and a half later, his mother remarried, ending a brief idyllic period of intimacy between mother and son. She married Colonel (later General) Aupick, a successful military man, later an ambassador, who was never to understand his eccentric stepson and came to represent all the bourgeois values Baudelaire was determined to flout.

A restless and undisciplined student, Baudelaire received his baccalaureat and was immediately sent to India by his family, who hoped that the trip would cure him of his odd taste in literature and friends. The long sea voyage included a stopover in Mauritius and ended in Réunion when Baudelaire insisted on returning to Paris. The exotic "splendor of the East," which forms the scenic backdrop for poems such as "Former Life" and "Invitation to the Voyage," was known to Baudelaire only through this abbreviated voyage undertaken reluctantly at the age of 20.

The Social Backdrop

On his return to France in 1842, Baudelaire settled in Paris and began the long process of defining himself as a writer. France was ruled at the time by Louis Philippe, the constitutional monarch who had succeeded Charles X in 1830. Known as the "bourgeois king," Louis Philippe encouraged industrialization; under his rule, an increasingly powerful upper middle class emerged. The growth of capitalism turned Paris into a cultural and economic center but left its poor people more wretched than ever as industrialization proceeded too slowly to supply jobs for the many workers who flocked there. A new and peculiarly urban form of misery was coming into being in the "swarming city" to be described by Baudelaire in his poems.

The compromise that had put a bourgeois king on the throne left an ideological vacuum in Paris life. No new idealistic vision had replaced the fervor of the revolutionaries or the loyalty of the royalists; instead, the imaginations of the newly prosperous middle-class French seemed dominated by greed and cynicism. In response, painters, sculptors, journalists, and poets formed a world of their own, mingling, quarreling, and regrouping, defining themselves and their aesthetics through allegiance to particular styles of dress, newspapers, and literary heroes—always in fierce opposition to the prevalent bourgeois values. Some chose the *vie de bohème*, leading chaotic, impoverished lives on the fringes of society. Baudelaire's initial allegiance was to dandyism, a style which, in a broad sense, he cultivated throughout his life. The dandy dresses and decorates his home with elaborate care. Assiduously self-observant, he creates his own persona as if it were a work of art, regarding artifice as a noble aspiration toward perfection.

Baudelaire saw this careful formation of the self as a worthwhile discipline, but his family saw only that he was exhausting his funds through the lavish decoration of his apartment and established a trust to administer his inheritance. Baudelaire was already deeply in debt and would remain so, since the interest on his debts accumulated rapidly while his income was reduced to a meager if reliable flow doled out by the lawyer Ancelle, who was to equal his stepfather Aupick as a target of Baudelaire's wrath. Embittered and humiliated by the establishment of the trust, Baudelaire dressed in black for the rest of his life.

Around this time, Baudelaire became involved with Jeanne Duval, an actress and the subject of many of his poems. Her exotic appearance inspired such poems as "The Jewels," "Hair," and "Dancing Snake." She was also—along with Aupick, Ancelle, and a mysteriously contracted case of syphilis—a source of persistent agony for Baudelaire. The relationship was stormy, and each attempt at cohabitation ended in estrangement.

Art Criticism and Discovery of Poe

Baudelaire's earliest published work included a novel, *La Fanfarlo* (1847), and remarkably astute articles on the salons of 1845 and 1846. (The salons were periodic exhibitions of paintings held under the auspices of the Royal Academy.) Throughout his life, Baudelaire wrote art criticism, praising painters such as Daumier and Delacroix and influencing Courbet and Manet. He sought in painting the same blend of realism and beauty for which he strove in his poems. "The real painter," he writes, "will be he who can seize the epic character of contemporary life and make us see and understand, through color or design, how great and poetic we are in our cravats and our patent leather boots."* An artist's experience of the era, Baudelaire felt, offers the only possible original subject for artistic work, and in his poems he answered that call for a painter of the "heroism of modern life," always anchoring his imagination in palpably commonplace modern things and scenes.

The age of the bourgeois king came to an end in 1848 with the violent and ultimately ineffectual uprisings of February and June. For almost four months, France appeared to be on the verge of socialism, a prospect that triggered Baudelaire's only known involvement in political action. He is said to have participated in some of the street fighting and, with friends, helped found a newspaper. But when the workers' movement collapsed in June with the estab-lishment of a conservative military government that faded into the Second Empire of Napoleon III, Baudelaire permanently left the realm of political action.

Baudelaire's political disillusionment coincided with his artistic peak. Soon after Louis Napoleon's 1851 coup, Baudelaire began to write articles about and translations of Edgar Allan Poe, the American writer in whom he found a kindred soul. Critics debate whether Poe actually influenced Baudelaire's ideas or simply stated what Baudelaire had long thought, but in any case this discovery of Poe was crucial to Baudelaire's poetic development. Like Poe, Baudelaire used the macabre and the grotesque to explore the depths of the soul while simultaneously suggesting another, higher reality that is elusive and tantalizing. But more important than this resemblance for Baudelaire was the fact that Poe

*Quoted in Lois B. Hyslop and Francis E. Hyslop, *Baudelaire as a Literary Critic*, 1964, p. 35.

provided, in essays such as "The Poetic Principle," a theoretical justification for his literary practices. Art, Poe writes, is "no mere appreciation of the Beauty before us—but a wild effort to reach the Beauty above." Art breaks through the natural to a "supernal," or heavenly, beauty beyond. Music is the least representational of all the arts. It does not refer to anything outside itself, the way a book conveys a story or a painting portrays a scene. Therefore, music comes closest of all the arts to re-creating this higher beauty, which cannot be represented but only suggested. In addition, Poe emphasizes the importance of the will in creating art. Not frenzied inspiration but intently applied consciousness is behind his own work, he says.

Whether Poe was voicing Baudelaire's thoughts or helping to formulate them, he seemed to endorse Baudelaire's preference for artifacts over nature, rejection of didacticism in art, and search for a musical poetry aspiring to unearthly beauty. He also made Baudelaire famous, for the translations of Poe— unlike his poetry—were immediately recognized as classics.

Fleurs du mal and Later Works

Les Fleurs du mal (The Flowers of Evil), Baudelaire's first and only book-length collection of poems, was published in 1857. Baudelaire had been writing the poems since the early 1840s and publishing them occasionally in newspapers, but now he brought them together in a carefully structured chronicle of his spiritual life. Into it, he said, he had poured his entire soul. The book was received unenthusiastically by the press and was prosecuted in court for offending "morality and decency." Flaubert's Madame Bovary had recently been acquitted of the same charge, but Baudelaire was not so lucky. He was fined and forced to remove six poems from the collection. A second edition, in which the condemned poems were replaced by thirty-five new ones, appeared in 1861.

During the late 1850s, Baudelaire began publishing prose poems, but the early readers found them boring, and they remained uncollected until after his death. Published first as Petits poèmes en prose and then as Spleen de Paris, they include ironic narratives and grim re-creations of Parisian street life. Baudelaire was not the first to write prose poems, but the sharp precision of his language, his peculiar tone—sometimes cynical, sometimes naive—and his realistic treatment of urban life gave the form a new clarity and power.

Somewhat more popular was Les Paradis artificiels, a series of articles about hashish and opium. Published in 1860, the book includes translated excerpts from De Quincey's Confessions of an English Opium Eater (1822; enlarged edition,

1856) as well as Baudelaire's own vivid descriptions of drug-distorted perception. The world seen by the hashish smoker turns out to bear a striking resemblance to the world seen by the poet. Each object is not merely itself but symbolizes a higher reality as well; plants and animals "lecture you through form and color." To the drug user, language becomes in itself a sensual object, what Baudelaire elsewhere calls an "evocative sorcery," conjuring up visions of another world. Baudelaire does not, however, advocate the use of drugs to attain the mystical unity and verbal sensuality evoked by his poems. Drugs, he says, destroy the will, which he considered a crucial element in poetic creation. The miracle of drugs, he concludes, mimics but does not equal the paradise sought more laboriously by poets and philosophers. What drugs offer is temptingly accessible but illusory, for drug users awake irritable and will-less, helpless against the "terrible tomorrow!"

By the early 1860s, Baudelaire's life as a writer was virtually over. Increasingly disabled by paralysis and harassed by financial problems, he spent two miserable years in Belgium, where he lectured on Delacroix and Gautier. He died in Paris in 1867.

Baudelaire's life appears to have been one of unremitting misery, yet his friends were among the most distinguished of his contemporaries, including the novelists Gautier and Champfleury and the painters Courbet and Manet. His artistic responses were deep and prescient; he was among the first to appreciate Wagner, who became the hero of the symbolists a generation later. However, he was underrated as a poet and often cruelly abused by reviewers, who questioned his motives and his sanity. Afraid of being prosecuted, editors bowdlerized his poetry or, when Baudelaire reacted angrily, refused to publish him at all. Two years after his death, publication rights to his work were sold, but they brought only a paltry sum. More than a century after his death, however, he is recognized as a major influence on modern literature and is probably the most widely read of all French poets.

Literary Antecedents and Followers

Baudelaire's precise place in modern literature is difficult to specify. While he was certainly influenced by the literary movements of his time, he was in many ways extraordinarily original. He was not technically innovative—his verse forms were traditional—for he believed that discipline and order were essential to art, yet his often bizarre subject matter and powerfully evocative use of language provoked startling transformations in French poetry.

To understand Baudelaire's place in literature more precisely, it is worth examining the three literary movements that seem to have shaped him—romanticism, *l'art pour l'art*, and realism—as well as a fourth—symbolism—on which he was a major influence.

Baudelaire's primary influence came from the romantics, among them Lamartine, Vigny, and Hugo, who began publishing in the 1820s. The romantics insisted on the poet's right to break the conventional rules of versification in order to explore and express the inner self. At first, they were extremely controversial; in 1830, the first performance of Hugo's play *Hernani* provoked a riot, so intense was the audience's disagreement over the author's innovative method and subject. But by the time Baudelaire reached adulthood, the romantics' innovations were so ingrained culturally that his first concern—as Henri Peyre points out—was to define himself against them. While he inherited an interest in the exotic and the grotesque from his romantic forebears, his interest in evil was original, as was his emphasis on discipline, intellect, and artifice in place of the romantics' emotional extravagance and love of nature.

Baudelaire's friend Théophile Gautier was also moving away from romanticism toward a more stringent conception of beauty and art. The phrase "art for art's sake" (in French, *l'art pour l'art*) was a condensed version of his aesthetic and, to a large extent, Baudelaire's. Supporters of *l'art pour l'art* argued against the presence of any didactic or ethical element in art. This doctrine permitted Baudelaire to take evil and, through the perfection of his poetry, turn it into beauty. The same doctrine sanctioned the classic and pictorial subjects of the Parnassians, a later movement that rejected the romantic emphasis on personality and unconventionality in favor of impassive and formally perfect versification. Baudelaire's "Beauty," which portrays its subject as a "dream of stone," hating movement and emotion, can be considered a proto-Parnassian poem, and, much later, Baudelaire contributed to the first series of *Le Parnasse contemporain*, a Parnassian journal, in 1866. But while Baudelaire endorsed the high role assigned to art by Gautier and Théodore de Banville, his verse and personality were too volatile to fit such rigidly classical models.

Especially in his early art criticism, Baudelaire reveals his leanings toward realism, the precise rendition of everyday life. In his verse, his depictions of modern Paris and his treatment of humble people and trivial objects owe a great deal to the realists, among them the painter Courbet and the novelist Champfleury, both of whom were close friends of the young Baudelaire. But with age, his enthusiasm for realism faded, and he found in Poe support for his contention that an overly inclusive and literal depiction of the actual is limiting and materialistic.

From each of these movements, then, Baudelaire took what he needed: emphasis on the exotic from the romantics, on the self-sufficiency of art from Gautier and his followers, and on the actual from the realists. His reformulation and integration of these elements in *The Flowers of Evil* produced something new: a formally beautiful yet clinically precise depiction of personal vision and experience. This synthesis seems inescapably modern and was hailed as such by the symbolists.

Since symbolism as a coherent movement did not exist until 1880, Baudelaire cannot accurately be termed a symbolist, but it was as a precursor to the movement that Baudelaire finally entered the mainstream of French culture. The symbolists, represented most prominently by Verlaine and Mallarmé, argued that poetry should be musiclike, evoking a spiritual state independent of literal meaning. They emphasized the suggestivity of synesthesia, which is the stimulation of one sense by another, as when, for instance, one hears a flute and instantly visualizes a particular color. They were fond of Wagner's music, as was Baudelaire, because it united poetry, music, and scenic art. They were called symbolists because they used concrete objects to suggest spiritual or psychic states, echoing Baudelaire's poem "Correspondances," where the individual walks through a "forest of symbols." Perhaps most significant was the idea they inherited from Baudelaire of language as something palpable. Words for the symbolists, as for Baudelaire, were weightier, more sensual, and more fertile than for earlier poets, radiating music and associations.

Most readers of modern literature expect a poem to be difficult, to have no single verifiable meaning, to express a uniquely personal vision. To some extent, these expectations are due to the work of Charles Baudelaire.

ESSAY QUESTIONS WITH ANSWERS

The Flowers of Evil

8.1 Baudelaire felt that his greatness as a poet rested entirely on *The Flowers of Evil*. He continued to write poetry after the book first appeared in 1857, but rather than publish the new poems in a separate volume, he inserted them into the original and published a second edition in 1861. Why did Baudelaire choose to unite all his poems under a single title?

Answer Baudelaire insisted that there was a "secret architecture" structuring his book, and the poems do seem to be thematically related. There is even a hint of a plot. In the first and largest section, "Spleen and Ideal," the poet seems torn between yearning for an unattainable beauty and immersion in an immediately available but sordid reality. "Parisian Scenes," "Wine," "Flowers of Evil," and "Revolt," the sections that follow, represent attempts to come to terms with these conflicting drives. The humble, the blasphemous, and the ugly are transmuted by the beauty and intensity of the verse, but repeatedly the poems end in anticlimax or despair. "This life is a hospital," Baudelaire writes in a prose poem, "where each invalid is obsessed with the desire to change beds."* Again and again, Baudelaire shows, human activities prove to be failed shortcuts to salvation from which the individual awakes, in a new bed perhaps, but in the same hospital and with the clock's hands still inexorably advancing. Only the final section, "Death," offers a definitive escape from the hospital:

> Pour us your poison, to comfort us!
> We want—this fire so burns our brains—
> To plunge to the bottom of the abyss, Hell or Heaven, what does it
>   matter?
> To the depths of the Unknown to find *something new!*

*Translated by Francis Scarfe, Baltimore, Penguin, 1961. All references to the poems of Baudelaire in this chapter are to the Scarfe translations. Some quotations have been amended by the author.

For the 1861 edition, Baudelaire inserted his more recent poems under appropriate headings and added "Parisian Scenes." Baudelaire's collection grew organically, united by the author's sensibility and by his obsession with time, remorse, and death.

8.2 In *The Flowers of Evil*, Baudelaire often sounds like a penitent sinner, and occasionally he even addresses God directly. Yet one prose poem asks, "What does eternal damnation matter to one who has found an infinity of pleasure in a second?" Do Baudelaire's poems have a religious message? If so, what is it?

Answer Almost every ideological faction has claimed Baudelaire as its own, but the central dispute has concerned Baudelaire's Roman Catholicism. Prominent Catholic critics have praised his moral insight, finding in his depictions of evil the horror of the penitent, not the glee of the blasphemer. The twentieth-century Catholic dramatist Paul Claudel said of Baudelaire that he "sang the only passion that the nineteenth century could experience sincerely, remorse." Baudelaire was raised a Roman Catholic, and though his specific beliefs remain unknown, his vocabulary and spiritual concerns remained Catholic. He has been called a Satanist ("The Litanies of Satan" provides support for such a view), but to a large extent, Baudelaire's evil derives its power from the moral force of the laws it transgresses. That these laws do in fact have force is not questioned.

Baudelaire was a firm believer in the existence of sin. People are torn, he believed, between two forces, one pushing them toward God, the other toward Satan. When Flaubert chided him for giving the devil so large a role in his poems, Baudelaire replied that only the existence of a devil could explain certain aspects of human behavior. "It's the Devil who holds the threads that move us," he writes in his prefatory poem, "To the Reader."

This devil bears some resemblance to Poe's Imp of the Perverse, which he describes in "The Black Cat" as a "primary faculty" of the individual:

Who has not, a hundred times, found himself committing a vile or stupid action, for no other reason than because he knows he should *not*? Have we not a perpetual inclination, in the teeth of our best judgment, to violate that which is *Law*, merely because we understand it to be such?

The narrator is explaining his reason for hanging his cat. The act is completely unmotivated and consciously cruel, explicable only in terms of "the unfathomable longing of the soul *to vex itself*—to offer violence to its own nature—to do wrong for the wrong's sake only."

Poe and Baudelaire were raised in different religions, but they shared a strong belief in original sin. Far from being naturally good, they felt, people have an inborn urge to do evil, finding a perverse pleasure in the betrayal of their better instincts. Such pleasure is most tempting to those who are insensitive to simpler joys, "the most indolent and dreamiest of beings," as Baudelaire calls them in "The Bad Glazier," those who cannot rouse themselves to perform ordinary tasks yet discover new reserves of energy when behaving dangerously, absurdly, or maliciously. "I was more than once a victim of these crises and bursts of energy," Baudelaire's narrator writes, "which justify our believing that malicious Demons slip inside us and make us carry out, in spite of ourselves, their most absurd whims." The narrator proceeds to drop a flowerpot onto the glazier's load, smashing his glass.

Perhaps the hint of freedom in that act makes Baudelaire seem secular and modern rather than traditionally Roman Catholic. The glass breaker's ecstasy is an affirmation of his ability to act, not merely a satanic pleasure in spiting God.

Is Baudelaire, then, entirely irreligious? Is he endorsing perversity? In one form or another, perversity pervades his poetry, yet critics still argue over whether he means to frighten or tempt with this spectacle of sin. The irresistible fascination he grants to horror has at least as much power as his warnings against it. There is clearly a Promethean urge in Baudelaire to be more than human, to stand outside the laws of God and of psychological motivation, to behave inexplicably and irreligiously. Yet what Poe calls "the unfathomable longing of the soul to vex itself" is remarkably close to what Claudel calls remorse. In both cases, the soul turns inward and inflicts pain on itself. As in so many other instances in Baudelaire, the Satanist and the Roman Catholic mingle.

8.3   Even those who have never read Baudelaire may associate an aura of morbid sensuality with the name. "Baudelairean" suggests a taste for the bizarre and the sordid, but most of all the sensual. Smells, sounds, and sights take on unprecedented importance in his poems. How does Baudelaire use physical experience in his poetry?

Answer   In "Correspondances," Baudelaire writes of a natural world where everything matches up. Scents, colors, and sounds "*se répondent*," that is, answer each other, or correspond. A certain fresh smell conjures up the feel of a child's skin; another, mellower one emits the sound of an oboe. Can a perfume's smell be matched to the sweet low tone of an oboe? Not demonstrably, of course, yet somehow the correspondence feels right.

Synesthesia, or the linkage of different senses, offers a path to the infinite, to an ecstasy of mind as well as body. In his emphasis on the spiritual implications of correspondences, Baudelaire appears to have been influenced by Swedenborg (1688–1722), the Swedish mystic who argued that nature was a book to be deciphered, offering spiritual truth to those who could "read" it. But Baudelaire's world is more a symphonic concert than a book; nature is a system not of hieroglyphics to be decoded but of suggestions to be evoked.

The last stanza of "Correspondances" is crucial in that it describes the process of expansion by which a thing moves its perceiver to both mental and physical ecstasy. In the process, the thing itself loses its physical reality. Baudelaire was not a nature lover ("I am incapable," he says, "of sentimentalizing over vegetables"), and his purpose in describing the physical world is to penetrate beyond it. Synesthesia is one way of doing this, for it violates the rules by which we ordinarily understand sensual experience and so forces us beyond it. Another way is to create a vivid physical and emotional context and then suddenly leave it. Proust pointed out that Baudelaire had a tendency to "cut the wings" of his poems, that is, to cut them off on a note of anticlimax. "The Swan," for example, a lengthy and moving depiction of exile, ends, "I think of sailors forgotten on an island,/of captives, of the conquered! . . . of many others, also!" The final words are too vague to give the ending immediate impact; instead, they force readers outside the physical world of the poem, into their own minds.

Baudelaire is concerned not with physical reality per se but with the power of physical reality to evoke another, more vague reality. Sometimes this movement from physical to spiritual is so abrupt and obvious that a moral seems to have been tacked on, as in "Carrion," which ends with the reminder that beautiful women, too, eventually die and decay. Elsewhere, the physical setting blends with a particular mood which gradually takes over, as in "Evening Twilight," which describes in great detail the arrival of evening in the Paris streets and then ends in introspection and compassion, substituting mood for physical setting. Similarly, "Song of Autumn" turns the vividly re-created sound of wood being chopped into a remorseless, ominous reminder of time. "Song of Autumn" works because the physical description is completely suffused with the poem's mood. The thud of logs recurs like the ticking of a clock, heavy and inevitable, while the poet's mental state is portrayed with the utmost sensual immediacy.

8.4 Poems such as "Jewels" and "Hair" suggest sexual desire, but the desire seems always to remain unsatiated since these poems end in anticlimax. Why does Baudelaire treat physical love so elusively and indirectly?

Answer Baudelaire's treatment of women is related to his treatment of nature. Women *are* nature in his view, and as such they are imperfect, sinful, and subject to decay. His retirement in the face of sexual climax is one aspect of his rejection of the finite and the physical.

Biographers of Baudelaire have suggested that his sexual peculiarities are responsible for the strangeness of his poems, and some have suggested that he never actually consummated a sexual affair. Baudelaire's relations with women were complicated and obscure. Besides Jeanne Duval, Mme Sabatier and Marie Daubrun were subjects of his poems, but it is uncertain whether either was ever his mistress. Mme Sabatier he loved from afar and idealized; when she offered herself to him, he fled. Toward Marie Daubrun he was more affectionate than passionate; to her he wrote "Invitation to the Voyage." As the mistress of his friend Banville, she was probably unavailable.

Only Jeanne Duval, then, stirred Baudelaire's physical passion, but not at all in a traditionally romantic manner. She is depicted in the poems as silent, lecherous, icy, inhuman, a "statue with jade eyes, great angel with a brow of bronze." She is desirous yet inscrutable. Her insatiable sexuality has nothing to do with emotion, and the poet's insatiable desire has nothing to do with physical possession. "I cannot," he writes in "Sed Non Satiata," "to break your courage and set you at bay,/become Proserpine in the underworld of your bed!" Neither has the power to satisfy the other.

The critic Sainte-Beuve accused Baudelaire of "Petrarch-izing about the horrible." Jeanne Duval is in a sense an inversion of Petrarch's Laura, and Baudelaire sings her praises almost as obsessively. He praises her bestiality, sensuality, and coldness, for only beauty tinged with its opposite excites him. "I climb to the assault," he writes, "like a choir of worms on a corpse," dropping a revoltingly physical simile into "I Adore You as Much," an otherwise graceful and elevated poem. The hint of imminent death and corruption somehow enhances the woman's seductiveness.

In his *Journaux Intimes*, Baudelaire compares love to a "surgical operation" or torture: "One of the two will always be calmer, or less carried away than the other. One is the surgeon or the executioner; the other is the subject, the victim." The desires of two lovers can never match up, and it is only the presence of that torture that makes love tempting: "the unique and supreme pleasure of love is in the certitude of doing *mal* ["pain" or "evil"]."

Thus in poems such as "Jewels" and "I Adore You as Much," the loved one is tantalizing and unavailable. The poet's love is a sea, while she is the cliff he can never quite reach. She *is* her jewels—hard, glittering, objectified; the grammatical subject of the second stanza of "Jewels" is the jewel's splendor, not the woman. Or she is depicted as an urn to whom he says, "I love, o beast implacable and cruel/even this coldness which makes you more beautiful to me!"

There is a hint of sadism here, of the lover so jaded that he is aroused only when desire is spiced with pain. In "Jewels," the loved one disappears amid a catalog of body parts. She is so absent as a human being that she seems to have been disemboweled. In fact, the poem ends, as Leo Bersani points out in *Baudelaire and Freud*, with an oblique "murder." The list of body parts ends with a rather tangential description of the dying flame of the lamp. As he does in "Hair," the poet retreats from the sexual encounter. But the dying lamp and the red color it throws onto his lover's skin also suggest a murder.

To see his mistress as a person would enmesh the poet in the immediate, the imperfect. By metaphorically murdering her, he frees himself from the danger of satisfying his desire. Unsatisfied, his sexual desire becomes a kind of generalized yearning akin to spiritual aspiration. Baudelaire's concern with unsatisfied desire, then, does not reflect his sexual hunger so much as his unending dissatisfaction with physical reality.

8.5 Baudelaire's poem "Hair," in which a woman's hair becomes a landscape, indicates how closely related are his views of women and of exotic locales. Like his women, these places are elusive and endlessly desired. They suggest a rich sensuality that is nevertheless ephemeral and ungraspable. What are the other characteristics of Baudelaire's landscapes?

Answer Baudelaire's actual voyage to Mauritius is generally seen as the source of his exotic eastern imagery, but his descriptions of faraway places bear little resemblance to any actual locale. The palms, black slaves, and other images do not identify a spot on a map but suggest a hazy region whose only characteristics are warmth, proximity to the sea, and sensual luxuriousness, fused—paradoxically—with an elegant sense of order.

In "Invitation to the Voyage," "Former Life," and "Hair," Baudelaire creates a vivid, Tahiti-like world that remains unmistakably unreal, an "Orient of the West," as he calls it in the prose poem "Invitation," "where Nature is reshaped by dream, where she is corrected, beautified, remolded." All of these poems invoke an elsewhere separated from the real world by time or space, at once a memory from the past and a dream for the future. This equivocation about the temporal situation of the landscape is part of its disturbingly unnatural quality. A lost past can be mourned nostalgically; a geographically distant present can be courageously voyaged toward, and a future paradise can be prepared for. But Baudelaire's landscapes stimulate none of these emotional responses, for they are all three. "I *will* go there," the poet says in "Hair," using the future tense, yet he concludes, "are you not the oasis where I dream, and the gourd/where I drink, in long draughts, the wine of memory?"

This temporal paradox is matched by the contradictory fusion of harmony and luxury offered by this imaginary world, where opposites do not merely attract but cling lovingly to each other. The "tranquil voluptuousness" that appears in both "Invitation" and "Former Life" joins the spiritual state of calmness to physical pleasure, restraint and serenity to liberty and disorder. "Luxury is happy to reflect itself in order," Baudelaire writes in the prose "Invitation." Sensuality embraces formal coherence joyfully, as if they belonged together.

Of course, this combination is not natural at all but emphatically artificial and unreal. In this mirrorlike world where everything could be merely a momentary play of light glinting off the sea, person and landscape are interchangeable. In "Invitation," the entire country resembles the poet's lover, who is herself—as his child, his sister—a reflection of him. In "Former Life," the sun and sky are visible as reflections on the sea, which are then mirrored in the poet's eyes. Both poems oddly subvert the independent reality of the landscape they describe by announcing its utter subjugation to human aims. Critics have long puzzled over the sad secret which ends—anticlimactically as always—"Former Life" and is the "only care" of the naked slaves. In "Invitation," the port is filled with ships which have come "to gratify your slightest desire." The slaves and the ships are at the service of the poet and his lover because they are merely projections, offering imaginary satisfaction to real desires.

"All that is beautiful and noble," Baudelaire writes, "is the result of reason and calculation." His imagined landscapes are artificial, not natural paradises. The thriving port of "Invitation" is actually a system of canals; singled out for praise is the bedroom furniture. There is a hint here of *fin de siècle* decadence. Baudelaire's dandyism, his dislike of nature and love of artifice, were to come into fashion toward the end of the nineteenth century, reaching their peak in Des Esseintes, the hero of Joris-Karl Huysmans's novel A *Rebours* (*Against Nature*, 1884), who so thoroughly abhors the natural that he bejewels a live tortoise's shell, orders flowers that look like metal, and finally comes to feed himself through enemas, grotesquely reversing the natural process. Baudelaire's concern with artifice is not quite so obsessive, but it haunts his landscapes, giving them rounded forms, soporific rhythms, and a hothouse climate.

8.6   The first and longest section of *Flowers of Evil* is called "Spleen and Ideal." Four of Baudelaire's poems are called "Spleen," and his collection of prose poems is entitled *Paris Spleen*. What are the characteristics of the mental state this word designates?

Answer   In an essay on Poe, Baudelaire writes of the "irritated melancholy" of a person "exiled in the imperfect, who would like to seize immediately, on this very earth, a revealed paradise." Spleen, as Baudelaire uses the word, is just this irritated melancholy; its victim is impatient, discontented, and will-less, incapable of changing his or her state of mind.

In medieval medicine, the balance of humors circulating through the body was thought to determine a person's health and temperament. Spleen was considered the source of melancholy or bad temper. The word retains a clinical aura, suggesting that Baudelaire dissects the mental state of spleen with all the objectivity and precision of a scientist. Designating both bodily organ and mood, the word "spleen" reflects an essential ambiguity of the mental state—the contradictory way in which it seems at once as involuntary as physical illness and as deliberate as a mental act. If a person feels sad, for example, everything that person sees will conspire to reinforce his or her mood: a worm crushed on the street, a wrinkled woman waiting at a bus stop, a whirl of brown leaves in the gutter. To that person it seems that he or she is merely seeing and responding to what is there. Yet by selecting and emphasizing certain details, that person is projecting personal sadness onto the world. Thus moods appear simultaneously to be inflicted by reality and to emerge from within.

This confusion between inner state and outer reality is an essential characteristic of the mental state Baudelaire calls spleen. "Spleen LXXVIII" perhaps provides Baudelaire's most accessible explanation of the problem. The poem stretches the central prison image, with its connotation of containment and contraction, to embrace the entire world as the vast sky shrinks into the lid of a pot. The poet complains that he is trapped, with his mind simmering beneath this lid, but at the same time, the lid is all there is. The mind is cut off from the world, and the most determined struggling will not free it; yet even as it complains of its powerlessness, it has in a sense vanquished the world. Like the invalid frantically changing beds, the poet discovers that there is nothing else. The prison cell outside, formed by streaks of rain, is the mirror image of the cell inside the brain where spiders weave webs. All possibility of action is gone; instead, there is only the angry clanging of a bell, as if even the poet's voice were no longer his but had been transformed into inarticulate clangor.

To the poet suffering from spleen, the expansion of inner space provides not liberation but a more pervasive confinement. Time can expand in a similar way, as anyone who has experienced boredom knows. "Nothing equals in length the limping days," Baudelaire writes in "Spleen LXXVI":

> When under the heavy flakes of snowy years,
> boredom, fruit of sullen indifference,
> takes on the proportions of immortality.

The sufferer from ennui is very old—for he experiences as decades what for others are days—and very young—for he has barely *lived* at all. He has thousands of years worth of memories ("Spleen LXXVI"), yet his blood is the green Lethean water of forgetfulness, not the red blood of experience.

Spleen is above all the absence of will. Baudelaire worried that he lacked the willpower necessary to accomplish his work. It is conceivable that the poetic techniques that give power to his work also exacerbated his sense of impotence. Baudelaire tends to reverse the field of reference in his poems, projecting his feelings onto physical phenomena and then experiencing them as an onslaught from without. The process resembles the pathetic fallacy of the romantic poets, who attributed human emotions to natural objects. But where the romantics' attribution of human qualities to inanimate objects suggests the power of personality to penetrate an environment, Baudelaire's variant allows the environment to penetrate the individual, who becomes the victim of his or her perceptions.

But more important than the pathetic fallacy to Baudelaire was his use of imagery that is at once precise and oblique. The accumulation of carefully selected details in "Spleen LXXV" creates a believable scene that is also charged with meaning. Associations gather around the mangy cat (sickness, restlessness), around the log (cold, damp, tearing eyes from the smoke), around the cards (age, the many, unknown, probably dead people who have used them, the boredom their use implies). The net effect is a world where the poet's state of mind seems a natural and inescapable product of objective reality.

Baudelaire's use of "spleen," then, suggests a weary, bored, apathetic yet irritable state of mind. People suffering from spleen are likely to confuse the contents of their minds with the world outside, and they probably feel that they are somehow to blame for this mood at the same time that it seems a completely undeserved affliction.

8.7   Sometimes Baudelaire writes poems and prose poems with the same title and with very similar contents. Were the prose versions preliminary sketches for the poems? Why did Baudelaire write prose poems?

Answer   The prose poems apparently were not composed as earlier versions of the poems; for the most part, they seem to have been written later in order to develop similar themes at greater length.

Baudelaire explains his reasons for writing prose poems in the preface to *Paris Spleen*:

> Who is there among us who has not, in his ambitious days, dreamed the miracle of a poetic prose, musical, though without rhythm or rhyme, supple enough and abrupt enough to match the lyrical movements of the soul, the waves of reverie, the leaps of consciousness?

Prose gives Baudelaire the flexibility to be absolutely precise. Everything extraneous is eliminated, and the poet's vision is so condensed as to be enigmatic.

The huge cities, Baudelaire writes in his preface, give birth to this obsession with lyrical prose. The cities separated his own age from the past and demanded a new form or at least a variation on the old, for Baudelaire attributes the idea to Aloysius Bertrand, whose *Gaspard de la nuit* had been published in 1842. Why would cities and prose poems go together? Obviously, prose seems more suited to the banality of the modern world, but more important, it allows the poet to come out from behind the scaffolding of the poem, to speak in a voice that is at once more human and less personal. The prose poems seem to impersonate various voices, each telling a part of the story, none definitive. They are fragments. No formal requirements dictate where they should end, and often they seem to end a split second before their meaning is divulged. They are like faces in a crowd, moving rapidly into sight, crystal clear for a moment and then vanishing, like the woman in "To a Passerby." In the prose poem "Crowds," Baudelaire writes of the poet's taste for disguise and impersonation, for a "saintly prostitution of the soul" which allows him to lose himself in the lives of others. The prose poem is the formal expression of that "saintly prostitution." Shaped into a poem with rhythm and meter, the material would seem the deliberate effort of an artist who had imposed his or her identity and poetic craft. In prose, the same material seems to emanate magically from the city streets. Because the artist's intervention is far less obvious, the prose poem facilitates impersonation. The poet seems to slip off technical skill and slip into the skins of his or her subjects.

R.H.

SUGGESTED READINGS

Balakian, Anna, *The Symbolist Movement* (1977).
Bersani, Leo, *Baudelaire and Freud* (1977).
Carter, A. E., *Charles Baudelaire* (1977).
Hyslop, Lois B. (trans. Francis E. Hyslop), *Baudelaire as a Literary Critic* (1964).
Peyre, Henri (ed.), *Baudelaire: A Collection of Critical Essays* (1965).
Praz, Mario (trans. Angus Davidson), *The Romantic Agony*, (1933).
Ruff, Marcel, *Baudelaire* (1966).
Starkie, Enid, *Baudelaire* (1933).

C H A P T E R 9

TOLSTOY

Background and Early Life

Leo Nikolaevich Tolstoy was born in 1828 at Yasnaya Polyana ("Serene Meadow"), the rural estate of his aristocratic family. His patrician background and life at Yasnaya Polyana left their mark on his character and career. We see their influence in his deep identification with the family traditions and country life of the old nobility, his respect for the peasants, his partiality toward the strenuous outdoor existence of the sportsman and hunter, his alienation from the progressive liberal intelligentsia who dominated literary life in Moscow and Saint Petersburg, and his distaste for the new class of bureaucrats and professionals who were so prominent in this changing time. Despite his voluminous writings, Tolstoy never thought of himself primarily as a writer but always as a landlord, a person of public responsibilities, and a patriarch, leader, and teacher.

Although Tolstoy's biographers have tended to divide his life into discrete stages, it is a mistake to underestimate the element of continuity in his development. Even in the first portion of his life, as a young man of means experimenting with the roles of soldier, sophisticate, and hellion, Tolstoy often felt the need to find a moral justification for his life, an issue that came to dominate him in later years.

After being orphaned at the age of 9, Tolstoy was sent to the eastern Russian city of Kazan to live with a genteel aunt, who later introduced him to the city socialite's life of balls, parties, and visiting. Bored by these frivolities, Tolstoy turned to the university, but he soon found that none of the disciplines he studied satisfied his need to find a direction in life.

Upon inheriting Yasnaya Polyana in 1847, Tolstoy suddenly acquired the opportunity to employ his energies on his first project as a reformer. He returned home determined to devote himself to the task of ameliorating the living conditions of his serfs. Much has been made of Tolstoy's early reading of Rousseau. The ideas of that philosopher—his belief in the individual's natural goodness and the availability of truth to the common person, his faith in the ultimate harmony of virtue and happiness, and his emphasis on the need to live simply and in accord with nature—are evident in Tolstoy's first idealistic project, as they are throughout his life.

Perhaps Tolstoy's most interesting endeavor at this time was the founding of a free school for his serfs' children, run on the principle, later to form the heart of his pacifism and anarchistic socialism, that compulsion of any sort is wrong. Children were free to study whatever they chose and were not subjected to discipline. Although the school was fairly successful, Tolstoy soon found himself lacking the patience to persist in renovating a way of life distorted by generations of oppression. Temporarily giving up the attempt, he began a four-year period during which he lived the more typical life of a young man of his background, moving in polite society but also indulging in gambling and whoring. Mixed with this dissipation were liberal amounts of the self-castigation and self-contempt that throughout his life accompanied Tolstoy's intermittent bouts of self-indulgence. Eventually, intent on escaping what he felt to be a vicious and purposeless life, Tolstoy joined the army and saw action in the Caucasus and, during the Crimean War, at Sevastopol.

Already we see the typical rhythm of Tolstoy's life: a moment of high resolve—some worthy project or vow–a lapse into indulgence or irresponsibility, and then, born of self-recrimination, the setting of a new task and a vow to do better in the future. The battle between Tolstoy's puritanism and what once would have been called his healthy "animal spirits" never abated, though in later years the sins for which Tolstoy excoriated himself were more often of the mind than of the flesh. It is clear that, as so often appears to be true, his public battles for social reformation originated in his inner conflict.

Literary Debut and Marriage

While in the army, Tolstoy did his first serious writing, publishing the semi-autobiographical *Childhood* (1852), *The Raid* (1853), *Boyhood* (1854), and the *Sevastopol Sketches* (1855–1856), which made his reputation. When he arrived in Saint Petersburg, he was greeted as a celebrity, but he quickly found the inbred life of the literary capital too limiting. He once more withdrew from society, this time to travel.

The great public issue of the day in Russia was the impending emancipation of the serfs and the future of this newly freed portion of the populace. Tolstoy had freed his own serfs prior to the Emancipation Decree of 1861, and in that year he returned from western Europe to Yasnaya Polyana eager to participate in the making of a new age. He again took up an active interest in the welfare of the common people, which he was to pursue in numerous ways for the rest of his life. He reopened his school; however, it was quickly closed again by pressure from the government, which viewed it as subversive. This incident contributed to Tolstoy's animosity toward the established institutions of society and the state.

The second major period of Tolstoy's life began in 1862 with his marriage to Sophia Behrs. His home life during this time was full and happy, an example of that devout domesticity which seemed to pass out of existence with the nineteenth century. The act of fathering and raising thirteen children seems to have had a fruitful influence on Tolstoy's writing as well, for in those years his two great novels, *War and Peace* (1865–1869) and *Anna Karenina* (1873–1877), were written.

War and Peace

If the novel is a form whose greatest virtue is inclusivity, the expansive ability to present experience in all its variety, *War and Peace* is surely one of the greatest novels. *War and Peace*, which is at once historical novel, discourse on the philosophy of history and military strategy, national epic, family chronicle, and *Bildungsroman* and which contains over 500 characters, defies summary. Even to say that it is about the Napoleonic wars (1805–1814) and Napoleon's invasion of Russia (1812) limits this novel unfairly. The dimension and variety of the novel are suggested by some of the phrases that have been used to describe it: "an oriental idol with three heads and a multitude of arms" (Constantine Leontiev), in construction a "loose baggy monster" containing "all human life" (Henry James), and presenting moreover "the totality of objects" (Georg Lukács, quoting Hegel's description of Homer). Arguments persist as to whether the book is sufficiently limited and unitary to be called a novel and whether it has a structure, a "center," or a specifiable theme. It is agreed, however, that its power and lifelike quality depend on Tolstoy's characteristic ability to render things in their individuality: to capture the nuance of gesture that makes a person a unique individual, the detail that marks the identifying quality of an object or experience. He has the ability to present the world with an immediacy which makes it seem both familiar and entirely new, as though being seen for the first time.

The lucidity with which Tolstoy renders psychological and physical reality and the purposely antiliterary quality of his writing—his avoidance of highly figurative language, polished syntax, and exaggeratedly complex plotting—have a tendency to disarm critics. Thus, Matthew Arnold on Tolstoy's second great novel: "But the truth is we are not to take *Anna Karenina* as a work of art; we are to take it as a piece of life. A piece of life it is. The author has not invented and combined it, he has seen it." Like many others, Arnold mistakenly confused the seeming artlessness of Tolstoy's writing with an absence of art. In fact, Tolstoy was a painstaking writer, working through numerous versions and revisions to achieve the effects Arnold so admired.

Insofar as one can summarize the theme of *War and Peace*, it counsels a joyous resignation, a willing cooperation with the natural forces of life. In the novel's historical drama, Napoleon, whom Tolstoy mercilessly debunks, makes the mistake of thinking he can bend the course of great events to his will, while the Russian General Kutuzov, whose only strategies are patience and intuition, defeats the French at Borodino by relinquishing his will and allowing the motion of history to play through him. Stated baldly—"the affirmation of life"—the theme of *War and Peace* may seem mystical or banal. However, the manner of Tolstoy's writing, his immense patience in rendering the look and feel of things, conveys a powerful, simple faith in the immanent meaning and value of life. The power of Tolstoy's affirmative vision is demonstrated by his ability to communicate it in a novel about war, the experience which to most modern sensibilities reveals all that is fundamentally and ineradicably wrong with humankind.

Anna Karenina

In a famous essay on Tolstoy's two predominant and conflicting habits of mind, Isaiah Berlin contrasted the hedgehog with the fox. The fox knows many things, but the hedgehog knows one thing well. According to Berlin, Tolstoy was a fox who wanted to be a hedgehog. That is to say, Tolstoy naturally tended to see the world in terms of individualities, as a world various, multiple, and incapable of being subdued to one principle or explanation. However, Berlin feels, Tolstoy still felt the need for some all-embracing principle or unifying faith. If *War and Peace* is predominantly the novel of Tolstoy the fox, the balance begins to shift toward the hedgehog in *Anna Karenina*.

As its famous first sentence—"All happy families are alike, but every unhappy family is unhappy in its own way"—announces, *Anna Karenina* is a novel about families. The novel has two main plots. The Kitty-Levin plot is a story of a family's making, and the Anna-Vronsky plot is a story of adultery. Anna's adultery poses a moral problem which Tolstoy worries endlessly in the novel, and he seems very much to want to find the moral principle which will resolve it once and for all. The Pauline epigraph, "Vengeance is mine; I shall repay," coupled with the fact of Anna's suicide, seems to suggest the solution, condemning Anna categorically. Yet even here Tolstoy's ability to render his characters with an individuality that allows them to escape all such general dicta asserts itself. He grants Anna a vitality and appeal which undermine his own efforts to capture her for moral judgment. The questions Tolstoy meant to answer about her behavior remain permanently unanswerable. In *Anna Karenina*, the hedgehog and the fox are at a standoff, although the former is beginning to get the upper hand, which it retained throughout the last stage of Tolstoy's life.

Tolstoy's Conversion

With the autobiographical *My Confession* (1879–1881), Tolstoy made the decisive transition to the simplifying dogmatism that dominated the last portion of his life. In this book, Tolstoy describes his spiritual development as a long battle between his confirmed early skepticism about orthodox Christianity and his constant fear that without some such faith his life would be devoid of meaning. He analyzes his early life, painting it, probably exaggeratedly, as irredeemably sinful and vicious, and he repudiates both his writing and his devotion to family life as mere makeshifts to hide from himself the emptiness of a purposeless life. He recounts his "conversion" to the practical religion which alone, he felt, could guide his life, his dawning recognition that "to know God and to live is one and the same thing. God is Life."

The "Tolstoyism" for which he became famous is not so much a religion as a rationalist ethos and a practical philosophy of life. Purged of mysticism and theology, the essence of Tolstoy's faith lay in his belief that moral law is absolute and unvarying and that its dictates are spoken through conscience, the instinctive source of all morality. The dictates of conscience are essentially those taught by Christ in the Sermon on the Mount: love, self-denial, humility, and the return of good for evil. From these commandments Tolstoy drew his fundamental rules for life: that one should live simply, that all have the duty to labor, that one should not take up arms against another, that private property should be relinquished, that all institutions of the state which usurp God's sole right to judge and direct life should be abolished. Thus, the political consequence of Tolstoy's religious conversion was a belief in anarchism.

Tolstoy attempted to arrange his life according to these precepts, working in the fields, making his own shoes and clothing, and paring his life down to a rigorous asceticism. In this endeavor, Tolstoy struggled constantly to remove himself from the more worldly life of his family that continued around him, while his wife battled to curb his eccentricities and keep him from giving away his property and copyrights. The animosity between them blighted his last years.

Final Years

During this time, Tolstoy strove to instill in his writings a simplicity and universality in accord with his ethics. He came to condemn his earlier works as frivolous at best, sinful at worst. In *What is Art?* (1898), he describes his ideal of a perfectly communicative art which would appeal to every audience and whose subject would be the great moral truths, rendered with the simplicity of a fable or biblical parable. In addition to numerous short pieces written in accordance with this model, his late writings include many exegeses of his ethics, tracts against such evils as tobacco and alcohol, dramas, and a number of courageous broadsides directed against the government as well as "The Death of Ivan Ilych" (1886), "The Kreutzer Sonata" (1890), "Master and Man" (1895), *Resurrection*, which was published to aid the Christian-communist Doukhobor sect (1899), and *Hadji Murat* (1904), a last novel vivified by some of the pagan energies Tolstoy tried so vigorously to subdue in his final years. While the didacticism of some of these works renders them unpalatable to modern tastes, their combination of passion and simplicity makes many of them as impressive as Tolstoy's early masterpieces.

By the end of Tolstoy's life, the translation of his works into other languages, the gathering to him of disciples from all over, his much publicized struggles with his wife, and his run-ins with the government and the Orthodox church (he was excommunicated in 1901) had made him a world figure. When, in 1910, having fled his intolerable relationship with his family, he fell ill and died in Astapovo, it was an event of international significance.

ESSAY QUESTIONS WITH ANSWERS

"The Death of Ivan Ilych"

9.1 "The Death of Ivan Ilych" begins with a short scene depicting the discovery of Ivan's death by his colleagues. What is Tolstoy's purpose in beginning the story this way?

Answer Death is nearly as inevitable in fiction as it is in life. It is equally essential to tragedy and to thriller, to novel, comic book, soap opera, and serial. Death is part of every writer's stock in trade.

Yet the place of death in fiction is paradoxical. There is a striking discrepancy between this proliferation of imagined death and our emotional response to it. How often does a fictional death really startle or touch a reader? The very quantity of the imaginary dead and our overfamiliarity with the three or four traditional literary ways our heroes typically meet their ends—the death in battle, the tragic hero's death, the frail heroine's demise—may make it difficult for us to care. If somehow we do find ourselves too uncomfortably saddened, we can always say, "It is only a story."

The special function of death in fiction may lie exactly in its doubleness, the way it allows us to encounter what we dread and dismiss it at the same time. Stories, like dreams, allow us to glimpse the intolerable without necessarily forcing us to face our fears. We develop a comforting familiarity with the threatening and unpredictable. After all, there is nothing more predictable than a shocker that shocks us in every second scene, finally dispatches the lurking evil, and sends us off with a happy ending, all in ninety minutes. There is even something reassuring, sad though it is, about the fact that King Lear must always die in the last act and Don Quixote on the last page. Fiction regularizes death, molds it into familiar forms, and to a great extent draws its teeth.

"The Death of Ivan Ilych" includes death as part of its action. However, Tolstoy has placed death at the very center of the story; he has written a story *about* death. This presents certain unusual problems. In order to succeed as a story, "The Death of Ivan Ilych" must avoid the literary conventions and clichés that often dull our sensitivity to the reality of death. It must overcome the defenses of imagination and denial that shield us from the truth that we must die. The beginning of Tolstoy's story suggests how he means to accomplish this task.

The title holds nothing back. The fact of Ivan's death is given bluntly, precluding many of death's usual literary uses. The story is entirely lacking in suspense and surprises. It does not pose the mystery story's usual whodunit question, nor is there any question about whether Ivan will somehow be saved. He will die, and Tolstoy's very simple story offers no distractions from this awful fact.

Not only does the story give away its ending, it actually begins after Ivan has died, and in a way that questions the significance of his death. We hear of Ivan's death as it comes to the attention of his colleagues literally by accident, as one of them, Peter Ivanovich, happens upon Ivan's obituary in the newspaper. It causes only the smallest stir: some murmured regrets, a recollection of the last time he had been seen, a perfunctory question about the widow. In addition, the story allows us to overhear his colleagues' unspoken thoughts as each considers what Ivan Ilych's death means for his own ambitions: a chance for promotion, a vacant position to be filled by a relative. But even the more candid thoughts of these men, interrupted in the course of business by news of their fellow's death, are strangely flat and uninflected. Their greed is nearly as pale and automatic as their sympathy.

It is appropriate that Tolstoy has Ivan Ilych's colleagues discover his death through the newspaper—the neutral impersonal voice of public events—for this suggests how remote they are from Ivan's death. It means very little to them. His death is no more than news, just one among the too-numerous and indistinguishable mishaps that fill the papers day after day. Thus, the thoughts of Ivan's colleagues as they return to work place a decisive distance between themselves and Ivan: "It is he who is dead and not I."

By beginning the story with the tepid and inadequate feelings of Ivan's colleagues, Tolstoy puts his readers in a curiously vulnerable position. We must feel superior to these uncompassionate men. Yet the very ordinariness of these men and their thoughts suggests a generalization which would necessarily include ourselves: This is how we often react to death. The story seems to pose a question for the reader: How would you react to the death of such an acquaintance? Might you not also congratulate yourself on your better luck? If we impute some greater sympathy to ourselves, the story seems to refute us. After all, Ivan Ilych can hardly test our real feelings because he does not yet exist for us. If his death is no more than news to his colleagues, his life and death are at this point in the story merely rumor to us.

In this first scene, then, Tolstoy presents death not as it usually occurs in literature—heroic or tragic, romantic or shocking, in any case, significant—but as it often appears in daily life: remote, half acknowledged, little felt. The death of Tolstoy's Everyman (the name Ivan Ilych is the Russian equivalent of John Doe) is simply not real to his colleagues, protected as they are by their complacency and the reassuring routine of work. However, by showing how easily and unthinkingly the reality of death can be dismissed and by hinting at the inadequacy of this response, Tolstoy's story begins preparing the way for a more authentic encounter with death.

9.2 It has been said that Tolstoy's writing combines the concreteness and particularity of a realistically imagined world with a broadly generalizing critical moral vision. In this combination, Tolstoy achieves his distinctive identity as a writer. We might call this combination of technique and theme "critical realism." How does Tolstoy achieve this combination in the first chapter of "Ivan Ilych"?

Answer The first chapter, in which Tolstoy follows Peter Ivanovich as he pays his respects to Ivan Ilych's family, elaborates the theme "it is he who is dead and not I." However, as the chapter proceeds, we recognize that this feeling represents not only one individual's complacency but a failure or unwillingness on the part of society as a whole to admit the fact of death in a more feeling way. By the end of this short chapter, we feel that we know this society and how it manages its feelings, and we sense what is false and shallow about it. Yet Tolstoy tells us none of this directly; we seem to find out by ourselves. Tolstoy uses several narrative techniques to convince us of the reality of this world's things, people, and events and at the same time to allow us to discover the nature of this society as a moral reality.

The story is told by an omniscient narrator who is privy to the thoughts and feelings of the characters. In an earlier version, Tolstoy wrote the story as a diary, recounted in Ivan Ilych's own voice. One can theorize that Tolstoy changed to an omniscient narrator because this method of narration allows greater flexibility. It can widen its focus to include an entire scene or group of people, as in the description of the collective response of Ivan's coworkers to his death, and it can narrow its focus to emphasize a single detail or present the feelings of a single character. In the second portion of the first chapter, the narration focuses on Peter Ivanovich as he pays his condolences to Ilych's family, and we see the scene as he sees it.

For Peter Ivanovich, the call is strictly a matter of propriety, a tiresome duty. He intends to go, make the gestures and utter the conventionalities that are expected of him, and leave as quickly as possible for something more pleasant: a round of bridge, perhaps. The tone of the scene is set by the discrepancy between the formal rituals of mourning Peter Ivanovich must perform and his lack of any real feeling, his distraction. He is not certain what he must do. As he approaches the bier, he wonders, Should I cross myself? Yes, he decides, "at such times it is always safe to cross oneself."* But is he supposed to genuflect? And if so, how? Toward the coffin? The priest? The icons?

These protocols of mourning are a standard of behavior; they represent what everyone is expected to do. They are the common coin of social life, and by putting them on display in this scene, Tolstoy allows us to feel that we are glimpsing society itself.

Peter Ivanovich seems to grant these social customs unquestioned authority. He is eager to uphold the standards of propriety, to do the right thing (whatever it is). But his concern is only for propriety. The forms of mourning, as they are mimicked by Peter Ivanovich and as they are more theatrically enacted by Ivan's widow, are entirely uninvested with real feeling. They are only forms. If we could judge this society by its customs, we could say that it has absolute authority—everyone acts as he or she should—but that it is at the same time a fraud, since its customs are merely dead husks of convention. They serve as masks for heartlessness rather than signs of concern. We get the sense that society is false and artificial. It stands apart from the people who animate it, as a mask rests in front of a face. Society is absolute; it displays itself everywhere, and it is a lie.

One of Tolstoy's characteristic skills is evident in the way he uses the physical trappings of society to help betray its falseness. Our sense of the tangible reality of this world is built up out of descriptions of the numerous objects that seem to come into view as Peter Ivanovich glances around Ivan Ilych's house: the coffin lid, with its decorative gold cloth and tassels; the ornately carved edge of a table which catches the widow's scarf as she walks by; the "clean cambric handkerchief" into which she weeps. When Peter Ivanovich and Ivan Ilych's widow talk in her well-furnished drawing room, Tolstoy directs our attention

*Translated by Aylmer Maude, New York, New American Library, 1960. All references to "The Death of Ivan Ilych" in this chapter are to the Maude translation.

to the furniture rather than to their conversation. Peter Ivanovich struggles with a hassock that squeaks and bounces under him. The two of them silently conspire, shifting the albums and sliding the ashtray under, to save the table from his cigarette ashes. The scene hovers on the edge of comedy as the sheer "thingness" of this overstuffed room, with its knickknacks and pink cretonne upholstery, intrudes on their efforts to play decently the roles of disconsolate widow and concerned friend of the family.

Tolstoy's ability to describe this scene in such detail makes it seem real, but its very tangibility makes a moral point. The materiality of the setting outweighs its humanity, making this society seem less human than it might be. Just as the forms of mourning are unanimated by true emotion, these objects seem not so much things among which a life is fashioned as obstacles which stand in the way of life. When Tolstoy lingers on the antique clock in the dining room which, he tells us, Ivan Ilych had liked so much, we sense the terrible inconsequentiality of such objects in relation to death, the emptiness of a life devoted to things. Tolstoy reinforces this irony when, later on, we find out that Ivan Ilych's illness had begun when he fell while redecorating his house.

9.3 "Ivan Ilych's life had been most simple and most ordinary and therefore most terrible." Tolstoy's story can be considered an exegesis of this startling declarative sentence, which begins the second chapter. How does Tolstoy succeed in presenting an entire life in the space of a few dozen pages? How does Tolstoy make present to us the terribleness which is the meaning of Ivan Ilych's undistinguished life?

Answer At the beginning of Chap. 2, the narrative leaves Peter Ivanovich, who drops out of the story, and focuses on Ivan Ilych. In a few short pages, his life history is recounted. His life is amenable to summary because it is so entirely normal, unmarked by adventure or disaster or any other feature that would distinguish it. His past seems to be composed from statistical norms: His father is moderately successful; the one brother who does well is balanced by the other who fails; Ivan Ilych is, of course, the middle son. School, graduation, a career, advancement, marriage, and children follow one after another smoothly and predictably. Ivan Ilych's life seems almost to be cut from a pattern, and Tolstoy turns again and again to the same word to describe it: "decorous." Ivan Ilych's decorousness lies in his unquestioning willingness to conform to what is expected of him, to take the path of least resistance. When political opinions change, he retailors his beliefs to suit the latest style. He marries not so much out of love as from the sense that it is the proper thing for a man his age.

But the decorousness of his life betrays its artificiality; like his overdecorated house, his life is populated by dead forms which weigh upon real life, inhibiting spontaneity and vitality. Tolstoy makes this point by hinting at what this evenly running life fails to respond to. In a single phrase, in the midst of an account of ordinary domestic affairs—a tight budget, a new job, a new house—we learn that two children have died, as if this were of no more importance than a raise in salary. The even tenor of this life seems to depend on the denial of those things which cannot be comfortably and undisturbingly assimilated to it. No fully lived life can be so orderly and unbedeviled as to allow such neat condensation: "So Ivan Ilych lived for seventeen years after his marriage."

Ivan Ilych coats everything in his experience—work, relations with family and friends—with the approved veneer of the pleasant, easy, and correct, and Tolstoy's uneventful story travels effortlessly over the smooth surface of his life. However, at a number of points Tolstoy purposely breaks through this even finish by using the omniscient narrator to comment directly on the action. After recounting the one ludicrously mild "difficulty" in Ivan Ilych's easy life and the triumph into which he turns it—a promotion and a new, opulently furnished house—Tolstoy takes the measure of Ivan's happiness with brutal precision:

> In reality it was just what is usually seen in the houses of people of moderate means who want to appear rich, and therefore succeed only in resembling others like themselves: there were damasks, dark wood, plants, rugs, and dull and polished bronzes—all the things people of a certain class have in order to resemble other people of that class. His house was so like the others that it would never have been noticed, but to him it all seemed quite exceptional.

The authority of the omniscient voice, its ability to step back and deliver a categorical judgment ("In reality . . ."), works here to savage Ivan Ilych's narrow, secondhand notion of the good life. The potency of such commentary is preserved by the sparingness with which Tolstoy employs it. When he uses it, he does so to effect; on one other occasion, he rounds on Ivan Ilych, capturing him in two brief phrases: "The pleasures connected with his work were pleasures of ambition; his social pleasures were those of vanity."

It is, of course, Ivan Ilych's illness which shatters the calm of his life and decisively indicts the conventional life which has no capacity to admit such fundamental realities as sickness and death. Here too Tolstoy's means of managing narration shapes the way we come to understand and feel the story's meaning. As Ivan Ilych declines toward death, the narrative comes more and more to focus on his silent thoughts. Accordingly, we start to see the world, which now looks so drastically different to the sick man, as he sees it, and we feel his progressive isolation. In this way, the narration accomplishes what amounts to a reversal of the earlier terms of the story. The defining element in Ivan Ilych's character had been his tendency to deny everything difficult or anomalous; in short, to deny everything other than himself. In his legal work, Tolstoy tells us, he had found a way to cut through all "extraneous" consider-ations, all the knotty problems of real human litigants, and reduce everything to the few forms of a mechanical process. The world of others is entirely external to him, and he manages his relations to it with an unfeeling dexterity. With his illness, he finds the tables turned. His doctor confronts him as though he, Ivan Ilych, were an importunate plaintiff, and Ivan finds himself treated with the same cool, professional impersonality with which he had minimized the reality of others. He is now the other.

Much of the terribleness of Ivan Ilych's life is apparent at this moment. The very way he has lived, now embodied in those around him, leaves him to die emptily, unpitied, with no one to share his suffering. His sins have been small and unextraordinary, but with the logic of religion and myth they damn him to an absolute condition of suffering and abandonment. Tolstoy unrelentingly brings home to us each moment of Ivan Ilych's pain. He is brutally explicit in giving the details of Ivan Ilych's decline: the wasted flesh, the sudden irrefutable glimpse of a change for the worse, the humiliation when he can no longer manage his body's functions, and the moments of frantic hope that subside helplessly into despair. We feel him dying. It is terrible that he has unthinkingly lived in such a way that there is now nothing to mitigate his horror. Our sense of terror may rise as we share his sense of this unfairness—how could he have known?—and sense the relation, both intimate and strange, between his mor-tality and our own.

In one sense, the "ordinariness" of Ivan Ilych's life lies in its conventionality, which is terrible in its failure to prepare him for the trial of dying. In another sense, the ordinariness refers to his life's universality, the fact that it is a life little different from many others we could imagine; in this case, its terribleness lies in the mere fact of his death, which is itself ordinary, universal in its significance, and quite horrifying. However, the significance of this Everyman's death extends beyond death itself; it bears on life and its conduct. For Tolstoy, it is most of all in its demands on the conduct of our lives that the terribleness—that is, the exigent and inescapable significance—of death lies.

9.4   As Ivan Ilych declines toward death, the dwindling life of this average man, which had seemed perhaps blander and less noteworthy than most, suddenly seems to be populated by absolutes; great issues are at stake in his last days. The death of this ordinary man leads us to an ultimate question: How should a person live? Does Tolstoy's story suggest an answer? Are there any characters or ways of life which seem capable of affirming the meaning and value of life in the face of death?

Answer   Exiled from his former life—the satisfactions of position and prestige, the pride of the householder and husband, the small pleasures of card playing and visiting—which now seems entirely hollow and devoid of significance, Ivan Ilych is able to see that life whole and judge it: It becomes "the Lie." He arrives finally at an all-embracing question: "Maybe I did not live as I ought to have done?" In the answer to this question, Tolstoy tells us, lies nothing less than "the sole solution of all the riddles of life and death." Tolstoy is careful to suggest an answer to this question in the later stages of his story.

Gerasim, Ivan's servant, and Vasya, Ivan's young son, both stand apart from "the Lie." Gerasim faces up to the fact of Ivan Ilych's death, neither denying it nor withdrawing. The dying man senses his honesty and sympathy, and it is from Gerasim alone that he is able to draw some comfort. Gerasim's attitude toward Ivan Ilych rests on his recognition of the simple fact of their shared humanity. The first words we hear him speak acknowledge the collective significance of death: "It's God's will. We shall all come to it some day." The crucial word here is "we," and throughout the story it is Gerasim alone who speaks it.

While Gerasim is the character who is capable of caring for Ilych, Ivan's son is the one who gives him, momentarily, the chance to care for another. At the very last, still tormented by doubts, asking, "What *is* the right thing?" the dying man feels his son kissing his hand and, in his first moment of self-transcendence, feels sorry for the boy. This instant of feeling for someone other than himself releases Ivan Ilych from bitterness and allows him to embrace death without dread: "How good and how simple!" His last words are, "Forgive me."

Both Gerasim and Vasya are untinctured by the hypocrisy, the "hiding of life and death," that characterizes the society in which Ivan Ilych has lived his life, because both stand outside this society. Gerasim is a peasant and worker, and he carries with him the aura of the more natural world of physical labor, "the pleasant smell of tar and fresh winter air"; he represents health and vitality to the dying man. Gerasim's relations with others have a directness and spontaneity that seem an extension of the natural world into society. He performs the unpleasant tasks of cleaning and caring for Ivan Ilych easily and cheerfully, accepting this too as a natural part of life in the body.

Like Gerasim, Vasya represents an imagined escape from the fraud of society. As a child, he is not yet fully a citizen of this lying world. Whereas Gerasim represents the hope for a natural life, Vasya offers a vision of the innocence in which, it is said, each of us begins.

Gerasim, Vasya, and Ivan Ilych in his last moments of achieved grace all embody the imperative that Tolstoy repeated again and again in his fiction and his didactic writings: We must live our lives for other people. For Tolstoy, only this self-abnegation can redeem life from the darkness that surrounds it.

9.5 What is the relationship between Tolstoy's techniques and his themes, between the realist's commitment to everyday life as it is lived in society and the moralist's desire to sum up this life and judge it?

Answer Gerasim and Vasya, the peasant and the child, who incarnate Tolstoy's notion of life as it should be lived, are idealizations, wishes as much as realities. Gerasim in particular can be seen to embody the familiar romantic wish for a presocial natural life purged of the compromises and inauthenticity of life in society. Since Rousseau, European thought has been tempted by the fantasy of the natural man, and Tolstoy's glorification of the Russian peasants—who, needless to say, had their own complex and troubled situation in life—is no different from countless other attempts to find the pure, primal human being in the noble savage, the humble proletarian, or the unsullied child.

The fact that Tolstoy is forced to look outside society for a solution to its problems and the extent to which he is willing to sacrifice his usually unerring imagination to wishful thinking indicate the extremity of his critique of bourgeois society. In imagining the appealing but impossibly good Gerasim (is it credible that Gerasim should be so kind to a man who must have been a less than beneficent master?), Tolstoy the realist becomes Tolstoy the romantic. As Tolstoy's plain tale expands into a repudiation of society as such, he is forced to look beyond it. Genuine life, for Tolstoy, lies elsewhere: in the fields, with the peasants, with the children, with God, and ultimately beyond our everyday, secular selves.

Here we see what is paradoxical in Tolstoy, consummately skilled in the realist's art of rendering the worldliness of the world yet insistent upon our need to transcend the world in which his art is so firmly rooted. It is this tension between Tolstoy's ability to present the world in all its vivid reality and his hunger to go beyond the merely real to the transcendentally true which eventually transforms Tolstoy from a realist into a sage, from a writer of great epics into a dispenser of what he felt to be the greater truths of moral philosophy. The same antithetical energies impel "The Death of Ivan Ilych." Its strength as art lies in its sure grasp of this world—the everyday world without belief or reverence that is so recognizably our own—but its aspiration lies beyond.

D.E.

SUGGESTED READINGS

Berlin, Isaiah, *The Hedgehog and the Fox* (1953).
Christian, R. F., *Tolstoy: A Critical Introduction* (1969).
Lukács, Georg, *Studies in European Realism* (1950).
Matlaw, Ralph (ed.), *Tolstoy* (1967).
Steiner, George, *Tolstoy or Dostoevsky: An Essay in the Old Criticism* (1959).

C H A P T E R   1   0

IBSEN

Background and Early Years

"Anyone who wishes to understand me fully must know Norway," Ibsen told an interviewer in 1902. The reader of Ibsen will come away with a vivid mental landscape containing long nights, thick mists, craggy fjords, and provincial towns of claustrophobic middle-class homes where the only entertainment is endless gossip. In general, the facts support this picture of Ibsen's mental landscape. At the time of Henrik Ibsen's birth in 1828, Norway had produced virtually no great writers and scarcely existed as an independent country. From 1387 to 1814, Norway had been under Danish rule, and it remained dominated by Danish culture through the nineteenth century. From 1814 to 1905, it was under Sweden's jurisdiction. Politically and culturally dominated, Norway was also economically underdeveloped; its towns were tiny, its farmers and fishers put at a disadvantage by their old-fashioned methods. Even its capital, Christiania (now known as Oslo), had a population of only 30,000.

Ibsen was born in the small town of Skien, 100 miles southwest of Christiania. His family was well-off, but his father, a businessman, went bankrupt a few years later, and the family moved to Venstøp, a nearby town, where they scraped by in poverty and social obscurity. At age 15, Ibsen escaped to Grimstad, where he worked as a pharmacist's apprentice. When not occupied filling prescriptions, he sketched, read, wrote plays, made a few friends, and impregnated a servant girl, whose child he supported but ignored for the rest of his life.

Ibsen had been studying to matriculate at the university in Christiania, and he moved there in 1850 to prepare for the entrance examination, which he failed. The same year his first play, *The Burial Mound*, was performed. The play was not a success, but in 1851 Ibsen was hired by the Norwegian Theatre in Bergen to write and produce plays. This theater was part of a movement to encourage the presentation of plays in Norwegian, dealing with Norwegian themes; the more established theaters still performed in Danish.

Ibsen was a sensitive but not particularly effective producer. Nor was he initially successful as a playwright. During his years at the Norwegian Theatre, five of his plays were produced, but none drew a large audience. His stint in Bergen gave Ibsen valuable experience, though, and allowed him to tour Germany and Denmark, where he absorbed current theatrical techniques.

In 1857, Ibsen moved to Christiania, where he was artistic director of that city's Norwegian Theatre, and a year later he married Suzannah Thoreson. Sigurd, their only child, was born in 1859. Ibsen continued to write plays, but recognition eluded him, and in 1862 his theater went bankrupt. When Ibsen received a small government grant in 1863, he left for Italy, where he was joined in Rome by his family. For the next twenty-seven years, the Ibsen family returned to Norway only to visit.

Brand and *Peer Gynt*

While the Ibsens settled in Italy, a complicated crisis was shaking Europe as the Prussian army invaded the Danish duchies of Schleswig-Holstein. Ibsen called for Scandinavian solidarity, expecting Norway to give its neighbor military backing against Bismarck's extremely effective army. But Sweden and Norway, while sympathetic, did not intervene militarily. The Danes were defeated, and Ibsen raged against Scandinavian complacency and hypocrisy, which were the national characteristics, he decided, of a people so unwilling to fight for a principle.

Shortly after the Schleswig-Holstein crisis, in 1866, Ibsen published *Brand*, a play about a fanatical preacher who lashes out at his townspeople for their compromises and smug mediocrity. Though in part an outlet for Ibsen's fury at his own country's compromise, *Brand* also exposes the limitations of fanaticism: Brand's austere faith, while awesome, is deadly and misguided, for it excludes love.

In *Peer Gynt*, published a year later, Ibsen portrays the other side of the coin: the limitations of compromise. Peer Gynt is the opposite of Brand, a charming, self-deceiving, compulsively compromising mediocrity who gladly accepts the slogan of the monstrous, subhuman trolls, "To thyself be—*enough*," in place of the human "To thyself be *true*." Both Brand and Peer Gynt fail in life, the one by expecting too much of himself, the other by expecting too little.

Ibsen described Brand as himself at his best moments, while at his worst he was Peer Gynt. These two poles recur throughout his work: the single-minded seeker of truth opposing the lover of social convenience. But Ibsen shifts his viewpoint from play to play, refusing to oversimplify; if compromise seems repellent and destructive in *Ghosts* (1881), it becomes necessary in *The Wild Duck* (1884), whose truth seeker, Gregers Werle, wreaks havoc where he means to sow revelation.

Abandonment of Verse: A *Doll's House* and *Ghosts*

With *Brand* and *Peer Gynt*, both of which sold well, Ibsen became well-known. These plays also marked the end of his efforts to write verse drama. More easily read than performed, both involved scenery and action on too vast a scale for the stage, and both were written in verse. With the *League of Youth* (1869), Ibsen abandoned verse for prose, aiming at more colloquial language in a more ordinary setting. In *The Pillars of Society* (1877), he went still further in eliminating such stylized theatrical devices as monologs and asides. From this time until his last plays, Ibsen wrote in colloquial prose about contemporary themes in Norwegian settings. His plays, in fact, were controversial for their ordinariness; one critic accused him of having "dramatized the cooking of a Sunday dinner." The socially constricted small-town drawing rooms and their hypocritical inhabitants seemed to Ibsen's audiences to have been transferred directly from life to art.

Ibsen had been living in Dresden since 1868; in 1878, he moved to Rome, where he wrote *A Doll's House*, the story of a wife's departure from her husband's home. The slam of the door behind the departing Nora at the end of the play created a scandal. No woman, people argued, would be so unnatural as to leave her children, and one actress insisted on performing the play with a happy ending. Greater still was the scandal surrounding *Ghosts*, in which inherited syphilis acts as a focal point for the destructive preconceptions and inherited tendencies that limit each generation's capacity for self-realization. Readers and viewers were shocked by what they regarded as a clinical depiction of venereal disease.

Later Years

Ibsen had become known primarily as a writer of plays about social issues, a reputation reinforced by *An Enemy of the People* (1882), in which a doctor insists on revealing that his hometown, a supposedly healthful seaside resort, is actually a health hazard because of the sewage polluting its waters. Despite his colloquial dialog, however, Ibsen had always been a poet, more interested in evoking moods and exploring the various aspects of a situation than in taking a particular stand. With *The Wild Duck*, this tendency became more pronounced. Here and in Ibsen's later plays, particular objects seem to radiate multiple meanings, as important for their evocativeness as for their literal role in the play. The wild duck, the white horses of *Rosmersholm* (1886), the sea in *The Lady from the Sea* (1888), Thea's hair in *Hedda Gabler* (1890), and the steeple in *The Master Builder* (1892) all have a mysteriously suggestive aura, indicating that what is not said is more important than what is, that what cannot be explained provides a more powerful motive than what can.

In his last plays, *Little Eyolf* (1894), *John Gabriel Borkman* (1896), and *When We Dead Awaken* (1899), Ibsen became progressively less concerned with re-creating realistic situations and conversation. His final play, like *Brand*, ends amid mountains with the burial of its central figures in an avalanche, a difficult scene to produce on stage. In 1891, Ibsen and his family returned to Norway for good. He died in Christiania in 1906.

Literary Affinities

Ibsen has been associated with two important literary movements: naturalism and symbolism. The French novelist Emile Zola, whose *Thérèse Raquin* appeared in 1873, was the major force behind naturalism. He felt that the writer should be a scientist, transcribing the actual, even gruesome details of life, showing how inheritance and circumstance determine the destinies of human beings. Ibsen's *Ghosts* was read by his contemporaries within this context.

Hand in hand with naturalism went a new realism in the production of plays. For the first time, real furniture was used on the stage, and stage props were no longer painted into the scenery. Acting became less stylized, and actors began to speak to each other on stage rather than to the audience. The theaters also began to support themselves differently. So-called independent theaters sprang up that relied on subscriptions rather than the unpredictable response to particular plays. This made possible the production of more experimental plays with limited audience appeal. Without these theaters—the Freie Bühne in Berlin, the Théâtre-Libre in Paris, and the Independent Theatre in London— Ibsen could scarcely have gotten the productions he deserved. Nor, without Ibsen, would these theaters have had the plays they required.

Ibsen's development as an artist, then, was intimately connected with the major literary trends of nineteenth-century Europe, first toward the increasingly realistic portrayal of everyday life and then toward the use of symbols, objects whose accreted meanings hint at spiritual truths that are inexpressible in literal terms. The Belgian playwright Maurice Maeterlinck (1862–1949) was the major proponent of symbolist drama, although Ibsen's Swedish contemporary August Strindberg showed a similar lack of concern for the literally plausible.

Ibsen was a tremendously influential force in the shaping of modern drama and literature. The young James Joyce wrote him awed, admiring letters. George Bernard Shaw treated him as a great social critic in *The Quintessence of Ibsenism* (1891). Feminists from the late nineteenth century on have embraced *A Doll's House* as a call for the liberation of women. The poet Rainer Maria Rilke portrayed Ibsen in *The Notebooks of Malte Laurids Brigge* (1910) as an example of the heroic artist struggling to express the intangible and find external equivalents for inner mysteries.

ESSAY QUESTIONS WITH ANSWERS

Hedda Gabler

10.1   *Hedda Gabler* bears its central character's maiden name, yet she has just returned from her honeymoon with Jörgen Tesman. Why is the play not called *Hedda Tesman?*

Answer   The title reveals two things: Hedda's utter lack of identification with her new life as the wife of Tesman and her persistent identification with her father, General Gabler.

Hedda cannot figure out what to do with herself, and her marriage provides no solution. She is married, probably even pregnant, but her identity as Hedda Tesman remains irrelevant and incongruous, an incongruity noticed by everyone but Tesman. Self-involved, Hedda has trouble being stirred by anything outside herself. Her emotions are untouched by life, her identity untouched by her marriage. "Now you're a part of the family," Tesman keeps telling Hedda in Act I, but she replies, "Leave me out of it." The name Gabler serves as a reminder of her isolation and of her continued identification of herself as General Gabler's daughter.

"Do you remember her riding along the road with her father?" Miss Tesman asks Berte. "In that long black habit? And feathers in her hat?"* Hedda's major source of identity lies in the past, in her apparently superior social position and her association with her father, presumably a man of action and distinction. Hedda's pistols had been his, and her attraction to violence is also probably a paternal inheritance. General Gabler's portrait dominates the back room where Hedda plays a wild tune on the piano before shooting herself with his pistols.

Elizabeth Hardwick points out that Hedda is more a man than a woman. Certainly in her society, egotism, curiosity, and drive would lead a man to success, while for a woman, whose life was so limited that she had to seek out

---

*Translated by Una Ellis-Fermor, Baltimore, Penguin, 1975. All references to *Hedda Gabler* in this chapter are to the Ellis-Fermor translation.

171

other people's experiences and achievements, these same qualities led only to frustration. Ibsen wrote to a young female friend that women's wills were undeveloped and unhealthy because women had to look outside themselves for sources of interest and identity, while happiness could come only through the exertion of one's own will. To a certain extent, then, Hedda's diseased will results from the fact that she is a woman, Hedda Gabler rather than General Gabler. If she were a general, her desire to bend others to her will would find a more direct and acceptable outlet. As Hedda, however, she can exert her will only subtly, vicariously, and destructively.

Thea Elstved is also frequently addressed by her maiden name. Tesman keeps forgetting that she is married and introduces her as Miss Rysing, ironically emphasizing the similarity of her position to Hedda's. Like Hedda, Thea does not love her husband, and so it is fitting that she retain her maiden name in the minds of others. But while Hedda has been committing herself to a lifetime of hypocrisy, Thea has courageously acted out her alienation from her husband by leaving him.

Just as Lövborg's addressing Hedda as Gabler indicates his unresolved previous attachment to her, Tesman's use of the name Miss Rysing suggests that his involvement with Thea is not entirely over. It points in fact to the end of the play, when the deaths of Lövborg and Hedda are counterpointed by the collaboration of Thea and Tesman, suggesting an eventual happy ending, when, well after the final curtain, Miss Rysing will perhaps become Mrs. Tesman, finally obliterating her maiden name.

10.2   For much of Act I, Hedda is absent, presumably asleep. But despite her absence, the audience gets a good sense of what she is like. How does the interaction of Berte, Miss Tesman, and Jörgen in Act I prepare for the action of the play and the entrance of its heroine?

Answer   Absenting Hedda from the opening scene is, of course, good dramatic strategy, for it gives her later entrance greater impact. It also suggests some of the force of her personality, for the absent Miss Gabler is very much present in the consciousness and conversation of those who are already awake and moving about the stage.

We learn that she has already forced various characters to do a number of uncharacteristic things. Miss Tesman has bought a new hat and parasol and had to return home the previous night with Judge Brack rather than her nephew as an escort. Berte, the maid, has removed the slipcovers from the drawing room furniture, must learn to address her master as "Doctor," and is clearly nervous about how she will please her new mistress. All three on-stage characters com-ment on the great quantity of luggage Hedda has brought with her from her honeymoon, which has forced Hedda to stay up late unpacking.

The luggage says a number of things about Hedda, suggesting a habit of luxury, a taste for fine clothes, and a disregard for others. It even suggests her tendency to define herself through style rather than substance, things rather than ideas. The overly fashion-conscious Hedda apparently cares more for the flare with which a thing is done than for the thing itself.

Hedda's force of will is indicated throughout Act I by the intensity with which her wishes are described by the other characters. She *had* to unpack immediately upon arrival. She *cannot* live with slipcovers on the furniture. She *had* to have the trip. All these imperatives, however, are applied to essentially superficial needs. Hedda had insisted upon a lengthy honeymoon because it was the fashion to go on lengthy honeymoons. Similarly, the covered furniture and unpacked clothes are matters merely of style; Hedda knows how she wants to live, but she does not know what she wants to do.

The evident change in the Tesman household's routine, the impressive quantity of her luggage, and the pressure she seems to exert even while sleeping all suggest that the impact of her actual presence will be forceful indeed.

10.3
Despite Hedda's force of will, there is something cowardly about her. Thea appears terrified of her, yet on hearing of Thea's leaving her husband, Hedda says, "How did you dare risk it?" Hedda admits to Lövborg that she is an awful coward, terrified above all else of creating a scandal and being ridiculed. Why should a scandal be the most fearful thing for Hedda?

Answer Hedda is afraid of committing herself to something irrevocable. Like Peer Gynt, the compulsive compromiser, she does not believe in burning her bridges behind her. She takes pleasure in Lövborg's accounts of his scandalous life because they allow her the illusion of experience without its price. She will commit no outward act of unfaithfulness, she makes clear to Judge Brack and Lövborg; though hollow, her marriage will be irreproachable. Nor had she been willing to go along with Lövborg previously, when their relationship had threat-ened to become "serious." Adultery, love, and scandal would compromise her in the eyes of others. For someone obsessed with style, the opinions of others count above all else.

As long as life remains for Hedda a spectator sport, she can have the illusion of living while maintaining an irreproachable composure. A scandal, though, would force her into the arena. Gossip, after all, is what the spectators do at the expense of the players. Once gossiped about, she would become a pawn to other people's conceptions of her.

Hedda is accustomed to being admired from afar. Her image has been impressive in the past. She is a "fine lady," Berte says in Act I, and Miss Tesman agrees. Her ability to awe onlookers has been her greatest source of satisfaction. In marrying Tesman, she has already sacrificed some of her distance and dignity. That is why she is so insistent on not having been changed by her marriage. She is terrified of anything that would encroach still more on her ability to excite awe and envy, for it is on this ability that her sense of identity is based. Were she to excite gossip, that ability would be lost forever.

"One doesn't do that kind of thing," Hedda says in Act I, speaking of Miss Tesman's leaving her hat out. This concern with what people do or do not do has a dictatorial power over characters in Ibsen's plays. "That's what one says but doesn't do," Judge Brack says skeptically of Hedda's melodramatic death threat. In the play's final words, after her death, he exclaims, "One doesn't *do* that kind of thing!" Hedda's suicide is the one thing she manages to achieve that "one doesn't do." Her triumph is that she manages it perfectly, shooting herself through the temple and killing herself instantly. It was the one thing she could do that would be at once an irrevocable act and stylistically perfect. It is so profoundly inexplicable that it is virtually beyond the reach of gossip.

10.4 Hedda speaks of Lövborg's returning from the party at Brack's with "vine leaves in his hair." What is the significance of this image?

Answer Hedda seems to have a fuzzy, sentimental notion of genius. In speaking of vine leaves, she refers to Dionysus, the god of wine, and her assumption is that intoxication and creative genius are linked. It is a romantic idea and a dangerous one if the genius happens to be an alcoholic, as Lövborg is. Hedda might defend herself as hoping to lead Lövborg not to his former life of dissipation but to joyous liberation and self-fulfillment. He will, she hopes, have the strength to combine freedom and discipline, to step outside the bounds of social convention without falling to pieces. This triumphant joining of surrender and control would be signified by the vine leaves, worn as symbols of joy, not dissipation.

But Hedda's notion of vine leaves derives from no great insight into the creative process and certainly from no knowledge of Greek religion. While feeling herself superior to her surroundings, she is actually echoing a conventional notion of creative genius. Lövborg, of course, has no moderation; the vine leaves are beyond him. In surrendering himself to alcohol, he loses himself and his manuscript.

At this point, Lövborg can redeem himself in Hedda's eyes only by transforming the loss into an act of will. As accidents, the lost manuscript and drunken orgy are humiliating, but willed self-destruction has a certain beauty. Over and over, Hedda insists he must "do it beautifully." The adverb is revealing; what matters for Hedda is style: not what is done but that it be done beautifully.

If Lövborg will only shoot himself, she believes, through the temple if possible, he will be doing something "irradiated with spontaneous beauty"—something done without the random and meaningless quality of ordinary actions, something that maintains the coherence and purity of a mental construct.

Because this suicide is important more as an assertive act of will than as a death blow to the body, the temple, seat of intellect and will, is the most logical place for the bullet to strike; this emphasizes the deliberateness of the action, suggesting a methodical self-execution. The heart, where Hedda next thinks Lövborg has shot himself, is a sloppier organ but still has enough symbolic import to make the death beautiful. But the actual wound to the bowels is irredeemably messy, suggesting all the chaotic, meaningless accidents of ordinary life.

Hedda's beautiful ideas cannot be put into action without being demeaned. The image of the vine leaves exemplifies this separation between idea and enactment. Intended to suggest joyful liberation from constraint, the vine leaves in fact signify only debauchery and self-destruction. The world will not cooperate with Hedda's efforts to shape and "beautify" it.

10.5   *Hedda Gabler* is a concentrated, tightly constructed play that ends with the death of its central character. To what extent could it be called a tragedy in the classic Aristotelian sense?

Answer   *Hedda Gabler* is not a classic Aristotelian tragedy. It is an odd combination of tragedy and comedy, mingling the dramatic portrayal of human destinies with a satiric depiction of contemporary manners, as when Hedda's suicide is immediately followed by Brack's "One doesn't *do* that kind of thing!" This final comment on appropriate social behavior jars ludicrously with the tragic self-annihilation that immediately precedes it.

In Act I of *When We Dead Awaken*, Ibsen's last play, the sculptor Rubek reveals the secret of his portrait busts. "On the surface," he says, "there's the 'striking likeness.' " . . . But deep down underneath, there's the pompous self-righteous face of a horse, the obstinate muzzle of a mule. . . ." On the surface, in other words, Rubek merely portrays the outward appearance of his sitter. But lurking within is a satirical portrait, an attack on the person he seems to portray objectively. This same doubleness is evident in Ibsen's plays, where characters seem at once heroic and ludicrous. Dr. Stockmann in *Enemy of the People*, for example, is a courageous scientist who dares to tell the truth about sewage polluting a seaside resort, even though he knows this will turn the community against him. But he is also an absurdly stubborn, arrogant bungler. Ibsen never allows a character to strike a heroic pose without undercutting it in some way.

Maurice Valency in *The Flower and the Castle* suggests that Ibsen attained this two-sided quality by writing his plays twice: first straightforwardly as virtual melodramas, without the deflating comic touches, and then more satirically, as he revised to undercut his characters' pretensions. In this sense, Valency points out, the plays enact Ibsen's critiques of his own romantic illusions.

The undistinguished bourgeois settings, the characters' concern with money and social convention, and the generally unadmiring view of humankind all keep Ibsen's plays from being in the classic sense tragedies. The suffering of an Oedipus evokes awe before its excessiveness, its undeservedness, yet its inexorable logic. Hedda's suffering, however, is trivial compared with Oedipus's anguish. Unlike Oedipus, she bears no relation to her community as either leader or scapegoat; she is simply an anomaly. Her fate seems to grow out of no coherent logic; no oracular warning gives it meaning, nor does it bring insight or relief to others.

It is part of Ibsen's point—and part of Hedda's frustration—that her world does not accommodate tragedy. It is too ordinary and confined. The entire action takes place in two small rooms in the aftermath, not the midst, of whatever passions might be aroused. Hedda has already rejected Lövborg and married Tesman. Thea has already fallen in love with Lövborg and left her husband. The conversation is colloquial and choppy. None of the characters has tragic stature. Thea, who might aspire to it, has only a limited understanding and the passions of a nurse more than those of a lover. Lövborg has the genius but not the dignity or self-control. Hedda lacks the depth. Nothing from without has ever aroused her, as Brack points out, and there can be no tragic heroine without passion.

Hedda seeks the beauty and grandeur associated with tragedy but lacks the inner resources and outer circumstances necessary to live it. Her tragedy, then, is that she has been done out of her tragedy. This is true to such an extent that even after giving up on Lövborg as an inept tragic hero, when she acts out the tragedy flawlessly, tragedy nonetheless fails her. The curtain does not fall immediately after the deadly gun shot, but after Brack's final, deflating comment. Nor does the plot seem to resolve itself definitively, for the audience can anticipate the union of Tesman and Thea and the publication of Lövborg's book.

These indications of a future leave the play feeling unfinished. There is no sweeping clean of the stage by death and no summing up by a chorus, only the cynical, debauched judge's "One doesn't *do* such things!" Like the chorus of *Oedipus*, Brack speaks not merely for himself but for his society. But that society has been degraded and trivialized since the time when a chorus could pronounce a deeply felt truth on its behalf, for example, *Oedipus*'s "moral man must always look to his ending." People have debated for centuries what Aristotle meant by catharsis. One possible means of defining it may be to point to the end of *Hedda Gabler* and say that it is precisely that feeling of resolution, relief, and communal emotion that the ending of *Hedda Gabler* does not provide.

10.6 Early readers of *Hedda Gabler* were mystified by its portrait of, in one critic's words, "a monster in female form." Others found more to sympathize with; the actress Elizabeth Robins describes Hedda as "pitiable in her hungry loneliness." Is Hedda in any way justified, or is she an inexplicably cold and destructive person?

Answer Certainly, Hedda's hostility toward her tedious, unimaginative environment is understandable. She is surrounded by extremely uninteresting and unappealing people, either shallow or corrupt. Judge Brack, for example, considering his profession, ought to represent his society's standards at their best. Instead, beneath his veneer of respectability, Brack is a cynical womanizer who would use his recognition of Hedda's pistol to manipulate her. As a purely negative force, then, Hedda seems to oppose this world and expose its mediocrity.

Hedda can also be seen as a feminist heroine, taking a stand against the stiflingly limited role available to her as a woman. As a man, she would have had an outlet for her fierce will. She could, perhaps, have been a general like her father, using her pistols within a more acceptable social context. As a woman, she can exert her will only through others.

To a certain extent, Hedda's destructiveness is an element in everyone's makeup, an integral part of the world as conceived by Ibsen. Explaining her cruelty to Aunt Julle in the hat incident, Hedda says, "That kind of thing comes over me . . . and then I can't stop myself." Ibsen himself once told a friend of his longing to "commit a madness," to do something outrageous, such as hitting a teacher or making a scene in the street.

There are dark forces within everyone, Ibsen felt, and Hedda can be seen in part as a personification of those dark forces, or "trolls," as he called them in an early poem: "To *live* is to war with trolls/in the vaults of the heart and the brain." In the mind, then, there are mysterious drives that may dominate our actions without our understanding them. This assumption becomes increasingly important in Ibsen's later plays, where the observable actions and dialog seem only fragments thrown out by the huge, hidden dramas beneath the surface of the characters' minds. Not surprisingly, Ibsen was much admired by Sigmund Freud.

In all these ways, then, Hedda makes sense. She seems alienated from a corrupt society, frustrated by her fate as a woman, and shaped by a psyche she cannot understand. But she is also an extraordinarily dislikable character, devoid of emotional or intellectual depth. She wants not to alter her corrupt environment but to dominate it. She is the most conventional of characters, and her passions tend to be even more trivial than those of the people around her, for example, her envy of Thea's luxurious hair. There is no comfortable way of looking at Hedda. She remains always partly justified and partly monstrous.

R.H.

SUGGESTED READINGS

Fjelde, Rolf (ed.), *Ibsen: A Collection of Critical Essays* (1965).

Hardwick, Elizabeth. *Seduction and Betrayal* (1975).

McFarlane, James (ed.), *Henrik Ibsen* (1970).

Meyer, Michael, *Ibsen* (1971).

Northam, John, *Ibsen: A Critical Study* (1973).

Valency, Maurice, *The Flower and the Castle: An Introduction to Modern Drama* (1975).

CHAPTER 11

RIMBAUD

Background and Childhood

> And the Mother, closing the exercise book,
> went away satisfied and very proud, without seeing
> in the blue eyes and bumpy forehead
> the soul of her son given over to loathing.*

So begins Arthur Rimbaud's autobiographical poem "The Seven-Year-Old Poets," written when he was 17. Throughout his poetic writings, Rimbaud was to remain the small, vulnerable, secretly defiant boy confronted by smug, hugely looming authority; notice that the mother's capital M and the fact that she is *the* mother rather than *my* mother give her an anonymous, stolidly wall-like quality. Rimbaud wrote all his poetry between the ages of 14 and 23, and as a result it retains all the fierceness of adolescence, the violent seesawing between extremes of adult corruption and childlike purity. There is something uncanny about a child endowed with such artistic power; he remains willfully a child yet expresses his vision with the power of an adult.

Rimbaud was born in 1854 in Charleville, a rural town in the Ardennes, in France. His father was an army officer who deserted the family when Rimbaud was 6 years old. His mother was a stern countrywoman whose narrow ideas and repressive child-raising methods have been blamed by many for her son's re-

*Translated by Oliver Bernard, Baltimore, Penguin, 1962. All references to the poetry of Rimbaud in this chapter are to the Bernard translations.

belliousness. She raised Arthur and his brother and two sisters sternly, for she valued conformity, social status, and religious devotion above all else. Ironically, her son became the great poetic rebel, an *enfant terrible* whose life was as shocking as his poetry.

Rimbaud received his education at the Collège de Charleville, where he won prizes and astonished the teachers with his brilliance. He read voraciously (one of his poems describes readers at the public library, where he must have spent a lot of time), but Charleville provided no outlet for his intellect. There were no literati-filled cafés where he could talk out his ideas, and perhaps as a result these ideas went directly into his life and work, though for a long time they simply went unvoiced. Until adolescence Rimbaud was a model student, cultivating only in secret the defiance expressed in "The Seven-Year-Old Poets."

Georges Izambard, a teacher at the Collège de Charleville, gave Rimbaud his first opportunity to discuss his reading and helped introduce him to the works of the poets then prominent: Banville, Verlaine, and the recently dead Baudelaire. But Izambard soon left the town, and the outbreak of the Franco-Prussian War in 1870 increased Rimbaud's isolation unbearably. He decided to run away from home.

The first time, he landed in a Paris prison, since he had boarded the train without enough money to pay for a ticket. Izambard rescued him and took him home to Douai, where Rimbaud lived for three weeks, tended by Izambard's two kindly aunts, who presumably removed the accumulated prison lice from his hair and so inspired the poem "The Lice-Seekers." He was returned to his mother, however, and his isolation resumed.

Literary Theorizing

In May 1871, Rimbaud wrote letters to Georges Izambard and to his friend Paul Demeny; these letters have become major documents of French poetry. The 16-year-old had developed a theory of the poet as *voyant*, or seer, which has been said to anticipate Nietzsche and Freud and which certainly exerted a tremendous influence on his own poetry and that of his successors. In these letters, Rimbaud says that the poet is a seer, a prophet who gains magical insight by deliberately abandoning himself to sensual experience. The exact method to be used is not specified, but drugs, alcohol, and sex are the most likely means. He calls the process "a long, immense, and deliberate disordering of all the senses." The process is a discipline, requiring suffering, perhaps ending in madness, but resulting in arrival at the "Unknown."

"*Je* est un autre," he wrote in the letters: "*I* is an other." The "I" who writes poetry is aligned not with the conscious, social self, which is rational, controlled, and moral, but with a vast subconscious cosmos, hallucinatory and amoral. Poetry is a kind of automatic writing dictated by this subconscious. The force moving the pen is not the obvious social self identifiable as Arthur Rimbaud but another self, invisible, capable of sending out messages and visions direct from the Unknown, undistorted by convention and reason.

Rimbaud's doctrine may owe something to Charles Baudelaire's *Les Paradis artificiels* (*Artificial Paradises*), in which Baudelaire describes the effects of hashish. The submersion of the drug user's personality in his surroundings, his passivity before his visions, resembles Rimbaud's other "I." "Now you soar through the azure of the hugely enlarged sky," Baudelaire writes. "You no longer struggle, you are carried away, you are no longer your master and you don't worry about it." The feeling of self-abandon is much like the mood of Rimbaud's "Drunken Boat." Of course, it was Baudelaire who urged in a prose poem, "Get drunk! From wine, from poetry, or from virtue, whichever you prefer."

Baudelaire's drunkenness, though, is less destructive than Rimbaud's. In *Artificial Paradises*, he condemns drug use as endangering the discipline poetry requires. For Rimbaud, however, danger is heady and stimulating; he seeks it out. Baudelaire, he felt, was the first seer but in the end was too traditional, too deliberate and self-conscious. Most of all, his poems were too formally perfect. If the unknown is formless, Rimbaud argues, the poet's work must reflect this. If the poet retains only fragments of visions, the poems will be fragmentary.

Poetry's formal structure places the poet's vision within a traditional framework, making it seem comfortable, pleasing, even familiar. Language itself tames experience, often robbing it of its most disturbing qualities. Rimbaud refused to let his visions lose their impact, their aura of the unspeakable. He would write, he said, in a new language that would place no barrier between vision and verbal rendition, a language "from the soul for the soul, containing everything, scents, sounds, colors, thought attaching to thought and pulling." He wanted to get across the experience itself, unadulterated by the grammatical and logistical demands of language or the formal demands of poetry.

Rimbaud and Verlaine; Rimbaud's Brief Career

Soon after his two "seer" letters, Rimbaud wrote "The Drunken Boat," probably his most famous poem. He then set off for Paris, invited by the poet Paul Verlaine, with whom he had corresponded. The two poets began a stormy and presumably homosexual relationship. It ended in 1873 when Verlaine shot Rimbaud in the wrist and was imprisoned for two years as a result. In prison,

Verlaine was converted to Roman Catholicism. Around the same time, Rimbaud completed his long prose poem *A Season in Hell* and probably wrote the *Illuminations*, a series of difficult, fragmented poems in prose and free verse. In 1873, Rimbaud had *A Season in Hell* reprinted in Belgium, but it was never distributed and received little attention. By 1875, he had ceased to consider himself a poet. No one knows why.

Rimbaud spent the rest of his life traveling through Europe and especially Africa. He settled in Abyssinia as a trader; at one point, he was even a gunrunner. He was almost completely cut off from the cultural life of France and remained indifferent to the growth of his fame in the 1880s, when Verlaine described his work in *Les Poètes maudits* (*The Cursed Poets*) and published his *Illuminations* in *La Vogue*, a symbolist magazine. Many in Paris believed him dead.

Soon after, in 1891, Rimbaud did in fact die, apparently of cancer. He was 37 years old.

Literary Influence

Rimbaud's concern with getting beyond consciousness, with preserving the chaos and fragmentation of his visions from another world, links him to the surrealist movement of the 1920s. Led by André Breton (1896–1966), this movement in both poetry and art saw dreams as a gateway into the same world Rimbaud reached through sensual disordering. Like hallucinations, dreams are unwilled, illogical, and vivid; they unroll inside the sleeper's mind yet seem dictated by an "other self" that is beyond the sleeper's conscious control. The surrealists were directly influenced by Freud and his followers, and they sought to give direct expression to the unconscious as described by psychoanalysis. They honored as their predecessors Gérard de Nerval, Charles Baudelaire, and Rimbaud, all of whom predated Freud yet seemed aware of that other level of consciousness which Freud was the first to define in scientific language.

Rimbaud's idea that the poet has to suffer for his or her vision has become part of our culture's understanding of the artist. The title of Verlaine's *Les Poètes maudits* provided an appropriate name for the syndrome; since the late nineteenth century, it has been assumed that the great writer may well be "cursed," paying for genius with personal suffering, often self-inflicted. The alcoholic or suicidal artist is a familiar figure in modern literature. Rimbaud's writings and life provided an influential model of self-destruction for art's sake.

ESSAY QUESTIONS WITH ANSWERS

"The Lice-Seekers"

11.1   Rimbaud's poem "The Lice-Seekers" describes an actual incident that occurred when the 15-year-old Rimbaud arrived at Douai, home of his teacher Georges Izambard, after staying briefly in a Paris prison. He was deloused there by Izambard's two aunts, the two sisters of the poem. Though the subject is rather sordid, the poem is strangely beautiful. What is there about the process of being deloused that stimulates such powerful emotions in the poet?

Answer   "The Lice-Seekers" is best read on a fairly literal level, for its imagery and emotional content derive their power from a very specific psychological state: that of the tired, frightened, rebellious child who expects only discomfort and hostility from the environment and whose defenses are gone when he meets unexpectedly with kindness.

A child is taken from his bed by two sisters, who seat him near an open window overlooking a garden and pick the lice from his hair. Their faces are close to his as they seek out the tiny lice; he hears them breathe and suck in the saliva that accumulates when, intent on their difficult task, they forget to swallow. He hears their eyelashes beat when they blink and the crackle of lice under their nails. The most striking aspect of these impressions is their astonishing precision. Smells, feelings, and sounds seem larger than life, as if seen under a magnifying glass, so that the subtlest nuances (the hiss of saliva, for example, or the sisters' perfumed breath) can be vividly specified. If all this seems imperceptible in real life, one has only to think of the absolute stillness and trancelike fatigue of a child roused from sleep and the precision sensual impressions have to a mind emptied of thought by exhaustion.

The poem is very much about a child. A child is small and vulnerable in relation to the environment, and thus perceptions tend to come to the child in pieces; the child is too small to see the environment as a whole, but what the child does perceive becomes disproportionately large and absorbing. In "The Lice-Seekers," only the parts of the sisters' bodies that enter the child's awareness are mentioned. He feels their fingers, sees their nails, hears their eyelashes, and smells their breath; each of these impressions comes to him sharply and separately. An adult would immediately grasp the whole picture, but the tired, perhaps feverish child does not integrate the impressions, and as a result they retain a primitive impact and a sensual definition unique to Rimbaud's poetry. Baudelaire had equated genius with "childhood rediscovered at will"; Rimbaud not only cultivates a childlike vision but manages to convey it in all its naive integrity.

Throughout the poem, the child is entirely passive, and this passivity reinforces the impact of his impressions. Rimbaud's use of "the child" rather than "I" in narrating what is apparently his own experience emphasizes this passivity; as narrator of the poem, the child would no longer seem so helpless. The child is curiously will-less, the object of the care of others. He is without a conscious, controlling self to order and integrate experience. As a result, everything that happens to him seems unmotivated and dreamlike. The two sisters do not simply walk into the room. In the French, "Il vient près de son lit deux grandes soeurs charmantes," they are not even the subject of the verb "come." The English "There come . . . two charming sisters," by inverting subject and verb, gives a similarly floating, undeliberate, and purposeless feeling to their arrival. In fact, their silvery nails could have materialized out of the white swarm of dreams.

The child's only activity is to receive impressions. The third stanza begins, "He listens," and the fourth stanza, "He hears." In each case, the remainder of the stanza describes the impressions themselves, not their perceiver, who seems to vanish under the weight of his perceptions. The poem was probably written before Rimbaud's two "seer" letters, but it anticipates his emphasis on the poet's passivity in transmitting visions. The child is made drunk by his weakness, his vulnerability, and the unexpected kindness of the two sisters; the result is a series of overwhelmingly vivid sense impressions bearing a family resemblance to those of "The Drunken Boat."

Finally, the hint of sexuality running through the poem helps further to turn the delousing process into a powerful emotional experience. As the child surrenders to his impressions and to the sisters, the poem accumulates a sexually charged tension. The beating eyelashes and electric fingers suggest a building rhythm that is released in the final stanza with its abrupt rhythmic break and emphatic assertion, with the phrase "Then the wine of Sloth rises in him" fading into the final desire to cry. The sisters' motherly kindness reaches him only through his senses. He is, after all, a rebellious child, unused to maternal caresses. But when the child finally feels desire, it is not for sex but for tears, as if the surrender to tears were the equivalent of sexual release.

Rimbaud has often been called a poet of adolescence. He wrote most of his poetry before reaching adulthood, and the poems emerge from a twilight world between childhood and maturity, where intense sexual feelings are expressed in a tone of startling naiveté. "The Lice-Seekers" re-creates the psychological state of a love-starved adolescent while embodying—in its emphasis on powerful, fragmented sense impressions experienced as near hallucinations—the poetic theory of a creative adult.

"The Drunken Boat"

11.2   Rimbaud's poem "The Drunken Boat" seems to be narrated by a boat. However, this boat has very unboatlike attributes, including the ability to know, see, dream, regret, desire, get drunk, and narrate a poem in the first person. Rimbaud could have described his travels *in* a boat; why does he eliminate the presence of a human being and describe the travels *of* a boat?

Answer   A friend of Rimbaud's was disturbed by this question and suggested that he explain what he meant by equating himself with a boat, but Rimbaud obviously chose to ignore the advice. Instead, the poem is narrated by an "I" that teeters back and forth between boat and person. It has a hull, rudder, and anchor, but its emotions are human. Rimbaud's ambiguous "I" is thus disorienting. Readers immediately find themselves in the middle of something, unable even to tell what it is that is taking them there. They are in unfamiliar territory, forced to shed their ideas of the possible before entering the world of the poem. From the start, then, the act of reading the poem mimics the boat's magical journey into the unknown. Once readers have accepted the premise that a boat can narrate a poem, they are ready for the relatively ordinary transformation that follows, when a river barge becomes an explorer of the seas.

But why a boat rather than a rock, for example, or a train? First of all, a boat moves, and unlike a train, it moves in harmony with its environment. A boat can drift, surrendering itself to the waves and currents. Water has always suggested maternal, life-giving qualities, despite its dangers, and a boat rocking on the sea suggests the peaceful oblivion of a baby in its cradle. A boat floats on the very element that threatens it. Its movement is inseparable from the risk of sinking, much as Rimbaud's poetic theory required him to risk self-destruction for the sake of his vision.

Since the *Odyssey*, the sea voyage has exemplified adventure. Baudelaire works with the same idea in "The Voyage," which clearly influenced Rimbaud.

"Our soul is a three-master seeking its Icaria," Baudelaire writes. And in "The Seven-Year-Old Poets," Rimbaud writes that he dreamed of travel as he read "lying on pieces of unbleached canvas, and violently announcing a sail!" To the child, sea travel promises an exotic liberation from restraint. "The Drunken Boat" was among the first poems Rimbaud wrote after his "seer" letters, in which he had announced his search for the unknown. Like a latter-day Columbus, he hoped to discover a truly new world, and, like Columbus, he would do so by boat.

Baudelaire's "Voyage" also describes a search for the unknown, but his sailors find only their own image and their own boredom wherever they go. Only in dying will they find something new. Rimbaud's humble barge, however, is more triumphant. "I have seen what man thought he saw," it announces, implying a newness, an unknownness so absolute that it can be spoken of only as the opposite of human conceptions. Such a vision must be enunciated by something other than a person, for it is a vision belonging to the other "I," the "I" that belongs not to human society, but to a nonhuman cosmos.

11.3 In "The Drunken Boat," Rimbaud mentions Redskins and Florida, references which suggest a journey to America, but for the most part the boat seems simply to be at sea, with no particular geographical location. Does the boat actually go somewhere? If the poem does not describe a journey to a particular place, what meaning do the boat's visions have?

Answer Rimbaud's geographical references and seafaring details are wholly literary, derived from writers such as Hugo, Chateaubriand, and Jules Verne. They do not point to a specific locale or indicate any experience with boats or voyages, except as portrayed in books. Yet Rimbaud does manage to create a sense of an other world. Whereas the barges of civilized Europe, guided by haulers, carry wheat or cotton back and forth in an endlessly circular process of trade, the boat's new world is reached only by breaking brutally from that circle.

The boat may not travel any recognizable route, but it does seem to move. It descends a river, and after ten days of purification (the sea washes away wine and vomit) it sets out to sea, where it has fantastic visions ("From then on, I bathed in the Poem of the Sea") that are awesome, ecstatic, and exhausting. The boat suffers from the force of its visions and yearns instead for the small, bounded puddle at home.

The entire journey seems to be a hallucination which is rejected at the end of the poem. But while it lasts, the hallucination represents a triumphant discovery of a new world, a tentative answer to Baudelaire's disillusioned boredom in "The Voyage," which he begins by announcing the smallness of the world, despite the illusions of children:

> For the child, in love with maps and prints,
> The universe is equal to his huge appetite.
> Ah, how the world is big in lamplight;
> In the eyes of memory, how the world is small!

To the child, the world is huge; to the adult, the world is small. The child looks through one end of a telescope, and the adult looks through the other. Baudelaire identifies with the adult, who looks back with the perspective of experience on a shrunken world that offers nothing new, nothing unknown.

Rimbaud, however, retains his childlike vision while escaping, imaginatively at least, from the restrictions of a child's life. The "I" of "The Drunken Boat" is in part the toy boat of the penultimate stanza, magically liberated from the puddle. To a tiny boat, as to a small child, the world is huge. Everything seen far exceeds the child-boat's ability to take it in, and the result is a chaos of images, profuse and enormous. Rimbaud is fond of describing excess; exaggeration of number and size is typical of a child's perception. "The Drunken Boat" is filled with plural nouns and gigantic objects; Floridas, glaciers, and behemoths.

The child-boat, then, has successfully escaped the bounds of the familiar. Bathing "in the Poem of the Sea," it merges with its surroundings and passively registers the sights around it. The stanzas begin repetitively—"I know," "I have seen," "I have dreamed," "I have followed"—and then open out into images which, like the sense impressions of "The Lice-Seekers," seem to overwhelm the boat with their impact, until finally it announces in surprise, "I miss Europe, with its ancient parapets!"

The boat has envisioned the new ("I have seen archipelagos of stars!" it shouts), but only the old offers safety. To the child-boat, the world is filled with wondrous sights and vast panoramas, and for a time it all constitutes a fantastic spectacle. But the vision of such a vastly exaggerated world takes its toll. The child's heedlessness gives way to the child's vulnerability. Unlike Baudelaire's sailors, this boat has found the world as large as it had dreamed, and the final result is exhaustion and terror. The world of "The Drunken Boat" is not too small to produce anything new but too big to be borne. Its narrator turns the telescope around finally, preferring to see the shrunken world of the past. The small scale and the boundedness of memory decried in Baudelaire's "Voyage" provide the drunken boat with its only haven.

The boat, then, does go somewhere. What it encounters there is overwhelmingly new and thus wonderful and frightening at the same time.

A Season in Hell

11.4 A *Season in Hell* consists of an untitled introduction followed by seven titled sections. While certain words and themes recur, it is not clear how these sections are connected. Nor is it clear at all times who is speaking. Conflicting points of view are presented within each section, and the narrator's tone shifts abruptly and unpredictably. One moment he sounds defiant and cynical; the next, exhausted and pitiful; then, resigned and tranquil. To what extent can *Season* be read as a coherent story with a plot uniting the sections?

Answer Like Baudelaire's *Flowers of Evil*, Rimbaud's *Season* is a spiritual autobiography, a fragmented but continuous attempt to find hope. Unlike *The Flowers of Evil*, however, it was written in a short time, during a period of spiritual crisis. As a result, it is more focused but also more compressed, explosive, and difficult to interpret. *Season* does seem to tell a story, but it dramatizes rather than explains. At times it becomes almost a play, with an ever-present but mysterious "I" playing all the parts at once.

Season opens with a brief introduction that mentions the narrator's loss of an earlier happiness. Disappointed by beauty, he chose instead hostility and alienation from society, but now he wants to find some way to return to the "banquet" (an image suggesting Christ's last supper) he had abandoned. He wants to stop being a "hyena" and become once more a guest at the common table. The remainder of *Season* describes the narrator's failed attempts to make sense of his life and find his way back to the banquet. He rejects both traditional Christianity and his own rebellion against it, which he ridicules as grandiose and misguided.

"Bad Blood," the section immediately following the introduction, establishes the futility of the narrator's revolt, since his heritage and his baptism trap him within the context of history and religion. By birth, he is a slave to the world and to the values which he had thought he could ignore. "Night In Hell" enacts the actual experience of the Christian hell, whose worst quality is that it does not provide, as he had thought, a way out of the world: "Ecstasy, nightmare, sleep in a nest of flames." As a mere inversion of Christianity, the hell vision provides no escape. "I am hidden and not hidden," he says. He has found hell but not oblivion.

"Delirium" is divided into two parts, each spoken by an inhabitant of hell. The first part is spoken by the "Foolish Virgin" concerning her "Infernal Bride-groom" (generally read as an impersonation of Paul Verlaine's self-pity and passion for Rimbaud), and the second is spoken by the poet, who denounces his past. This second section, "Alchemy of the Word," is generally interpreted as Rimbaud's rejection of his own work and poetic theory. "I prided myself on inventing a poetic language accessible some day to all the senses," the narrator announces, echoing his 1871 "seer" letters, but then he brutally deflates his own past pretensions: "I reserved translation rights." The section contains ex-cerpts from Rimbaud's 1872 poems—exquisitely beautiful evocations of perfect beauty—and then concludes: "That is over. Today I know how to greet beauty." Whether his new view of beauty is dismissive or simply different remains un-certain.

"The Impossible" and "Lightning" explore alternative philosophies: the mys-ticism of east and the promise of science. Both options are rejected, however, for they ignore two vital facts. First, the poet is irrevocably western; second, he lacks the discipline and patience required for the pursuit of scientific progress. With "Morning," though, comes a gleam of hope. The language becomes more tranquil. "I have forgotten how to speak," he writes, but then he asks, "When will we go, beyond the beaches and mountains, to hail the birth of the new work, the new wisdom, the flight of tyrants and demons, the end of superstition, to adore—the first!—Christmas on the earth!" The possibility of beauty is established not as something describable or even attainable but as a question and a possible future.

In "Farewell," the poet renounces magic, much as Prospero does at the end of Shakespeare's Tempest. His poetic theory had been based on his self-identification as a seer with magic access to the unknown and the immortal. Now he gives up his "eternal sun"; for the time being, he is embracing the seasons, the ordinary passage of time, and the great expanse of human history: "I who called myself magus or angel, exempt from all morality, I am thrown back to the earth, with a task to seek and rough reality to embrace!"

The poet, then, seems to reject both the banquet and the hyena—Chris-tianity and its opposite—as deluded efforts to escape time and history. "Each is right," Rimbaud writes, "scorn and charity," that is, defiance and submission. But neither defiance nor Christianity can subsume the other; both are trapped in the "Forward, march!" of progress. Like rafts on a river, they can collide with each other, but neither can mount the bank and alter the river's flow.

Season as a whole—as suggested by the title and the references to spring, summer, winter, and fall—insists on the inescapable reality of time. The only vision of beauty it offers is the offspring of time: the future tense. The only hope *Season* presents is to be found not by a vertical leap into magic but by remaining on earth and moving methodically onward into the future.

11.5   The language of *Season* is explosive and often discordant, with little of the verbal beauty characteristic of Rimbaud's other poems and the *Illuminations*. For the first time, Rimbaud seems to be concerned with ideas rather than sense impressions. Connections between ideas seem to matter. The young Rimbaud rejected logical continuity. Why does he seem to seek it here at the expense of poetic beauty and magic?

Answer   On the draft of "Night in Hell," Rimbaud wrote, "One isn't a poet in hell." The oppressively stabbing, broken quality of the language in *A Season in Hell* represents a deliberate renunciation of verbal magic. It is poetry only by virtue of its power and compression. Rimbaud rejects his own verbal facility, blaming it for the failure of his life. "Who made my tongue so perfidious that it has guided and preserved my sloth up until now?" the narrator asks in "Bad Blood." In "Alchemy of the Word," he explicitly rejects his earlier poetry and its magical use of language.

In the past, Rimbaud had made things with words. He put words together, and forms and colors appeared instantly. He made metaphors (as when he equated himself with a boat) and then acted them out in his poems as if they were real (as when the boat embarked on a voyage and saw fantastic things), thus turning figures of speech into hallucinations. Through the disordering of his senses, he could reverse this process; drunk or simply exhausted, he would actually hallucinate, and from these hallucinations he would derive metaphors for his poems. "I grew accustomed to pure hallucination," he writes in "Alchemy." "I saw quite frankly a mosque in place of a factory." The poetry that resulted had a shimmeringly real quality. He fulfilled the goal he set himself in the "seer" letters of finding a new language that would present vision without the intervention of logic.

But in *Season*, Rimbaud rejects that "alchemy of the word." No longer does language create experience. Instead, the experience described in *Season* exists outside the poem and overshadows it. The poet seems to use language to enact a preexisting drama rather than to create a new one. "Night in Hell" in particular is more an act of purgation than poem—a verbal spewing out of spiritual pride, the poison he had swallowed.

Rimbaud's narrator plays a different role in *Season in Hell*. The "I" is not dissolved into its visions but remains, despite its instability, a self coherent enough to surface again and again, perhaps in a different guise but always seeking integration (that is, a full understanding of the self in relation to history), not dissolution. In giving up verbal sorcery and reentering the world of seasons and sustained effort, Rimbaud has subjugated his words to the logical continuity of his ideas and his narrative identity to the chronological continuity of time.

11.6 The last section of *Season* is entitled "Farewell." This is generally interpreted as announcing Rimbaud's retirement as a poet. His alternative to poetry is often stated in Christian terms. He frequently mentions charity, for example, and looks ahead to a "new Christmas." Is Rimbaud in fact rejecting his poetic theory as blasphemous and embracing Christianity instead?

Answer Rimbaud is rejecting his poetic theory and embracing a more humble approach to life, but not really a Christian approach. *Season* is filled with religious terminology, and there is some speculation that after he was shot by Verlaine, Rimbaud considered converting (though baptized, he had not been a practicing Roman Catholic for some time), but there is no evidence that he did so.

Livre Nègre or *Livre Paien* (*Negro Book* or *Pagan Book*) were the titles Rimbaud originally considered giving *Season*. The section "Bad Blood," which was written first, reflects his early intention to write about the binding implications of baptism as opposed to the pagan's freedom from the concepts of good and evil. Rimbaud had wanted to live entirely outside the moral strictures of his religion and society, as if they did not exist. Instead, he finds that he has merely defied them, thus acknowledging their power. Even the pagans, whose ignorance of religion has allowed them to escape moral concerns, are doomed to share his knowledge. "The white men are landing," he writes. "We will have to be baptized and put on clothes and work. I have been shot in the heart by grace. Ah! I had not foreseen it!"

The decision that he cannot live as a pagan, however, does not make Rimbaud a believer. He has accepted the Christian vocabulary, but with it he constructs his own vision of salvation. When Jesus appears in "Night in Hell," it is right after Satan himself, and his voice merges indistinguishably with the narrator's. All three—Satan, Jesus, and the poet—are masters of hallucination, sharing a language without sharing a faith. Rimbaud's "new Christmas on earth" is hypothetical, posed only as a question in the future tense, and the salvation he seeks calls for freedom and the joining of body and soul rather than their separation.

While not requiring an actual conversion to Christianity, Rimbaud's new vision does require a renunciation of the poet's old self. "I have to bury my imagination and my memories!" he writes. "A fine reputation of an artist and story-teller lost sight of!" These lines have traditionally been read as a literary letter of resignation which predates, according to some critics, the writing of many of the *Illuminations*. (The relative dating of the two works remains controversial.) In any case, *Season* bids farewell more to a self-image than to writing itself. The poet is essentially rejecting his past claims of exemption from the common fate and the common language.

The voice speaking in "Night in Hell" is that of a man recognizing his irrevocable estrangement from the world at the same time as he recognizes that he has never left it. He has always understood its language and will endure its judgment forever. When he returns in "Farewell" to the world's language and rejects his own, he makes a last effort to reshape that judgment, to offer himself and the world some hope of the salvation he had thought he could eschew.

At the end of *Season*, the poet writes, "There is nothing behind me but that horrible tree." He refers apparently to the tree of good and evil in the Garden of Eden, with which he has had a fierce spiritual combat, confronting it at last on its own terms. He is exhausted, lonely, and without assurance of triumph, for "the vision of justice is the pleasure only of God." But he seems now to be cultivating patience and humility in place of magical omnipotence. Magic is outside time and this provides an immortality of sorts, but it is sterile and solitary and provides only an illusory escape from the judgment of God. As prophet, he could conjure up new worlds; as human, he accepts the slim hope offered by the old one. As prophet, he could conjure up new images; as human, he borrows images from Christianity. His use of Christian imagery, then, is an indication of his new humility, but it does not suggest a specific religious content.

Illuminations

11.7 Rimbaud's *Illuminations* are strikingly violent. The very idea of illumination has a violent quality. Like a blow, it arrives suddenly and obliterates what was there before. But Rimbaud's prose poems also portray a literal violence: "Story" chronicles a series of murders, and "Morning of Drunkenness" ends with the announcement "Behold the age of the Assassins." In his "seer" letters, Rimbaud had announced that he would become a poet by disordering his senses, and he had acknowledged that suffering might be involved. How is Rimbaud's view of art and of the artist's suffering connected to the violence of *Illuminations*?

Answer   For Rimbaud, art is a negation of the actual. To reach the world of the other "I," he must break down the ordinary, social "I" through a self-destructive process of sensual disordering. The world with which he is then put in touch permits no compromises with the ordinary. Illuminatory flashes of pure vision are impossible to sustain or describe except as the disruption and destruction of the ordinary. When the Genie of "Story" arrives, he is described as "*un*speakably," "*un*admittedly" beautiful, promising a happiness "*un*speakable, *un*bearable" [emphasis added]. A representative of that other "I," he is describable only as the negation of commonly known qualities.

To reach the realm of pure vision, the present world must be destroyed, a process described in "After the Flood." After the biblical flood, the poet complains, the mediocrity of daily life rose up again and obscured the secret of true life. Only a new flood will reveal it. "Waters and sorrows," the poet urges, "rise up and bring back the Floods."

In "Story," the prince attempts his personal version of the flood. He is looking for that lost secret: "He wanted to see truth and the time of full desire and satisfaction." His first step, taken in a mood of Baudelairean ennui (similar to the destructive impulse of "The Bad Glazier"), is to wipe out the ordinary pleasures of wives, companions, and servants. The word "essential" is the key here. He wants the "hour of essential desire and satisfaction" as opposed to the meaningless, accidental, contingent pleasures of day-to-day life. Essential pleasure would be lasting and significant, the completion of a profound need—a kind of permanent orgasm—rather than the random pleasures of excess.

The prince, like the assassins of "Morning of Drunkeness," must clear out the nonessential to make room for "the superhuman promise made to the created body and soul." When the Prince and the Genie die "in essential health," they have for a moment reached that promise. But like orgasm (their relationship certainly suggests sexual union), the moment cannot last. The deaths dealt out by the Prince are ineffectual. Life—trivial, boring, contingent—springs up once again, as it did after the flood. The executions must take place over and over again.

This repeated effort to go beyond the conscious world is a kind of poison because its aim is to kill the poet's ordinary self and because its effect is to alienate him from a world which does after all exist. "Morning of Drunkenness" can be read as a reply to "Night in Hell" (or vice versa, since the order in which the poems were written remains controversial). Here, the poet exalts his suffering and reaffirms his "method," that is, the process of sensory disordering which is to bring him to this other, magical world. "We have faith in poison," he writes.

Most critics interpret the word "poison" as referring specifically to hashish. The French word for "hashish user" is *hachichien*, which in both French and English is etymologically related to the word "assassin," referring to a medieval Muslim sect whose members committed political murders under the influence of hashish. In announcing the time of the assassins, Rimbaud is both reaffirming his poetic method and calling for a new flood. It is time to wipe out the old, he is saying, and ourselves as well, through the use of the poison of hashish and the less literal poison of wholesale negation. The resultant torture is disturbingly close to ecstasy, for destruction on the "magical rack" also bears the potential for a new creation.

11.8 The language and imagery, as well as the content, of many of the *Illuminations* is tortured. Occasionally, Rimbaud uses incomplete sentences, and sometimes it is hard even to tell what a poem is about: "Flowers" may actually be about a theater, and "Seascape" may be about a plow. In "Barbarians," exclamation points, repetition, and single-word ejaculations disrupt any possibility of logical interpretation. Is this linguistic violence related to the more literal violence of "Story" and "Morning of Drunkenness"? What is the purpose of this twisted syntax?

Answer Rimbaud's twisted and incomplete sentences suggest that what he attempts to convey in *Illuminations* is essentially foreign to language itself. When Verlaine published the *Illuminations*, he gave them the subtitle "Colored Plates." Since "plate" can mean a sheet of metal or a printed engraving, among other things, the subtitle hints at the poems' metallic quality, the intensity of their colors, and their strong visual orientation. Both title and subtitle reveal a tension between what Rimbaud was trying to do and the linguistic medium in which he had to do it. The process of understanding language requires time and conscious thought. Illuminations—or colored plates—are, however, seen instantly and comprehended without the intervention of thought.

To retain the illuminatory qualities of his vision, Rimbaud must do violence to language. Complete sentences suggest temporal duration and allow abstract conceptualization, since a reader can process a sentence and retain its meaning independently of the actual words on a page. Thus Rimbaud moves away from complete sentences, preferring clusters of nouns and adjectives. He tends to eliminate main verbs or deemphasize them, because it is precisely the act of predication—of saying something about something—that he hopes to eliminate from his poems.

Rimbaud is not trying to say something *about* illuminations but to create them out of words. They are glimpses whose meaning adheres to the actual words he uses, not to a separate system of meaning already familiar to the reader. For this reason, Rimbaud must dislodge words from their ordinary function of referring to something outside themselves. If a writer says "star," for example, the idea of a star is conveyed; the reader can point upward at night and say, "There is a star." But if the writer says "the dripping star," something new is created for which there is no outside referent, no object to which one can point and say, "That is what the writer means." The object exists only in the words and cannot be abstracted from the words. Thus, Rimbaud's almost indecipherable pictures of flowers and plow disrupt our ordinary associations with these objects and replace them with a word picture that refers to nothing outside itself.

"Bridges" not only exemplifies these linguistic oddities but treats them thematically. The poem is about the building of objects out of words. The qualities of the words seem to determine where the poem goes; the words do not describe preexisting objects but conjure up new ones. Rimbaud uses the phonetic resemblance between the words *accords* ("chords") and *cordes* ("ropes") to move from visualized bridges to heard music while suggesting an association between the crisscrossing lines and a stringed instrument. This scene of bridges exists only as an interplay of purely verbal associations.

Similarly, the two sentence fragments with which the poem opens suggest that a scene is being created, not commented upon. In naming objects, the poet conjures them up but refuses to say anything about them (an act which would grammatically complete the sentences), because for the poet—as for many primitive peoples—the mere act of naming has magical power. In the poem's final line, which completely erases the scene, the poet exposes his own magic trick. He has built a scene that has no existence outside the words he has used; like a house of cards, it can be toppled in an instant.

This sudden obliteration of the poet's construction has some of the violence of "Story," which is also in a way about the momentariness of the poet's magic. "Story" weaves and unweaves its plot as it goes along, predicating events and then undoing them. Whatever the Prince kills, revives in the next line. Even the Prince's death is revoked. Thus, the *Illuminations* annihilate one world, construct a new one, and then annihilate that world too.

There is the suggestion of a progression in all this, from the assassinations

of "Story" and "Morning of Drunkenness," to the verbal murder of "Bridges,"
to the world of "Barbarian," which is "far from the former assassins." In "Barbarian," the language is at its most violent, the images limited to extremes of
fire and ice, red and white, or to one-word exclamations and repetitions of "O,"
suggesting that whatever is happening is not easily contained by language. Over
and over, opposites are juxtaposed, their contiguity creating a sense of violent
ecstasy, an orgasmic fusion of opposites.

Miraculously, "Barbarians" presents an ecstatic peak that lasts. The repetition and the repeated refrain which ends the poem suggest that it could go
on forever, for its last line could also be its first. Here the poet is finally past
the need to obliterate either the world as it is or the vision that replaces it.
The poem describes another time and place where none of that is necessary:
"Far from the old places and the old fires we hear and smell." The sights described
need not, like those in "Bridges," be dismantled; the poem is cyclical, and the
sights "do not exist." In this world of essentials, existence would be superfluous;
magically potent names are enough.

All of this is, of course, next to impossible to discuss in words. The barbarity
of "Barbarians" lies in its strangeness and in the utter uncouthness of its language,
which make it all but impossible to discuss in sensible, utilitarian prose. Here
the vision of "Story" seems to be completed and the "essential health" of the
Prince-Genie sustained. The result is in effect the replacement of "Story" by
its opposite. Even though it made little sense, "Story," had the pretense of a
plot; "Barbarians" instead has only stop-action utterances. "Story" was filled
with violent events: "Barbarians" has no events, only violent language. "Story"
ended by negating itself as a story while allowing its characters to live on;
"Barbarians" ends by negating its characters ("they do not exist," it keeps saying)
while allowing the poem itself to live on (the suggestion of a cycle is contained
in the last line).

Far more characteristic of Rimbaud are those poems which end in a retreat
from or a destruction of the vision presented. "Barbarians" provides a rare glimpse
of the "hour of full desire and satisfaction." All the violence intrinsic to Rimbaud's illuminations has been absorbed by language, which is here on the verge
of exploding into babble yet somehow refrains from doing so.

                                                                    R.H.

SUGGESTED READINGS

Bonnefoy, Yves, *Rimbaud,* translated by Paul Schmidt (1973).
Cohn, Robert Greer, *The Poetry of Rimbaud* (1973).
Fowlie, Wallace, *Rimbaud* (1966).
Houston, John Porter, *The Design of Rimbaud's Poetry* (1963).
Starkie, Enid, *Arthur Rimbaud* (1961).
St. Aubyn, F. C., *Arthur Rimbaud* (1975).

C H A P T E R 1 2

CHEKHOV

Social Background and Youth

Anton Chekhov was born in 1860 in Taganrog, a port city on the Sea of Azov in southern Russia. Like Lopahin in *The Cherry Orchard*, he was the son and grandson of serfs; his grandfather and father had bought their freedom several years before Anton's birth. In 1861, serfdom was abolished by the decree of Czar Alexander II. The emancipation was a long overdue step toward modernity in Russian social, political, and economic life. For the educated class, the institution of serfdom had always served as a kind of historical Rorschach test, an image in which they saw a complex and often contradictory picture of their own social position and responsibility toward the nation.

Unfortunately, the emancipation did not prove to be the panacea for the nation's ills that many had hoped. Instead, it made for new problems by creating a class of freed men and women who owned nothing and no longer had a secure place in society. Amid the doubts and recriminations that followed the emancipation, those who had championed reform became even more uncertain about their own social identity and their relationship to the newly freed Russian masses. It was into this unsettled climate that Chekhov was born.

During Chekhov's childhood, his father was a shopkeeper of modest means. When he went bankrupt, the family was forced to flee to Moscow to avoid their creditors. Anton was left behind in Taganrog to finish his schooling, and until he rejoined his family in Moscow three years later, he learned of their hard times through harrowing letters from his brothers.

Upon coming to Moscow in 1879, at the age of 19, Chekhov entered upon medical studies. In this choice of a profession, he discovered what many educated young men of the time claimed they wanted but seemed unable to find: a way to work honestly and usefully for their fellow human beings.

Early Works

In medical school, Chekhov began to submit short stories and sketches to the Moscow and Saint Petersburg journals. His amusing, often satirical pieces were successful with editors and readers, and he soon earned an enviable reputation under one of his pseudonyms, Antosha Chekonte. Chekhov lived these Moscow years with great vitality, combining his medical studies with writing and nightly explorations of the bohemian side of the city's life.

The two recurrent themes of Chekhov's early pseudonymous stories are the foolishness of bureaucrats and the need for money. Chekhov and his family felt the press of poverty, and despite the earnings from Chekhov's stories, not until 1884, when he earned his medical degree and began to practice, did their fortunes improve. It was with great pride that Chekhov, who was now the family's main support, bought them a small house in Moscow.

Chekhov's first ambitious literary work, the drama *Platonov*, was written during the early Moscow years; however, it was rejected for performance and was published only long after Chekhov's death. This failure, along with the frivolity of his early prose pieces, convinced Chekhov that he had no talent beyond the knack of amusing an undemanding audience. Nonetheless, his reputation grew; after he was taken up by some of the leading figures in the Russian literary establishment, he was persuaded to take his work more seriously. The first noteworthy product of this change is the novella "The Steppe" (1887).

Humanitarian Efforts

In 1889, Chekhov suffered the first attack of tuberculosis, the disease which was to shorten his life and cause him a great deal of pain. From the first, he saw what his attacks meant, but his considerable courage and stoicism allowed him to continue to live as fully as possible. In fact, Chekhov was more stoical about his illness than he was about his misadventures as a dramatist. Although some of his early comedies were popular successes, his first attempts at drama, including *Ivanov* (1887), were all failures in their initial performances, and more than once he came close to abandoning drama entirely. Disgusted with his audience and disappointed with himself, he soon looked for another task in life.

In 1889, Chekhov conceived the idea of a journey to the northern Pacific island of Sakhalin to investigate conditions in the notorious Russian prison camps there. After traveling for months, he arrived in Sakhalin in 1890. He found the camps to be even more ghastly than their reputation, and he spent three months investigating living conditions in detail. In prison life, Chekhov found a formidable challenge to his belief that literature can be a force for truth and change. He wrote about his discoveries in a book (*Sakhalin Island*, 1891) that, in fact, led to reform of some conditions on the island.

Upon his return to Russia, Chekhov bought an estate in Melikhovo, a town south of Moscow, and in the cherry orchard there built a small studio in which to write. He also continued to practice medicine, often treating the poor for free. When cholera broke out in 1891–1892, he was appointed health inspector for his district. For Chekhov, realism was more than a literary credo; it represented a commitment to living on intimate terms with the harsher realities of life.

The Moscow Art Theatre

Although Chekhov appeared incapable of failing in fiction, he seemed equally unable to succeed in drama, the form he respected most. In 1897, *The Sea Gull* was staged at the Imperial Alexander Theatre in Saint Petersburg. Its reception was so harsh—the audience hooted from the very first scene—that Chekhov vowed never to write another play.

Nevertheless, Vladimir Nemirovich-Danchenko and Konstantin Stanislavsky, the two directors of the Moscow Art Theatre, tried to persuade Chekhov to hazard another performance of *The Sea Gull*. Although he refused, they went into rehearsal anyway. To Chekhov's great surprise, the Art Theatre's production of *The Sea Gull* was a huge success. However, Chekhov never approved of that company's overly literal realism. Although his later plays were staged by them, he was always somewhat unhappy with the Moscow Art Theatre, especially with Stanislavsky.

Another significant result of his dealings with the Moscow Art Theatre was Chekhov's meeting the actress Olga Knipper, who became his wife in 1901. Unfortunately, their marital life was marked by separation, the tensions born of their respective careers, and Chekhov's illness.

Despite terrible health, Chekhov completed *The Cherry Orchard* late in 1903. In 1904, it was staged by the Moscow Art Theatre with Olga Knipper in the role of Ranevskaya. Its directors planned the premiere as a celebration of Chekhov's forty-fourth birthday and twenty-fifth anniversary as a published writer. It was only with the greatest effort that Chekhov was persuaded to attend the premiere. When he entered the theater, he was greeted by a great ovation, followed by speeches, wreaths, and gifts. Chekhov was thoroughly embarrassed and barely able to hide either his chagrin at this overelaborate homage or his displeasure over what he felt to be Stanislavsky's unsatisfactory staging of the play.

Chekhov spent most of his last days in Yalta, where his doctors hoped the climate might help reverse his decline. In March 1904, he traveled with his wife to Germany, and he died in Badenweiler on July 15.

Major Works

Chekhov's greatest achievement in fiction is the group of short stories he wrote in the years following 1889, including "A Dreary Story" (1889), "The Duel" and "Ward Six" (1892), "The Black Monk" and "The Teacher of Literature" (1894), "Three Years," "Anna on the Neck," and "Ariadne" (1895), "My Life" (1896), "Peasants" (1897), "The Darling," "The Lady with the Dog" (1899), "In the Ravine" (1900), "The Bishop" (1902), and "The Betrothed" (1903).

The formal hallmark of these stories is an impeccable economy and simplicity of construction. Most of them deal with ordinary people—domestic servants, teachers, doctors, small landowners—in ordinary situations. Chekhov portrays these characters with a keen psychological sense that sees every human failing but is never unsympathetic. He is always alive to the familiar pathos of self-knowledge and self-deception, aspiration and impotence, isolation and the wish for intimacy. We get a sense from these stories that people face life alone, with little hope of mastering their imperfect and contradictory circumstances. This perception marks Chekhov as a precursor to the existentialists of the twentieth century. However, his capacity for acceptance and even optimism measures the temperamental distance between Chekhov and these later, much harsher writers.

Chekhov's dramatic masterpieces are, along with *The Cherry Orchard*, *Uncle Vanya* (1899) and *The Three Sisters* (1901). These plays share certain formal and thematic similarities. They are concerned most of all with the passage of time and the way in which time erodes human aspirations. Each play is haunted by the specter of the wasted life. However, the tragedy of lost possibilities is played out in a minor and frequently comic key. Chekhov's people are caught by life's lesser snares: unclarity, indecisiveness, loyalty to the wrong cause. The impotence of Chekhov's characters is reflected in the static quality of his drama, which subordinates action to the creation of mood. The characteristic mood here is a sweet, almost aching sadness that has come to be known as Chekhovian.

Literary Ideals

In 1886, at the age of 26, Chekhov jotted down a short list of literary ideals that can be taken as his personal manifesto: "(1) Objectivity, (2) truth in the depiction of people and things, (3) maximum brevity, (4) boldness, (5) compassion." These were the qualities Chekhov strove for and largely achieved in his short stories and plays. Chekhov is often spoken of as a realist, but this classification is not very helpful. Every writer who hopes to get at the truth can in some sense be called a realist, and each is likely to have an individual theory of how best to achieve true "realism." The truth that Chekhov sought to express is less available in ideas than in feelings, less evident in the grand moments than in the small. It is allusive, intimate, and best approached elliptically and hesitantly. Unlike the realism of Zola and the naturalists, which took scientific description and explanation as its model, the realism of Chekhov is embued with a lyricism which makes it akin to music and poetry.

ESSAY QUESTIONS WITH ANSWERS

The Cherry Orchard

12.1   A grand and noble old estate is about to be auctioned. A beloved son has drowned. The child of serfs is about to supplant his parents' masters. A young man speaks boldly of revolution. An aging and profligate noblewoman makes a last attempt to restore her life to health and wholeness. This is the stuff of melodrama. But can one call *The Cherry Orchard* a melodrama?

Answer   A series of potentially melodramatic occurrences does take place in *The Cherry Orchard*, yet Chekhov handles them in a way that is the opposite of melodramatic. He could have us wondering anxiously if the estate will be saved; he could prolong the suspense and then save the family in the nick of time. But Chekhov does not choose this approach. Instead, from the first act it is clear that the cherry orchard will not be saved. In fact, Ranevskaya and her brother Gayev, the two characters who have the most to lose, do almost nothing to save the estate. They talk vaguely about borrowing some money from a relative who, they admit, is not very kindly disposed toward them. Gayev dreams about Anya's somehow marrying money, but there are no suitors on the horizon. When Lopahin urges them simply to try to save themselves, he ends up tearing his hair in frustration. At times, Ranevskaya and Gayev seem not to care what will happen to their beloved home. If the sale of the cherry orchard has the potential for melodrama, Chekhov does not exploit it.

The same is true of other incidents in the play. Ranevskaya's young son, Grisha, drowns, but, like the actual sale of the orchard, this happens offstage and long before the play begins. When Ranevskaya is reminded of her lost son, his death comes to her not with the bathos of melodrama but with the sweet sadness of an old heartbreak.

Although Lopahin dispossesses Ranevskaya and Gayev, he is not the typical sneering villain who forecloses mortgages in melodramas. In his early attempts to get the family to save themselves, he seems more solicitous of their interests than they are. What kind of villain would reintroduce himself to Varya by sticking his head through the doorway and bleating like a lamb, speak of the beauty of poppy fields, and go to pieces when Ranevskaya cries?

Although Trofimov speaks the rhetoric of revolution and at times paints a stirring picture of a life devoted to high principle, he is as much a fool as a firebrand. He is a "mangy master" who, after his dramatic exchange with Ranevskaya in Act III, tumbles down the stairs. He spends the last half of the play looking unsuccessfully for his galoshes.

Nor is the matter of Ranevskaya's Parisian lover handled melodramatically. His only appearance in the play comes by means of the pleading telegrams he sends from Paris. Ranevskaya's affair with him seems a shabby business, more pathetic than romantic.

If *The Cherry Orchard* is not a melodrama, what kind of play is it? This question has dogged *The Cherry Orchard* since its composition. In its first production by the Moscow Art Theatre, Stanislavsky directed it as a tragedy, but Chekhov was incensed by what he felt to be the distortion of his play. While writing it, Chekhov spoke of *The Cherry Orchard* as a comedy, even going so far as to call it a farce. When reviewers referred to it as a drama, he felt that the play had failed or missed its audience.

It is not hard to understand the confusion that attended the initial production of *The Cherry Orchard*. If we focus on the actual loss of the estate as the heart of the play, there is no denying the mood of sadness and loss. Yet the play is also funny. Just think of Yepihodov, "Two and Twenty Troubles." With his pratfalls and long face, endless tales of woe, and mournful guitar playing, he makes sadness itself funny. Simeonov-Pishchik too is a character from comedy. He is not above playing the buffoon, as when he swallows a handful of Ranevskaya's pills in one gulp or when he claims to be descended from Caligula's horse. With his constant faith that something will turn up to save him from ruin, he is a latter-day Micawber. And when something does turn up (valuable minerals are discovered on his land), it is both amazing and perfectly right—Simeonov-Pishchik is watched over by the providence that protects children, fools, and other innocents. In a tragedy, nothing would have turned up for Simeonov-Pishchik.

Charlotta too would seem entirely out of place in a more serious drama. Her magic tricks, her rueful and slightly bristling self-regard, and the air of alienation that hovers around her make her a strange bird indeed. Yet this woman of (odd) parts seems perfectly at home in Chekhov's quirky, hard-to-characterize play.

However we finally categorize *The Cherry Orchard*—it has been called a tragicomedy, a "theatre-poem," and even a vaudeville—we have to take into account its full range of seriousness and playfulness.

12.2   What is the main action of *The Cherry Orchard*? Does the play focus on the fate of a single important character, or is there some other pattern to the way it unfolds?

Answer   The play is structured around its single significant event: the sale of the estate. In the first act, which takes place in the early hours of a May morning, we learn the precise date on which the estate is to be sold: August 22. Act II takes place on a summer evening; Act III, on the day of the sale; Act IV, in October. Thus, the play proceeds from spring to fall, from the season of beginnings to the year's end.

  In terms of the characters' movement through the play, *The Cherry Orchard* is structured as an arrival, a gathering, and a departure. The play begins with the arrival of Ranevskaya, Gayev, and Anya along with their small entourage, Yasha, their valet, and Charlotta, the governess. Lopahin and Trofimov have come to the estate and waited until morning to greet Ranevskaya on her return after five years of absence. Act II and Act III are social occasions which bring all the characters together. In Act IV, after the sale of the estate, the characters are dispersed in different directions by ones and twos. Thus, the play tells the story of a group of people, their relations with one another, and their fate as a group. There is really no single hero or heroine, although some characters, such as Lopahin and Ranevskaya, may strike the reader as especially important.

12.3   Far more important than any single character in *The Cherry Orchard* is the group as a whole. Chekhov selects and portrays these characters so that in their diversity and representativeness they create an implied picture of Russian society as a whole. How does Chekhov structure this group portrait?

Answer   What all the characters have in common is their relationship with each other and with the cherry orchard. Their history together and their intertwining relationships make them into an ensemble, and within this ensemble there are subgroups of various kinds. Grouped by social class, there are the landowners—Ranevskaya and her daughters, Gayev, and Simeonov-Pishchik—along with their servants—Yasha, Dunyasha, Charlotta, Yepihodov, and Firs. Lopahin has climbed beyond his origins in a way that puts into question the entire traditional class structure. The son of serfs, he has become a successful merchant. By the end of the play, with his purchase of the estate, he too has become a landowner, but of a very different sort than Ranevskaya and Gayev. Unlike them, he will squeeze a profit from the old estate, which he will subdivide and sell as lots for summer houses. Charlotta is classless or declassed; she is educated but has no money and no way to live without taking on the quasi-dependent role of governess. Varya, who is Ranevskaya's adopted daughter, is becoming like Charlotta. She can no longer look to her family for support, and after Lopahin fails to propose to her, she has no choice but to hire herself out as a governess.

The characters may also be grouped by age or generation. The oldest is Firs, who remembers the old days when the cherries were picked, dried, made into jam, and sold at the market. But not even the recipe remains from that grand old time. The youngest are Anya and Trofimov, whose lives are all ahead of them. When Anya and Trofimov speak, it is almost always of the future, their own and that of society. The members of the middle generation, Ranevskaya and Gayev, dwell in the past. It is no accident that the play begins in the room that is still called the nursery, since for Ranevskaya and Gayev the old house is synonymous with the very origin and course of their lives. In the last act, which again takes place in the nursery, Gayev looks at the window seat and remembers sitting there when he was 6 years old, watching his father walk to church on Whitsunday.

Many of the characters can also be grouped in pairs of lovers, each of which rings a change on the theme of love. Anya and Trofimov are young, eager lovers; they represent love under the sign of hope. Lopahin and Varya are older, more tentative, self-conscious, and inhibited. At the end of the play, it seems that their inhibitions have cost them their chance for love. In some ways, they duplicate in love the helplessness and incapacity that Ranevskaya and Gayev show in relation to the cherry orchard, and this is as sad in its own way as the loss of the estate. The triangle of swoony Dunyasha, bottom-pinching Yasha, and the long-faced Yepihodov play love as farce. Here, as so often in *The Cherry Orchard*, a theme is played out as it shifts between shades of dark and light, sadness and levity.

12.4 The cherry orchard bears a rich variety of meanings for Chekhov's characters. What does it mean to Trofimov? To Lopahin? To Ranevskaya and Gayev?

Answer In a sense, the cherry orchard is a mirror. Each character's vision of it embodies in some way his or her sense of self as well as his or her memories and aspirations. For some it stands for more: the identity and destiny of Russia. This grand old estate that is about to pass from the hands of the family that built it and has always owned it is a linchpin in history, tying past to future, and so it does not come as a surprise when Trofimov represents it as an incarnation of Russian history. In Act II, he asks Anya ". . . aren't human beings looking at you from every tree in the orchard, from every leaf, from every trunk? Don't you hear voices? Oh it's terrifying!"* For Trofimov, the orchard is inseparable from the system of serfdom, abolished only forty years before, that had made it possible for a few families, like Anya's, to live graciously while thousands toiled for little reward and without the rights of free people. For Trofimov, the orchard represents a shameful chapter in history that must be expiated and finally overcome in a happier, more honorable, and more socially just future.

Lopahin's first reference to the house, which occurs early in Act I, also relates to serfdom. Standing in the nursery, he remembers the time when he was 15 years old and his father, who before the emancipation had been a serf on the estate, punched him and bloodied his nose. He remembers how Ranevskaya, herself a young woman then, tried to comfort him, saying, "Don't cry, little peasant. It will heal in time for your wedding." Lopahin admits that he, like his father, was a peasant, and now, despite his money and fine clothes, he still considers himself a peasant.

To Lopahin as to Trofimov, the cherry orchard speaks of class relations, but in a very different way. Lopahin remembers an instance of kindness that for him is unmarred by any resentment at the touch of self-conscious *noblesse* in Ranevskaya's words to "the little peasant." Lopahin's recollection of the cherry orchard shows an aspect of class relations not represented in Trofimov's stark, black-and-white vision of history and injustice. Lopahin's connection to the past, via the cherry orchard, is more personal, more complex and modulated, than Trofimov's. The fall of the cherry orchard corresponds to Lopahin's rise from peasant to merchant. However, Lopahin does not see in this, as Trofimov might, the workings of history or progress. It seems instead to Lopahin like a private dream come true: "I'm asleep—it's only a dream—I only imagine it— It's the fruit of your imagination, wrapped up in the darkness of the unknown!"

Lopahin clearly cares about the estate, in his own way, as much as anybody. But that does not stop him from participating in its destruction, replacing the orchard with summer bungalows for vacationing city folk. This is, in his view, the practical thing, what any person who worked for a living and had a little common sense would do.

For Ranevskaya and Gayev, the estate is virtually synonymous with their

---

*Translated by Avraham Yarmolinsky, *The Portable Chekhov*, New York, The Viking Press, 1947. All references to *The Cherry Orchard* in this chapter are to the Yarmolinsky translation.

lives. It is rich with memories of their childhood and youth, the time when, as Firs says, everyone was happy without knowing why. When Ranevskaya looks out the nursery window and sees the trees with their white blossoms, she sees, unchanged, a vision from what she calls in Act I "my innocent childhood." But the unchanged tableau of the orchard also reminds her of how things have changed, of how far away those innocent days are. The past is not entirely benign; it includes an unhappy marriage and the death of a son. Ranevskaya's reverie, inspired by the orchard, ends: "If only I could free my chest and shoulders from this rock that weighs on me; if I could only forget the past!"

But the essence of Ranevskaya and Gayev is that they cannot forget the past, cannot be anything but what their lives have made them. With all their weaknesses, they are imperishably, even nobly, themselves. Gayev recognizes his own foolishness, but he cannot refrain from eulogizing bookcases, lecturing waiters on the decadents, and making imaginary billiard shots. His weakness is inseparable from his charm. We may cherish Ranevskaya too for her weakness. It is love and generosity above all that have ruined her life. And though we wish her happier, we do not wish her different. It is a triumph of identity that Ranevskaya and Gayev have survived so long and remained so totally themselves in a world that is hard on such guileless, generous, impractical folk.

Their individuality, maintained in equal parts by their courage and by their simple inability to change, is echoed in the individuality, the specialness, of the cherry orchard. When Lopahin suggests that the orchard be sold so that the house may be saved, they quite literally do not understand him. How can they sacrifice the marvelous orchard, which embodies the identity of the estate, their lives, their selves, in order to save themselves? It makes no sense to them. They can no more save the estate by changing it than they can change themselves. Ranevskaya and Gayev's tragedy, as well as their attractiveness, lies in their fidelity to themselves. Like all people who cannot change, they suffer; but they also win our affection and respect.

12.5 Soviet critics, as well as some other readers, have claimed that *The Cherry Orchard* is a play with a political message. Trofimov has frequently been identified as the spokesperson for this message, which is interpreted as a clear-eyed farewell to the old corrupt order, symbolized by the cherry orchard, and a welcoming salute to the new men—like Trofimov and, perhaps, Lopahin—who will build a new, more just Russia. In this view, the play is a prophecy of the revolution that was just a few years away. How accurate and complete is this view?

Answer   There is no denying that *The Cherry Orchard* is a play concerned with history and so with politics in the broad sense. Chekhov has taken pains to locate his play amid specific social and historical circumstances. The setting of Act II, the telegraph poles and the city that looms on the horizon, the fact that Simeonov-Pishchik has sold part of his estate to the railroad, the story of Lopahin's rise, and Firs's nostalgia for the days before "the Freedom" all locate the play at a crux of history, between the old Russia that had remained essentially unchanged for hundreds of years and the new Russia that was rapidly joining the modern world.

Perhaps the most vivid embodiment of the historical situation can be seen in the tramp who appears at the end of Act II. He is the only character who is not part of the ensemble but an interloper, entirely divorced from the web of relationships which ties Chekhov's characters together. He makes one vaguely menacing appearance and then leaves the play for good. The tramp is a creature of the new Russia. In times gone by, he would no doubt have been a serf, tied to some estate or village, but now he wanders in a changed society where there is no longer a place for him. Revolutions are impossible without such disenfranchised people, and to the degree that the tramp summarizes some of the play's concerns, it may be correct to call *The Cherry Orchard* prophetic.

If *The Cherry Orchard* is in some sense a political play, self-consciously concerned with Russia's historical situation, does Trofimov express Chekhov's views on these matters? Trofimov's liberalism and rationalism, commitment to work, sympathy for the dispossessed, and impatience with bourgeois complacency are indeed attitudes shared with his creator. Trofimov would have approved of Chekhov's medical work and visit to Sakhalin.

However, it is less clear what Trofimov would have thought of Chekhov the artist. In turn, Chekhov the artist is less than entirely accepting of Trofimov, making Trofimov's inadequacies vividly apparent. If Trofimov sees the historical picture more clearly than any of the other characters, he is also more deluded than most. He believes that he is "above love." As Ranevskaya points out in Act II, his clarity and conviction are linked to his ignorance and sterility:

> You settle every great problem so boldly, but tell me, my dear boy, isn't it because you're young, because you don't yet know what one of your problems means in terms of suffering? You look ahead fearlessly, but isn't it because you don't see and don't expect anything dreadful, because life is still hidden from your eyes? You're bolder, more profound, more honest than we are, but think hard, show just a bit of magnanimity. . . .

The abstract truth of Trofimov's formulations pales beside the earned truth of Ranevskaya's lived experience. Trofimov's ideas are not wrong, but they are wrongheaded, heartless and thin. Ranevskaya's speech is not a rebuttal of Trofimov's ideas but an *ad hominem* attack; his ideas are inadequate because in some way he is.

This may strike us as unfair. However, in theater ideas come in three dimensions, embodied by the people who believe in them. Whatever merit there may be in Trofimov's ideas, it is Ranevskaya's vision of fully felt experience and fully expressed identity that is at the emotional heart of the play.

12.6 If the moral values embodied by Ranevskaya lie at the heart of *The Cherry Orchard*, what effect do these values have on the style and structure of the play as a whole?

Answer No one word can completely capture the panoply of values associated with Ranevskaya. However, if one were forced to select a single word, "aestheticism" might be a good choice. The values that Ranevskaya stands for— authenticity, depth of feeling, the preciousness of identity, in sum, her emphasis on the quality of experience and feeling—amount to an aesthetic view of life. In its beauty and singularity, the cherry orchard is the emblem of Ranevskaya's aestheticism. Saving the estate means nothing to Ranevskaya if the manner of doing so defiles it, if it is, as Ranevskaya calls Lopahin's plan, "vulgar."

Ranevskaya herself embodies the antithesis of vulgarity: nobility. She is noble in every sense of that archaic-sounding word. The idea of nobility expresses at once a political and an aesthetic vision of life. It suggests the proposition that the good, the beautiful, and the powerful are ideally one and the same and that they can be united and embodied in the lives of a nation's highest citizens. The noble or aristocratic way of life is an aesthetic put into practice. It represents both the views of particular classes at particular times and a vision of perfection and wholeness shared by all.

The Cherry Orchard shows the end of nobility in all its senses as a historical possibility. Lopahin is not by any means a bad man, but he is incomplete. He can fulfill his social role as Lopahin the merchant only at the expense of destroying the cherry orchard. The beautiful and the socially necessary have gone their separate ways.

The Cherry Orchard takes its form from Ranevskaya's aestheticism. Like Ranevskaya, the play cares more for the texture of experience than for its ultimate significance. The play's constant oscillation between comedy and pathos suggests that our experience of these feelings is what really counts. It is the flow and feel of experience that is important, not its distilled meaning. Like Ranevskaya, who is committed to the aesthetic of nobility, the play is devoted to aesthetic experience as an end in itself. *The Cherry Orchard* is closer to purer, nonnarrative artistic forms—the lyric, the idyll, impressionist music and painting—than to any more familiar genre of drama.

D.E.

SUGGESTED READINGS

Hahn, Beverly, *Chekhov: A Study of Major Stories and Plays* (1977).
Hingley, Ronald, *Chekhov: A Biographical and Critical Study* (1966).
Jackson, Robert (ed.), *Chekhov: A Collection of Critical Essays* (1967).
Magarshack, David, *Chekhov the Dramatist* (1952).
Simmons, Ernest J., *Chekhov: A Biography* (1962).

Part Three

THE MODERN
WORLD

INTRODUCTION

Since people in every age see their own time as "modern," the term is technically undefinable. It is commonly used in this century, however, to describe the era since 1914. The modern era, then, spans the time between Proust, near the start of the century, and Beckett, our contemporary. What qualities and events characterize this era? Most strikingly, two world wars, a radically new understanding of the self and the universe, and a wave of artistic experimentation bearing the fuzzy label "modernism."

Proust's *Swann's Way* appeared in 1913, Kafka's "The Metamorphosis" was published in 1915, and in 1914 World War I began. If modernist literature did not directly result from World War I, it nonetheless emerged from the same atmosphere and first presaged and then reflected the social disorder and dislocation the war left in its wake. World War I brought to an end a time of European optimism during which it was believed that life and human beings might continually improve. Inventions such as the telephone, automobile, and airplane had seemed to suggest a future of moral and technological progress. However, the war revealed a huge gap between the two kinds of progress, as technological developments were harnessed to destructive ends in the form of tanks, submarines, and poison gas.

Along with the illusion of progress, the war shattered European illusions about warfare. Concepts such as nobility and heroism came to seem anachronistic and irrelevant when a line of advancing soldiers could be suffocated by a cloud of mustard gas or mowed down by machine guns sheltered within trenches. Paul Fussell in *The Great War and Modern Memory* argues that a characteristically modern form of irony emerged from World War I: a perception of the gap between intentions and what actually happens, between noble words and sordid reality. The unprecedented destructiveness of World War I indicated that moral progress was not at all inevitable and that the traditional values of western culture—courage, civility, social and intellectual cultivation—were vulnerable indeed. Skepticism and pessimism, qualities associated with modernism, can be traced in large part to the mood of disillusionment surrounding World War I. The worldwide economic crisis of the 1930s, followed by a second world war more horrific than the first, reinforced this sense that neither the world nor human impulses were even close to being understood or controlled.

Also shaping modernism were the contribütions of three major thinkers: Nietzsche in philosophy, Freud in psychology, and Einstein in physics. All three, different though they were, seemed to call into question the tenets of traditional morality; for example, the belief that clear guidelines for proper behavior have been given to humankind and that acts can be definitively judged as either good or evil. Nietzsche had denounced morality outright in *Beyond Good and Evil* (1886), and Freud's depiction of the psyche as largely driven by instinctual forces appeared to ignore or at least diminish the importance of moral choice. (Freud, however, was deeply interested in the ethical implications of his theories, which he explored in such works as *Civilization and its Discontents* [1930]). Finally, Einstein's theory of relativity, first formulated in 1905, was popularly interpreted to mean that even those physical laws commonly regarded as unshakable are in fact flexible, changing according to circumstance.

All these intellectual developments appeared to replace absolute standards with uncertainty. Whether it was Nietzsche's "will to power" or Freud's "libido" that dictated human behavior, it was certainly not any external force such as an omnipotent God or a timeless moral standard. The very existence of what is commonly called reality seemed to be called into question; if Einstein had found that the world's physical qualities alter according to the circumstances of the perceiver, could there be such a thing as "objective" reality?

Proust's answer to this philosophical question is a simple no. He insists that each person creates his or her version of the world and lives accordingly. The result of this extreme subjectivity is extreme isolation since no true communication is possible between different worlds. Mann and Kafka, too, create characters for whom the world is essentially a projection of their minds; Aschenbach's wanderings through a corrupt Venice and Gregor Samsa's transformation into an insect enact their internal desires and fears. The modernist's concern, then, is often less with representing "reality" (an impossible task, since either there is no such thing or it is too formless to be described in coherent language) than with dramatizing the inner workings of the mind.

This emphasis on subjectivity has implications for characterization and plot. For the modernist, a character is defined by the way he or she sees the world rather than by any easily nameable character traits or physical attributes. Characters thus defined may seem open-ended or incoherent. In modern fiction, plotting may reflect illogical psychological associations rather than traditional chronological order. The author may make no pretense of creating a convincingly real world and may, as in the case of Brechtian theater, openly admit the use of artifice in order to force the audience out of the conventional role of spectator.

If the work of art cannot hope to duplicate reality, neither can language itself. A pained consciousness of the limitations of language and a consequent involvement with words as things in their own right rather than as representations of other things are both characteristic of modernist literature. The almost meaningless babble of Beckett's characters, like Marcel's longing for a place that will live up to the magic of its name, suggests that language can only seduce and deceive, hinting at a coherence which it is powerless to produce or convey.

The typical protagonist of modernist fiction or drama has sometimes been called the anti-hero, so direct is the opposition between the qualities of such a protagonist and those traditionally associated with the hero. Like Gregor Samsa, the modern hero may be totally ordinary, as are the tasks he or she has to perform. The modern hero's most striking quality is helplessness; such characters seem to have no control over what happens to them. An outsider even at home, the modern hero has no refuge—except perhaps the mind—in which he or she can act effectively. Such a character could scarcely be more different from the traditional hero who overcomes gigantic obstacles as representative of the culture's highest values. Interestingly, many modern writers have themselves been cultural outsiders. Samuel Beckett, a native English speaker writing in French; Marcel Proust, a bourgeois Jew infiltrating the French aristocracy; and Franz Kafka, a German-speaking Jew living in Prague were all exiles of sorts, even in their native lands.

Modernist authors have been accused of seeking to destroy western humanistic values and of being destructive and depressing. Certainly, modernist literature suggests a shrunken view of the importance and dignity of human beings. But at its best it does so with a great deal of humor, affection, and sympathy. In dramatizing human vulnerability, depravity, and futility, modernist writers such as Proust, Kafka, Mann, Brecht, and Beckett offer an unflattering but recognizable picture of ourselves. In acknowledging its truth, we transcend those barriers between one mind and another whose power the work itself may assert. This is the paradox of modernist literature: that it asserts, with Beckett, "I can't go on; I'll go on."

C H A P T E R 1 3

PROUST

Early Life

"How I hate old Proust," says a character in Aldous Huxley's novel *Eyeless in Gaza* (1936), ". . .forever squatting in the tepid bath of his remembered past. . . . There he sat, a pale repellent invalid, taking up spongefuls of his own thick soup and squeezing it over his face." So vividly repulsive a picture is gripping and not entirely misleading. Disabled by asthma, which he treated by piling on overcoats no matter what the weather, isolated by his habit of sleeping during daylight and writing at night, insulated by the cork- and tapestry-lined walls of his Paris apartment, and troubled by his homosexuality, which he never publicly avowed, Marcel Proust was a notoriously eccentric man whose way of life should have condemned him to solitude and self-obsession. Yet in *Remembrance of Things Past*, he created a huge, various, and keenly observed world whose inhabitants range from the residents of relatively rustic Combray to the artists, aristocrats, and bourgeoisie of Paris.

Proust's genius is often attributed in part to his mixed parentage. His parents' marriage, which united natives of provincial Illiers (the novel's Combray) and cosmopolitan Paris, resembles a Proustian metaphor linking apparently unrelated worlds. His father, Adrien Proust, a distinguished doctor, was the first of his family to leave Illiers; his mother, Jeanne Weil, was a Jewish Parisian. Proust was born in 1871, the older of two children.

At age 9, Proust had his first attack of asthma, which was to keep him pampered and hypochondriacal for much of his life. The illness apparently receded, allowing him to attend the Lycée Condorcet and even to serve for a

221

year in the military. While at school, he began to frequent artistic and aristocratic gatherings, with his schoolmates often providing an entrée into otherwise
unapproachable salons. Parisian society in the late nineteenth century was rigidly
stratified; largely devoid of political power, the aristocracy cultivated prestige,
with the guest list as its most potent weapon. Their clannish parties, lovingly
chronicled by Paris newspapers, created and maintained minute social distinctions. The members of the *ancien régime*, for example, whose titles derived from
the Middle Ages, could look down their noses at the less exclusive newcomers
who owed their nobility to Napoleon. The moneyed upper middle class, professionals, and artists all tended to have their own salons, each presided over by
a hostess who was in turn socially defined by her guest list.

These are the distinctions re-created so precisely by Proust, whose fictional
Guermantes family, of course, possesses the most *ancien* of titles. Aided by his
classmates, his intelligence, and his somewhat mannered charm, Proust was
able to penetrate a wide range of salons, including those of the faubourg Saint-
Germain, the Paris neighborhood traditionally favored by the nobility, whose
name became synonymous with the most exclusive segment of aristocratic society. What he saw there became the substance of his novel, where he portrays
the aristocracy as he knew them: enchanting but shallow and self-deceived snobs
who were themselves the victims of their rigidly stratified hierarchies.

Proust studied as well as socialized, briefly attending the Sorbonne, where
he heard the lectures of the philosopher Henri Bergson (1859–1941), whose
theories of time and memory appear to have influenced him. He also briefly
held a job at a library that involved only minor duties, which he nevertheless
failed to perform. He was rejecting the possibility of a conventional career in
favor of a more mysterious vocation: writing. His only visible activities, however,
were occasional articles on the arts and frequent socializing. In 1896, he published *Pleasures and Days*, an elaborately produced but fragmentary collection
of stories and poems interspersed with his friends' illustrations and musical
compositions.

Proust seemed at this point a mere dabbler and aesthete, a typical 1890s
figure devoted to delicate sensations and exquisite *objets d'art*. The impression
was created in part by his friendship with the comte de Montesquiou, whose
elaborate dress, second-rate poetry, and exaggerated sensibility made him the
1890s aesthete *par excellence* (he was the model for Huysmans's decadent Des
Esseintes in the novel *A Rebours* [1884] as well as—much later—for Proust's
Charlus). There was little outward sign of the intellectual and literary groundwork Proust was laying for the eventual creation of his masterpiece.

Middle Years: Ruskin and L'Affaire Dreyfus

From 1896 to 1901, Proust worked erratically on *Jean Santeuil*, an unfinished, posthumously published novel that resembles an embryonic *Remembrance*. During the same period, he was discovering the English writer John Ruskin and in the process developing his own theory of art. Ruskin wrote about painting, architecture, and social problems. His elegant literary style, worship of art, and emphasis on seeing as a rigorous and illuminating experience appear to have influenced Proust, who immersed himself in Ruskin's prose and translated into French *The Bible of Amiens* (1880–1885) and *Sesame and Lilies* (1863).

Another important influence on Proust—and on France—during this time was the Dreyfus affair, the ten-year furor surrounding the wrongful conviction in 1894 of a Jewish army officer, Alfred Dreyfus, on charges of spying for Germany. By 1896, evidence had surfaced proving that Dreyfus was innocent, but a forged letter was used to acquit the real spy and keep Dreyfus in prison. By 1897, France had split in two. Those who supported the military (generally conservative and often anti-Semitic) were violently estranged from those who supported Dreyfus. In 1899, Dreyfus was freed, but it was not until 1906 that his sentence was reversed. As a partly Jewish writer with aristocratic friends, many of whom were promilitary, Proust, himself pro-Dreyfus, was intensely aware of how the Dreyfus affair had split French society. The affair appears in *Remembrance* as the catalyst and symbol for the aristocracy's collapse into moral bankruptcy.

Early Writings

In 1903 Proust's father died, and two years later came the far more devastating loss of his mother, with whom Proust had had an intensely close relationship. His idiosyncrasies had always mystified his parents, who had continued, somewhat uncomfortably, to support and house him. Their death left him at once freer and more obligated: freer to live in an unconventional manner but more obligated by a guilty sense of the sorrow he had brought them to produce some work to justify their pain. After a month-long stay in a sanatorium, Proust moved to a Paris apartment at 102 boulevard Haussman and devoted himself to writing.

This time, he produced a conglomeration of essay and narrative entitled *Contre Saint-Beuve* (*Against Sainte-Beuve*). Sainte-Beuve was a nineteenth-century French critic who took a biographical approach to literature, placing what Proust regarded as a disproportionate emphasis on the life rather than work of the writer. *Against Sainte-Beuve* argues that the life is irrelevant to the artist's work. It also includes early versions of some of the most famous episodes of *Remembrance*. The most important of these is the story of the *madeleine*, which apparently refers to an actual biscuit tasted by Proust as well as a crucial turning point in his artistic and psychological theories.

Proust and Involuntary Memory

Sometime around 1909, Proust ate a *madeleine* which he had dipped in tea. The incident gave rise to the moment in *Remembrance* when a grown Marcel, tasting the same tea-dipped biscuit, discovers the origin of its eerily familiar taste: As a child, he had been served the same combination of tea and *madeleine* by his Aunt Léonie. Out of this recognition grows a chain of fantastically vivid memories, unsought and entire. The whole town of Combray, which the narrator then proceeds to describe, appears as an emanation from this experience.

This uncanny and exhilarating release of past memories by the accidental repetition of a sense impression became known as involuntary or instinctive memory. Voluntary memory, Proust felt, is groping, incomplete, and abstract. Involuntary memory, though, reproduces the past with such sensual immediacy that it seems to be reexperienced rather than merely remembered. In this 1909 experience, Proust found a way of exploring and recapturing the past; through the literary re-creation of involuntary memory, he could reproduce both the fleeting passage of time and the special moments at which it is caught, held, and transcended. Earlier writers had exclaimed over the power of a flowery smell, for example, to evoke with strange clarity a long-past summer. But when Proust based his entire aesthetic and even his philosophy of life on the evocative potency of certain sense impressions and the access they provided to the past, he was doing something new.

Remembrance of Things Past

In the years that followed, Proust worked with a new intensity and sense of purpose. In 1913, he submitted *Swann's Way*, the first volume of *Remembrance*, to publishers as the first in a series of three volumes. The publishers (among them, on behalf of the publishing house Gallimard, the novelist André Gide, who was soon to regret and then retract his decision) were reluctant to take a chance on a work they regarded as obscure and meandering; Grasset finally published the book at the author's expense.

At this point, World War I intervened, preventing publication of the second volume. While Proust waited for peace, he revised and expanded the remaining manuscript, a process that once begun appeared to have no end. He incorporated the war itself into his novel, which mushroomed from the original three books to seven. As he brought the world at large into his manuscript, the world paid him increasing attention. A repentent Gide led Gallimard's eager and finally successful negotiations for the publication rights to the second volume, *Within a Budding Grove*, which appeared in 1919. It won the Prix Goncourt for that year, and Proust's fame as a peculiar but masterful and brilliantly innovative writer was never after in doubt. The remainder of *Remembrance* appeared sporadically throughout the rest of and after Proust's life.

The work's original French title, *A la recherche du temps perdu*, means literally "in search of lost time." Its volumes are *Du côté de chez Swann* (*Swann's Way*); *A l'ombre des jeunes filles en fleurs* (*Within a Budding Grove*); *Le Côté de Guermantes*, parts one and two (*Guermantes Way*); *Sodome et Gomorrhe*, parts one and two (*Cities of the Plain*); *La Prisonnière* (*The Prisoner*); *Albertine disparue* (*The Sweet Cheat Gone*); and *Le Temps retrouvé* (*The Past Recaptured*). *Sodome et Gomorrhe* was the last part published during Proust's lifetime. He died in 1922 while revising the final volumes.

ESSAY QUESTIONS WITH ANSWERS

Remembrance of Things Past

13.1   The plot of *Remembrance* is often described as circular, for it tells the story of a boy who wants to be a writer and, at the book's climax, seems to be about to begin composing the very book in which we have read about him. Such a circular plot suggests a tightly constructed book whose essential subject is the act of writing. But *Remembrance* is over 3000 pages long, stuffed with characters, realistic details, and social commentary, appearing at times to be almost formless. Why does Proust make his circular plot so huge and involved?

Answer   Early in *Swann's Way*, Marcel, who is the novel's narrator and is not necessarily to be identified with its author, Marcel Proust, describes the long walks on which his father would take the family. Starting from the front door of the house in Combray, they would wind along unfamiliar paths until Marcel's mother was completely disoriented and convinced they were lost. Just at the moment when exhaustion caused her to wonder how they would ever get home, Marcel's father would reveal the door of their house, unfamiliar at that angle but a stone's throw away.

These Sunday walks of Marcel's childhood bear a striking resemblance to the plot of the novel. *Remembrance* is the story of a young man who wants to be a writer, has a series of experiences that convince him he cannot, and finally, having reached middle age, realizes he can. His pursuit of the aristocracy and his obsessively jealous love for Albertine have ended in loss and disillusionment, but these disappointments are now to become the substance of the novel he thought he could not write. His apparently aimless wandering through life has led him back to his own door, to the triumphant decision to be a writer.

In the meantime, there are lavishly detailed portraits of Paris society, which dissolves as the novel progresses amid the crumbling of social distinctions resulting from increasing financial pressures and World War I. Marcel appears to verge on despair as he paints the increasingly garish dissipation of the aristocracy and the indiscriminate destruction caused by the bombs. But just when his world and his vocation seem irrevocably lost, Marcel discovers their potential for redemption and the subject of his novel.

The decisive moments come at the end of *The Past Recaptured*, the last volume, when Marcel, after a long absence from Paris, attends a party given by the princesse de Guermantes. Just before entering the salon, he experiences a series of involuntary memories and for the first time understands their significance. Tripping on an uneven paving stone in the street, he suddenly finds all of Venice resurrected in his mind, because he had tripped in an identical way on the uneven stones outside Saint Mark's. This mental resurrection floods him with the same inexplicable joy he had felt almost 3000 pages earlier on tasting the *madeleine*. This time, though, he understands that the source of his joy is not the content of his memory but the act of remembering. When, through memory, he joins past and present in his mind, he is triumphing over time and creating a moment that transcends time.

This discovery endows his imagination with a new power and a new task. The power consists in the ability to re-create the past in a present sense impression, allowing him to savor a moment imaginatively at the same time that he is literally experiencing it. The Venice of his memory, poeticized by its distance in the past, coexists for an instant with its physical evocation, the paving stone. When Marcel recognizes the resemblance between these moments and the experiencing of a work of art, he has understood his task. For this, he realizes, is the same satisfaction he feels while listening to the Vinteuil sonata (composed by his neighbor in Combray), which he, like Swann, loves so much. The pleasure comes from sensing the individual notes that are sounding in the immediate present yet are overlaid with the formal structure of the whole.

Deciding joyfully that these moments and the past that emerges from them can form the substance of his novel, he steps into the salon, eager to greet the old friends with whom he now plans to populate the novel. He is shocked to find, however, that he recognizes no one, and for a moment his work seems once more in jeopardy. The guests seem to be comically attired in wrinkled masks and white-haired wigs. Gradually, the grotesque disguises are recognized as the inevitable work of time. The unfamiliar faces are in fact Marcel's friends; they have simply grown older.

As Marcel gropes for the connection between his memory of his friends and their present wrinkled incarnations, the reader performs a similar act of mental transcendence, searching through his or her memory of the more than 200 characters peopling the novel, trying to remember who is who, and finally joining name to face in a victory over forgetfulness. How Proust's readers feel while reading *Remembrance* is an essential element in its construction and provides one explanation for its length. If the fruit of Marcel's experience is a sense of timelessness, the tree from which that fruit is plucked is time—long stretches of elapsed time. The fruit cannot be plucked without a long and painful climb involving intense effort. For readers to say, like Marcel at his door, "So that is where we are! We were never lost at all!" they must first feel that they have traveled a long way.

13.2   *Remembrance* is narrated in the first person by an "I" who remains mysterious even though the entire novel unfurls from his consciousness and is ostensibly the story of his life. On the two obscure occasions when this narrator is named, it is as "Marcel," the author's name, suggesting that author and narrator are one and that the novel is a disguised autobiography. Is this so? If not—if the mysterious "I" who tells the story is not Marcel Proust describing his own life—who is he?

Answer   One of Proust's biographers has suggested that every character in *Remembrance* can be traced to some actual person on whom his or her traits are based. Illiers, for example, is now visited by Proustian pilgrims as the original Combray, and an old family friend, Charles Haas, is reputed to be one of several models for Swann. But the vast majority of these places and characters can be traced not to one model but to several. Proust seems to have synthesized his memories of several people, using their actual characteristics as building blocks and adding others that are wholly fictional in order to create a new whole. Autobiography hardly seems an accurate term for a work so consciously constructed and carefully plotted.

This means that the "I" of the narration is not simply Marcel Proust, aged 42, lying in bed and writing his life story in notebooks. The "I," which has been the subject of endless critical analysis, is generally seen to have at least two component identities: the older, experienced narrator, who has already lived the life he is describing, and the character Marcel, who is living it out before our eyes in ignorance of its outcome. Marcel acts, while the narrator occasionally brings his superior knowledge to bear on those acts, interpreting and analyzing with the insight that age allows. The distinction is comparable to that between Marcel and his father during their Sunday morning walks. While Marcel wandered, intently smelling flowers and watching clouds and just as intently believing himself lost, his father both wandered and led, experiencing the same impressions but also knowing the shape they would take as a whole. Together they wandered through a kind of maze, but one had a map. Similarly, the "I" who recounts *Remembrance* has mastered its shape; his knowledge is the home to which the "I" who lives *Remembrance* will unknowingly return.

13.3 Most of *Remembrance* consists of Marcel's re-creation of his life and environment. Yet inserted into *Swann's Way* is a kind of mininovel, "Swann in Love," in which a virtually absent narrator recounts events that occurred well before his birth. It is not that the narrator has changed his identity or vanished; rather, he has changed his method, receding unobtrusively and allowing another major character to take center stage, the position reserved throughout the rest of the novel for Marcel. Why is this self-contained story inserted into *Swann's Way*?

Answer There is some speculation that "Swann in Love" was originally intended as a separate novel and was blended into *Remembrance* well after it was written, but this does not mean that *Swann's Way* is a carelessly assembled patchwork. Even if its presence was originally an afterthought, "Swann in Love" is an integral part of the novel, reinforcing Swann's role as a failed version of Marcel. Just as Swann is a talented connoisseur but not an artist, the novel he dominates is a kind of rehearsal for *Remembrance*.

Like Marcel, Swann has been accepted into the faubourg Saint-Germain. Like him, he falls obsessively in love with a woman who offers nothing but a blank screen on which his imagination can project its tantalizing images. Like Marcel, Swann is deeply moved by art: the prose of Bergotte, the paintings of Elstir, and especially the music of Vinteuil. Yet his only act of creation other than the daughter he has with Odette is an essay on Vermeer.

Swann is unquestionably one of the most likable characters in the novel—sensitive, intelligent, and refined—but he is nonetheless the failure Marcel has avoided being. He has failed because he has never pushed his understanding far enough. At moments, he perceives the futility and artificiality of the society he frequents or the absurdity of his passion for Odette. His understanding leads him as far as dismissal and disgust but stops short of Marcel's probing self-analyses. His experience is a series of dead ends, for he lacks the crucial insight of Marcel. He has not understood the true role of art; he has bound his artistic sensibility to his sense of self.

Swann falls in love with Odette because she reminds him of a Botticelli painting. He loves the Vinteuil sonata because it reminds him of Odette. Thus, he is using art as a symbol of his own experiences and a receptacle for his own emotions. Swann's misapprehension is a common one. Most people listening to a popular song, for example, instinctively project their own emotions onto the words and melody and feel moved as a result. Popular music invites this response as a result of its stereotypical descriptions of love and loss. Listening to the infinitely more complex music of Vinteuil, Swann performs a similar mental act.

Marcel, however, sees that the work of art is not an object to be exploited emotionally by its perceiver but a way of seeing, utterly resistant to any other use. The artist does not convey truths, nor does the appreciator of the artwork take possession of them. Both together are translators, the artist putting the world into an individual "language" and the audience "reading" it. The artist's genius lies in his or her ability to re-see the world, as if the artist were wearing magical glasses that could see through commonplaces. The audience also slips on those glasses, sharing in the miraculous distortions of this new language and style.

When Swann attends Mme de Saint-Euverte's party and sees her footmen as wild animals, he is seeing the world as an artist would. He is wearing the magical glasses that allow him to see the familiar transposed into a new key, translated into a new language, stripped of its functionality. His acquaintances' features are suddenly not "symbols of practical utility in the identification of this or that man" but "measurable by aesthetic coordinates alone, in the autonomy of their curves and angles."* A man with a monocle becomes a fish carrying a piece of the aquarium wall before his face. The world re-seen without preconceptions is a world of optical illusions and joltingly incongruous juxtapositions.

But Swann is able to do this only because his desire for Odette has made him lose all interest in society, granting him the disinterestedness necessary for perception of this kind. He lacks the artist's ability to bring this same intent scrutiny to all his relations with the world; that would mean understanding simultaneously the meaninglessness of society, the hollowness of his love for Odette, and the egotism underlying his love of art.

If "Swann in Love" is oddly self-contained, with its opening description of the hermetically closed "little clan" of the Verdurins and its depressingly final invocation of futility at the end, this is perhaps because Swann himself, for all his attractions, is doomed to self-containment. While listening to the Vinteuil sonata at Mme de Saint-Euverte's, Swann is overcome for a moment by memories

---

*Translated by C. K. Scott-Moncrieff, New York, Random House, 1982. All references to *Remembrance of Things Past* in this chapter are to the Scott-Moncrieff translation.

of Odette. His eyes mist, and he removes his monocle to wipe it. "And doubtless," the narrator comments, "if he had caught sight of himself at that moment, he would have added to the collection of the monocles which he had already identified, this one which he removed. . . ." But Swann did not catch sight of himself at that moment, for it is precisely his inability to see himself, paired with his inability to forget himself, that separates him from Marcel. Throughout that brilliantly hilarious discussion of monocles, Swann was himself wearing one, yet he neglected to think about it, as Marcel would have done.

13.4 In the first three sentences of *Remembrance*, the word "time" appears three times. It also appears, capitalized, as the last word of the novel, and the original French title, of course, includes the word "time." Proust described his novel as portraying "psychology in time," indicating that he meant to explore the passage of time as experienced by human consciousness. What exactly does Proust mean by time?

Answer Proust's concept of time is generally thought to have been influenced, or at least anticipated, by the philosopher Henri Bergson in his distinction between *la durée*—lived time—and objectively measured time. Bergson felt that earlier philosophers had distorted the notion of time by treating it as an artificially static, spatial construct when in fact time is constant movement, indescribably mobile and elusive. Proust, like Bergson, rejects the mechanistic definition of time measured solely by the clock. To Proust, time has meaning only as it is experienced by human consciousness. The clock, from Proust's viewpoint, is irrelevant. What counts is how time's passage is felt by a particular individual.

Time, then, has no objective existence or continuity, since it is evident only as a series of personal and momentary experiences. But such a perception of time has vital implications for human identity. The Proustian personality does not grow and expand continuously over time; instead of a steady development, there is an endless series of suicides and rebirths. Each person is a succession of selves having no more direct access to past or future selves than to the selves of others. Swann's reluctance to fall out of love with Odette is in part a disinclination to suicide. To stop loving her, he must kill the self to whom she is all that matters, and as long as he is that self, he cannot conceive of the new self that will take its place. While listening to the Vinteuil sonata, he remembers the days when Odette loved him, and he pictures as the object of her love a man whom he only vaguely recognizes as himself.

Time, then, happens inside the mind, which experiences it not as a continuous thread linking past and present but as a succession of moments that leave only faint traces behind them, except when reincarnated by involuntary memory. The result is a world filled with uncertainty, for it is being reborn at each moment. No wonder Proust's characters grasp nervously at any hope of certainty, trying to fit everything and everyone into preconceived patterns. When the comtesse de Monteriender tells Swann of the Vinteuil sonata, "It's astonishing! I have never seen anything to beat it . . . since the table-turning!" she is succumbing to an understandable if silly need to classify, to state the new in terms of the old even though those terms are necessarily irrelevant.

Proust's conception of time is an essential element in the construction of his novel, which rejects traditional notions of character and plot, a rejection in which he was followed by novelists such as Virginia Woolf and James Joyce and which identifies Proust as a decidedly "modern" novelist. Traditional characterization presented clearly defined personalities whose motivations might be complex but were always decipherable; traditional plots presented events in chronological order, implying that time has meaning and continuity.

For Proust, however, the only unified and definable personalities are those created and worn like masks, stiffly confining and distorting the endlessly shifting shapes behind them. His characters seem often to be caricatures because for him there is no difference between character and caricature. Anyone concerned with presenting a particular face to the world—and almost all his characters, with their avid social grasping, are—will unavoidably exaggerate, overact, and wind up looking peculiar. Where his characters are not caricatures, their traits and motivations are subjected to such intense scrutiny that they tend to vanish as the narrator suggests explanation after explanation, each reasonable but none certain.

Like character, plot has no objective validity in Proust's novel. It has meaning only as a series of mental acts, not as a succession of events. Incidents are reported as they surface in a human mind, evoked by the association of similar sensations or ideas. Proust, along with many other modern novelists, moves away from the traditional novelistic presentation of events in chronological order. Instead, there are flashbacks, chronological gaps, and wide variations in the pace of the storytelling, indicating that how things happen in terms of objectively measurable time has nothing to do with the way time is experienced in the human consciousness.

13.5 Class snobbery is a major theme of *Remembrance*. The young Marcel is literally obsessed with titles, and huge sections of the novel take place at upper-class parties. Why does Proust depict this pervasive concern with class distinctions?

Answer When Marcel first sees the duchesse de Guermantes, she is kneeling in her family chapel in the church at Combray beneath a stained glass window depicting her ancestor Gilbert the Bad. Underneath her are the bones of her relatives, the old counts of Brabant, all descendants of Geneviève de Brabant, who received absolution from Saint Hilaire. The scene illustrates the way in which an ancient title radiates beauty for Marcel, to whom it is inseparable from these strangely romantic associations. An ordinary name, like Smith, though it may originally have designated the village blacksmith, has long been separated from its meaning; the average Smith must feel that his or her name is a fairly arbitrary label affixed for no particular reason. A Guermantes, however—or so Marcel at first believes—inherits a tradition, a place in society, and an identity, all magically fused in the name.

Proust's provisional title for the first volume of *Remembrance* was "The Age of Names." By this he meant the time when names seem magically to evoke the essence of what they designate. Balbec, for example, the seaside town where Marcel vacations, conjures up for him images of gothic architecture and stormy seas until he goes there and learns to distinguish name from place. Similarly, the name Guermantes appears to him inseparable from ancient battles and chivalric deeds. Because of the power and privilege historically granted to holders of titles, the aristocracy serves as a particularly vivid example of the illusory union of name and thing.

Maturity brings the realization that all names are arbitrary. The Guermantes family is seen to be as commonplace as any other; their ancient heritage gives them no special aura as individuals, nor does the actual Balbec dwell in a gothic haze. Name and thing are not connected, and the pilgrim who seeks in the thing itself the name's magical evocativeness will be disappointed. Marcel learns this lesson when he finally realizes that the exclusive soirees he attends are indeed boring and that the aristocracy holds no tantalizing secrets.

Besides revealing to Marcel the illusory nature of names, the aristocrats in *Remembrance* also serve another purpose. They act out in the most visible way the need all Proust's characters have for certainty, especially in the form of a counterfeit self. Amid the uncertainty of the Proustian universe, no one can be quite sure who anyone else is, and the result is a compulsive need to place people in social categories. Everyone in *Remembrance* seems to be squinting anxiously at everyone else, trying to make out who they are and how they can best be labeled and filed away (hence the satirical emphasis on monocles at the marquise de St.-Euverte's concert). The careful distinctions of a traditional class system provide reassurance that there is order in the world and that each individual has a clearly defined status and identity. For the aristocracy, placed by the system at the top of society, the social ritual and ludicrously codified behavior dictated by their social status are tempting escapes from uncertainty.

As important as categorizing others is defining oneself. The most common plagiarism, the narrator comments, is the plagiarism of oneself. People invent or borrow rigid identities to which they then mold their personalities and even their bodies, as in the case of the marquise de Gallardon, whose posture is compared to a tree growing backward at the edge of a precipice. She has aped disapproval and condescension for so long that her body as well as her mind have been warped. She has forgotten that her lack of an invitation, not her fear of meeting Princesse Mathilde (the holder of a Napoleonic title and thus an upstart), is her true reason for not visiting her relative the princesse des Laumes. People figure out what they need to believe in order to fit the roles they invent for themselves, and then they believe it, whatever the price.

Even so prestigious a figure as the princesse des Laumes is not above this anxious reaction to uncertainty; she tries ludicrously to adapt her behavior as unobtrusively as possible to the latest rules. As she enters Mme de St.-Euverte's concert, she is not sure whether the energetic rhythmic nodding of Mme de Cambremer is a new style to be imitated or simply a particularly gauche response to Liszt. Alternately fixing her hair and rapping out a beat or two, she manages to avoid the appearance of either error or doubt. Thus in an effort to systematize their own protean personalities, Proust's characters are constantly composing their features and behavior to match their rigidified self-concepts. Nowhere is this rigidity and the human price it extorts more clear than in the ancient rituals of the aristocracy.

13.6   "What I call love here," the narrator of *Remembrance* comments rather casually in the middle of the novel, "is reciprocal torture." Yet almost constantly throughout the novel Marcel is in love with someone—with his mother, with Gilberte, with the duchesse de Guermantes, with Albertine—and the novel within a novel "Swann in Love" is a variation on the same theme. Why is Proust's idea of love so persistently pessimistic, and why does he dwell on it so insistently?

Answer   For Proust, love, especially sexual passion, is essentially a way of portraying the inevitable subjectivity of human consciousness in the most vivid and startling colors. "Love," the narrator comments, "what is it but space and time rendered perceptible by the human heart?" Similarly, for Proust, space and time are only the barriers separating each person's version of the universe from everyone else's. These barriers are also, of course, the conditions essential to the exercise of imagination, but here we come full circle, for imagination is at once the source of love and its doom.

Imagination gives birth to desire, but since it also depends on distance between the lover and the object of love, the longed-for fulfillment turns instead to disillusionment. Swann loves Odette because she resembles a figure in a Botticelli painting, because other men desire her, and because she is inscrutable, but at the moment he possesses her she is only Odette possessed by Swann, not the mysterious woman of his imagination. For the lover to get what he desires *at the moment he desires it* is all he wishes, but it is by definition impossible. What the narrator says of Albertine is true as well of Odette: "She was merely, like a stone around which snow has gathered, the generating centre of an immense structure which rose about the plane of my heart." Yet she is also tantalizingly separate. Swann can know Odette only as she appears in his own heart, but the inkling he has of her autonomous existence acts as an anchor thrust out ahead, pulling him after.

Swann is obsessively curious about all the circumstances of Odette's life apart from him. Perhaps because he realizes how much of her existence for him is the construction of his own heart, he is most attracted by the aspects of her that escape him. Just as Marcel finds it easiest to love Albertine when she is sleeping, since that is as close as he can come to seeing her when he is not there, Swann wants to see Odette as she is for others, unadulterated by his presence. Obviously, such a desire is doomed.

The same fate is enacted in *Remembrance* on a broader scale. Swann's failed attempts at objective knowledge of Odette echo Marcel's futile efforts to gain objective knowledge of the world. Just as time is measurable only as it affects human consciousness, so reality is perceptible only as a series of interpretations by individuals. No external standards are available to verify any person's sense of the way things are; every individual has his or her own version of reality, each equally true but equally removed from objectively valid truth. But the young Marcel wants desperately to get at a reality independent of his consciousness. "When I saw any external object," the narrator complains early in *Swann's Way*, "my consciousness that I was seeing it would remain between me and it, enclosing it in a slender incorporeal outline which prevented me from ever coming directly in contact with the material form. . . ."

The problem of Proust's narrator resembles that formulated by the physicist

Werner Heisenberg, whose indeterminacy principle seems to describe much of what modern literature is about. In part, this principle states that an atomic particle's position and momentum (data essential to a description of the particle's physical state) cannot be measured simultaneously, giving rise to an inevitable element of uncertainty. To the literary-minded, this has come to mean that a purely objective perception of the world is impossible, because the human mind always interposes itself between consciousness and the object it perceives.

In *The Captive*, the narrator comments sadly on a failed attempt to achieve communion with the sky through flight in an airplane: "however high one flies, one is prevented to some extent from enjoying the silence of space by the overpowering roar of the engines." The efforts of human understanding emit a roar of their own that disturbs what we seek to embrace undisturbed.

Thus, for Proust, love is a most poignant and painful demonstration that no communion between human consciousness and anything outside is possible. Love mobilizes the imagination (for the love object is an imaginative construct) at the same time that it most desperately longs to dispense with imagination, to possess the loved one without the intermediary that in fact makes her existence possible. This is why the narrator of *Remembrance* calls love "reciprocal torture."

13.7 Proust is famous for having written some of the longest and most intricately constructed sentences ever printed and for using some of the strangest imagery, comparing a footman to a greyhound, for example, or a monocle to a shell splinter. What is the purpose of these complicated sentences and disturbingly unfamiliar metaphors?

Answer There is a poster for sale that portrays a diagram of one of the longest sentences to appear in *Remembrance*. Its 958 words cover the entire poster, with the sentence's complexity revealed by the countless twiglike offshoots that indicate subordinate phrases and clauses. No one would claim that such sentences are invitingly readable. However, they are essential to the novel's meaning, and their effect on the reader has been carefully calculated. Faced with 900-word sentences, with profuse subordination forcing one to pause, to absorb, to postpone understanding, and to wait patiently for the main clause that alone will allow the pieces to fall into place, the reader undergoes a lesson in patience, subtlety, and, ultimately, perception. The sentences are difficult because reader as well as writer must do the work of seeing.

For Proust, the world is a complicated place. Everyone experiences the world differently, and one's experiences may change radically from one moment to the next. Yet language implies a certain fixity; to name something is to make it stand still, to make it seem definite. Proust's problem, then, is twofold. He must present the world in all its temporariness and uncertainty if he wants to avoid betraying its complexity. At the same time, he wants to create something permanent, something outside time in the same way that Marcel's moments of involuntary memory are outside time.

Proust was concerned with this problem, and as a result his style is inseparable from what he has to say about the world. His sentences are long because they are hesitant and careful, preserving alternative possibilities and spurning conclusiveness. He rarely says "because" without a "perhaps" before it and often follows it with "or perhaps because." His narrator is devoid of the sense of certainty—or arrogance—that presumes to explain another human being definitively.

In a sense, Proust's sentences unravel the act of perception. Ordinarily, people fit whatever they see into a system of preconceptions. But suppose that instead of seeing something one immediately labels "fork," one sees a silver rod with four toothpicklike projections at the end and only a moment later, recognizing it, says, "A fork!" This is analogous to Swann's experience at Mme de St.-Euverte's, when he sees General Froberville not as the old friend who got him into a club but as a "common, scarred, victorious, overbearing face" with a shell splinter stuck in the middle. Proust's sentences thus present a string of phenomena that only gradually acquire a familiar shape. He turns the most commonplace encounters with the world into slow-motion recognition.

"We feel in one world," the narrator writes early in Swann's Way, "we think, we give names to things in another." Only the artist can rejoin those divorced worlds by paradoxically articulating the world before it has been named, before it has been distorted by our need to classify it. But how can language be used to describe a newly created and prelinguistic world? Proust's answer is metaphor, or the equation of apparently dissimilar things, which alone, he wrote, "gives a kind of eternity to style." At twilight, a woman on the street may look for a moment like a lamppost. A second later we recognize her as a woman; of course, she is not a bit like a lamppost. But for a moment she was, and it is as a lamppost that Proust would describe her. The stylistic equivalent of involuntary memory —metaphor—joins disparate impressions on the basis of an underlying similarity. M. de Bréauté's monocle is equated with a slide prepared for the microscope; linking the two incongruous images is the sense of a flat glassy surface with something floating behind it. Similarly, Marcel as a child served tea by his Aunt Léonie is equated with Marcel the adult; here the common element is the taste of tea and *madeleine*.

Given Proust's sense of the world, with its pervasive temporal flux and inevitable subjectivity, the only truths that hold still long enough to be worth stating are connections. Each linkage of monocle and slide, of past and present represents the rescue of a moment from the flight of time. But this rescue is the work of reader as well as writer. Just as the reader joins Marcel in his struggle to recognize his old friends at the princesse de Guermantes's party, the reader joins Proust, sentence by sentence, in the difficult work of making connections. Proust's style, then, serves as the magical glasses he felt great art must be. In a sense, no one can read Proust without understanding him, because to absorb one of his sentences is to see the world as he does.

R.H.

SUGGESTED READINGS

Brée, Germaine, *The World of Marcel Proust* (1966).

Girard, René (ed.), *Proust: A Collection of Critical Essays* (1962).

Girard, René (trans. Yvonne Freccero), *Deceit, Desire, and the Novel* (1965).

Painter, George D., *Proust: The Early Years* and *Proust: The Later Years*, 2 vols. (1959, 1965).

Poulet, Georges (trans. Elliott Coleman), *Proustian Space* (1977).

Shattuck, Roger, *Marcel Proust* (1974).

Shattuck, Roger, *Proust's Binoculars* (1963).

C H A P T E R   1 4

MANN

Early Life and Works

A child of the nineteenth century who unblinkingly confronted the spiritual and political calamities of the twentieth, Thomas Mann offers authoritative testimony about the transition from Victorian to modern culture. He was born in 1875 in the old Hanseatic city of Lübeck. His father, a prosperous grain merchant and senator, was descended from a patrician Lübeck family which, generation after generation, had produced men of substance, leaders in business and public life. Mann often contrasted the solid, bourgeois strain he felt he had inherited from his Prussian father with the exotic, artistic element he credited to his mother, who had been born in Brazil of German-Creole parents.

Mann began publishing stories in his early twenties, and his first (and recurrent) theme is precisely this conflict between the ordinary, "healthy" life of the bourgeoisie, which his father's family had brought to a kind of perfection, and the strained, antagonistic outsider's life of the artist. Both *Buddenbrooks*, the 1901 novel that established his reputation, and the 1903 novella "Tonio Kroger" deal with this conflict. Subtitled "The Decline of a Family," *Buddenbrooks* chronicles four generations of a family much like Mann's father's as they and their business deteriorate through financial reverses, imprudent marriages, and physical debilitation. However, the decline in *Buddenbrooks* is more than that of a single family; it is that of nineteenth-century civilization itself: its virtues of hard work, prudence, and self-respect, and its moral and metaphysical certitudes. The later Buddenbrook children, Christian the misfit and Hanno the artist, go wrong because for them, as for Tonio Kroger and all heirs to dying traditions, "there is no such thing as a right way."

While Mann lovingly evokes the high bourgeois tradition represented by the Buddenbrook family, he does not view its loss as an unmitigated disaster. Mann is fully aware of the hard-driving business habits and philistine narrowness that made the bourgeois world secure. Nor does he view the later Buddenbrook descendants solely as failures; they are gifted with an originality, an artist's pitch of perception, that their elders lack. In *Buddenbrooks*, then, Mann maintains an attitude of ambivalence that was to become a hallmark of his work, viewing with a detachment that approaches irony both the bourgeois sunk uncritically in the stuff of daily life and the too-conscious artist alienated from it.

Perhaps the most impressive aspect of *Buddenbrooks* is the artistic maturity of this very young man's first novel. It is written with a patience, a Tolstoyan care for rendering the texture of daily life, that shows complete mastery of the classic realist novel, a form which until Mann had never been successfully developed in German. Even in this first novel, Mann showed his characteristic ability to both master a traditional form and modify it, in this case introducing into the novel an irony and a subtle play of ideas—Schopenhauer, Wagner, and Nietzsche leave their mark on almost all his writings—unusual in a realist novel. Already in *Buddenbrooks* one encounters Mann's tendency to consolidate the traditional in subject and style while troubling it with the modern.

The Years of Conservatism

In 1891, after the death of his father, Mann and his family moved to Munich. After the publication of *Buddenbrooks*, Mann's life in that Bavarian city was graced by fame, a happy marriage, and continued literary productivity. In 1903, he published *Tristan*, a collection of novellas that includes "Tonio Kroger." In 1909, he issued the lighthearted novel *Königliche Hoheit* (*Royal Highness*), which seems to affirm the possibility of a happy reconciliation between art and life. However, in 1912, in the masterful novella "Death in Venice," he again posed the problem of the artist cursed with a febrile sensibility, alienated from everyday life, and burdened with the duty to create.

With the outbreak of World War I, Mann temporarily abandoned fiction for essays, often of a patriotic stamp. Several of these were published together in 1918 as *Betrachtungen eines Unpolitischen* (*Reflections of an Unpolitical Man*). If this is propaganda, it is propaganda of a most troubled and scrupulously thoughtful sort. It is in fact a meditation on German cultural history—on German music and the nature of Germany's contribution to European culture and religion—as well as the general problem of art and culture in the modern world. The position that Mann reaches is a general defense of inwardness and spirituality against rationalism, an espousal of tradition and authoritarianism against a facile liberal faith in progress. One of Mann's philosophical antagonists in these essays was his brother Heinrich, a spokesman for the liberal democratic point of view and a writer of stature. It can be argued that Mann's writing in *Reflections* is not so much political argumentation as an attempt to clear a space for the writer to pursue his work outside the realm of politics. However, what Mann apparently did not realize or would not admit at this time is that escape from politics is itself a political act, since it lends implicit assent to the powers that be. This was the last time Mann was to take such an apolitical position. His political thinking moved progressively to the left and in later years he became a vocal defender of the liberal and democratic values he had excoriated in *Reflections*.

The Magic Mountain

World War I interrupted Mann's work on a novella he had planned as a companion piece to "Death in Venice." When it was finally published in 1924, *Der Zauberberg* (*The Magic Mountain*) had grown into his most ambitious novel, a summary of his thinking up to that time, and a complex response to the turbulent epoch through which Europe had just passed. The story of Hans Castorp, a German Everyman who goes to a Davos tuberculosis sanatorium for a three-week visit and stays seven years, *The Magic Mountain* is both a *Bildungsroman* (a novel of education or personal growth) in the tradition of Goethe's *Wilhelm Meister* and an audaciously experimental novel. As Castorp pursues his moral and spiritual education at the sanatorium under a variety of odd tutors in such subjects as medicine, politics, philosophy, psychoanalysis, and music—that is, western culture—*The Magic Mountain* widens into a novel of ideas, and its method becomes symphonic, a weaving of leitmotifs and themes, shifting between serious and satirical modes. The sickness that afflicts Hans Castorp and his fellow patients is not so much tuberculosis as *Liebestod* (the love of death), an ailment Mann found in himself, in German romantic culture, and in the disastrous recent history of Europe. The intent of the novel is to effect a kind of homeopathic cure through an intensive exposure to this love of death as it infects (often comically) sex, art, and politics.

Two of the characters in *The Magic Mountain* who fight the battle between life and death—and for Castorp's soul—are Settembrini and Naptha. A representative of the Enlightenment and a democrat, Settembrini values reason and progress and possesses an optimistic faith in humankind and its culture, the same values Mann had criticized in *Reflections*. Naptha, Settembrini's more complex but ultimately repellent antagonist, is a spokesman for totalitarian politics, terrorism, and a dark and disturbing irrationalism. In their duel at the close of the novel, each enacts his philosophy. Settembrini, noble but impotent, fires into the air. Naptha, committed to death and trapped by his own logic, shoots himself. Here and in the novel as a whole, the forces Settembrini represents win a cautious and much qualified victory.

At the end of the extraordinary chapter "Snow," in which Castorp nearly loses his life, he speaks the life-affirming words that could well stand as the novel's motto: *"For the sake of goodness and love, man shall let death have no sovereignty over his thoughts"* (italicized in the original). At the conclusion of *The Magic Mountain*, Castorp does indeed choose life. He descends from the sanatorium to the "flatland" to enter the world. But the year is 1914, and we last glimpse Castorp a moment before he disappears into the mud and smoke of a Flemish battlefield. Although his education has in a sense been a success and he has chosen life, history has the last thunderous though ambiguous word.

It is appropriate that *The Magic Mountain* end inconclusively, for the sickness of modern European history had not nearly run its course. In late January 1933, Hitler became chancellor of Germany. A few days later, Mann, who had registered his opposition to fascism in the powerful 1930 novella "Mario and the Magician" and campaigned courageously against national socialism in speeches and essays, left Germany for the rest of his life.

Years in Exile

After living for some years in Switzerland, Mann came to America in 1938, living first in Princeton and then, from 1941 to 1952, at Pacific Palisades, California. In 1944, he became a United States citizen. Throughout the war, Mann was a prominent representative of "the other Germany," recording anti-Hitler radio speeches for broadcast to Germany and serving as a rallying point for German émigré culture in America. Already a figure of international renown—he had won the Nobel prize in 1929, largely on the strength of *Buddenbrooks*—he became something of an American hero as well.

In the years before the start of World War II, Mann had completed two novels set at a great distance from current events. The four-part *Joseph and His Brothers* (1933) is a novel of myth and history inspired by the Old Testament.

Lotte in Weimar (1939, published in America as *The Beloved Returns*) describes an imaginary encounter between the aged Goethe and Charlotte, the heroine of Goethe's *The Sorrows of Young Werther*. In 1943, Mann began work on *Doctor Faustus* (published in 1947), a novel in which he struggled to express the meaning of recent German history.

Like *The Magic Mountain*, *Doctor Faustus* is both the story of one man and a collective history. Into the making of Adrian Leverkühn, the tormented hero, Mann put all his knowledge of German culture in addition to the fruits of fresh research into the Faust legend, the writings of Luther, the works of the great German printmaker Dürer, avant-garde German music, and the lives of Nietzsche and Wagner. Mann's protagonist is a composer of literally demonic ambition; he makes a pact, perhaps hallucinated, perhaps real, with the devil. With his overweening pride, his brutality, his crushing solitude, and his desolation of spirit, Leverkühn is Mann's picture of Germany brought to its then-tragic condition. An anatomy of the German soul, *Doctor Faustus* also became a brutal self-examination. The difficulty for Mann of so scrutinizing himself and his cultural heritage is registered in the shape of the novel—the way it piles irony upon irony, plays assertion against retraction against ambiguity so that its sense becomes infinitely problematic, knotty, and tortured. In form as well as subject, the novel points toward apocalypse; the end not only of Germany but of the novel form and of western humanism is within its imagining. Yet even in this terribly despairing book there is vitality and even warmth hinting at hope, as in Mann's portrait of his humble, pedantic narrator, Serenus Zeitblom, D.Phil.

In some ways, *The Confessions of Felix Krull, Confidence Man* (1954) is the only novel that the ever-ambivalent Mann could have written after *Doctor Faustus*. While Adrian Leverkühn is the artist as barbarian, combining the highest ambition with the lowest amorality, Felix Krull is the artist as comic rogue. Like the *pícaros* (those shifty vagabonds of the early Spanish novel) who are his ancestors, Krull survives through a cheerful cooperation with his victims' worst tendencies. He represents a particularly lighthearted conclusion to Mann's lifelong meditation on the nature of the artist.

During his last years, Mann traveled and lived in Europe. Although he visited both East and West Germany on several occasions, he never again lived in the homeland whose culture and trials so absorbed him. His last residence was Zurich, where he died in 1955.

ESSAY QUESTIONS WITH ANSWERS

"Death in Venice"

14.1 Gustave von Aschenbach, the protagonist of "Death in Venice," derives his identity entirely from his all-consuming work as a writer. What is the relationship between Aschenbach's identity, particularly his moral code, and his art?

Answer For Aschenbach, art is the product not of a sudden flash of inspiration but of a long and arduous effort in which the artist shapes himself as well as his or her artifact. The masterpiece is achieved through a process of self-mastery. "Duty," "discipline," and "will" are Aschenbach's key words. His motto is "Hold fast," and he is described by an acquaintance as a perpetually clenched fist, lacking the ease and indulgence of the open hand. The image of the clenched fist captures not only the tensed exertion of Aschenbach's will but the way it opposes and excludes. For Aschenbach, everything great, including his own art, is "great in despite"; it is won in opposition to "affliction and pain, poverty, destitution, bodily weakness, vice, passion, and a thousand other obstructions."* By suppressing these inner weaknesses, the artist achieves both the work of art and the heroism of unbending resolution. And in this victorious self-conquest the artist creates himself or herself as a moral being and creates a moral art.

Now in his maturity, after years of struggle in the service of his demanding muse, Aschenbach has become a conscious moralist in his art. He has abandoned the subjectivism, cynicism, and excessive intellectualism of his youthful writings for a literature that embodies the imperative to high moral resolve. Turning away from the preoccupation with the extreme and abnormal which characterizes much of modern literature, Aschenbach has withdrawn imaginative sympathy from characters (Dostoevsky's, for example) who are mastered by their passions and victimized by their irrationality. He condemns the claims made on behalf

---

*Translated by H. T. Lowe-Porter, New York, Vintage, 1966. All references to "Death in Venice" in this chapter are to the Lowe-Porter translation.

of such anti-heroes as mere moral equivocation. Aschenbach firmly "rejects the rejected, casts out the outcasts," and opposes writers drawn to "the abyss," which represents to him all that is irrational, instinctual, and chaotic in humankind.

As a literary moralist, Aschenbach has become something of a cultural hero. He has become famous; his writings have been anthologized in schoolbooks, and the values he supports seem to be the official values of his society. His code of conduct as a writer, his commitment to vocation, and his vigorous self-control embody the characteristic virtues of the bourgeoisie. As the narrator points out, Aschenbach has much in common with the stolid Prussian businesspeople and burghers who are his ancestors. But he is also an artist. As his writing has become increasingly high-minded, it has become all the more beautiful, displaying the perfect purity and simplicity of classic form.

The narrator asks rhetorically what moral sense one can make of the exaggerated beauty of Aschenbach's late style. He finds it both moral and immoral: moral in that it exemplifies Aschenbach's extraordinary self-discipline but immoral—that is, indifferent to morality and perhaps hostile to it—because its beauty is an end in itself and serves nothing but itself. We are pleased by the perfect pace and balance of artful sentences whether they describe good deeds or atrocities. The irony to which the narrator calls our attention is that Aschenbach's carefully crafted, hard-won moral art has, precisely by virtue of its formal perfection, escaped his own intention and become morally ambiguous. The further implication around which Mann builds his story is that Aschenbach's credo of moral resolution and strenuous self-conquest may also be dangerously flawed, undermined by tendencies that escape his militant will.

14.2 Mann depicts Aschenbach with a thoroughgoing and persuasive psychological realism, and he describes Venice with an exacting circumstantial realism that vividly renders the look, feel, and even smell of the place. However, at numerous points in the story, Mann relinquishes this realism for the fantastic. One such uncanny incident occurs at the start of the story, when Aschenbach encounters a mysterious stranger in the Munich cemetery. What is the dramatic significance of this encounter and the several other fantastic meetings with strangers that follow it?

Answer The appearance of the stranger in the Munich cemetery at the start of "Death in Venice" seems to carry a special if uncertain weight of meaning. Even though the stranger is described realistically and at length, a number of details combine to make him seem uncanny: his sudden appearance on the steps of the mortuary chapel, his indeterminate foreignness, his physical anomalies—

the prominent Adam's apple, the perpendicularly furrowed brow, the bared teeth—the way he glares at Aschenbach.

As Aschenbach turns and walks away, all but forgetting this odd apparition, he is suddenly smitten with the desire to travel; he fantasizes an exotic jungle land of rotting vegetation, tropical birds, and stalking tigers. With this odd encounter, then, begins Aschenbach's trip to Venice, during which he will encounter several other such uncanny strangers: the goat-bearded, oddly melodramatic ship's officer who with elaborate ceremony signs Aschenbach on board; the grotesque "young-old man" who is a decayed, rouged, and wigged homosexual roué; the muttering gondolier who shares the Munich stranger's snub nose and bared teeth and who obstinately rows Aschenbach out of his way and then vanishes; and the lascivious street singer who alternately fawns on and mocks his audience and who also displays the prominent Adam's apple and horned brow of the cemetery stranger.

By the time the reader meets the last of these figures, it is clear that each has been a portent of Aschenbach's impending degradation and death. What is the Munich stranger, with his horned brow, death's-head leer, and walking staff, but an incarnation of the demonic? The goat-bearded ship's officer is a satyr-devil who, with a flourish, signs Aschenbach to a devil's pact and a passage to hell. The repellent "young-old man" prefigures the moment when Aschenbach, in ardent pursuit of Tadzio, will have his hair dyed and his face made up, becoming himself the stranger by submitting to the strangeness within himself. The implacable gondolier in his black coffinlike boat reminds us of Charon, the mythological oarsman who ferries the dead to Hades. The street singer who panders obscenely to the audience he despises represents the final defilement of Aschenbach's ideal of the artist as guardian of morality. Neither entirely real nor fantastic, these figures disappear and reappear, merge with each other and share each other's features with the logic of a dream. Like a dream, they also express aspects of Aschenbach's self that he has suppressed in his carefully managed waking life: homosexual desire, a fascination with shame and self-abasement, and a wish for death and release.

As dream figures, these uncanny strangers seem to issue from Aschenbach's unconscious, but they are at the same time familiar figures from stories, myths, and legends: angels of death, devils, attendants in hell, satyrs. These eerie creatures are citizens in good standing of our common culture; they populate serious art and literature as well as tall tales, and they demonstrate that our culture is pregnant with forces as deeply irrational as any in our personal dreams. Aschenbach's rationalist art not only denies the unconscious in himself but refuses to acknowledge the irrationalism which lies close to the core of art and the collective imagination. By flooding his story with the fantastic, Mann demonstrates precisely what is lacking in Aschenbach's philosophy both as personal credo and as aesthetic theory. The final measure of the inadequacy of Aschenbach's aesthetic is that he could never imagine a story like the one in which he appears, darkly alive with the uncanny and the irrational.

14.3   What qualities does Venice possess that make it an apt setting for the novella's themes and actions?

Answer   The most exotic of western European cities, as strange as it is splendid, Venice saturates the novella with its atmosphere. Virtually every aspect of the city contributes to the themes of the story. Its fantastic architecture, its labyrinthine alleys and canals, its fluid population of strangers, and its sheer foreignness all give it an air of mystery that Mann exploits.

As a resort city, Venice constitutes a special province of idleness and pleasure, removed from the restraints of the workaday world. Like all resorts, it is populated by strangers who, suddenly granted anonymity, are free to indulge themselves in ways forbidden at home. A Venetian holiday offers the opportunity for dissipations large and small: a voluptuous indulgence in sea and sun, the casual voyeurism and exhibitionism permitted the sunbather, chance encounters and erotic adventure.

From the moment Aschenbach debarks in Venice, he is swayed by its enticements. Ferried toward shore in a gently rocking gondola, he lapses into a pleasant passivity. Seduced by the southern temper of the city, his rigid Prussian self-control relaxes, and he allows himself to drift psychologically, open to new possibilities. The ocean itself, which flows through and around the canaled city, is the perfect image for his slackened restraint. In its "immeasurable, eternal . . . nothingness," its perfect formlessness, the ocean promises to release Aschenbach from his endless striving toward perfect artistic form.

In this newly disarmed state, Aschenbach encounters Tadzio, and what begins as a connoisseur's appreciation of the boy's beauty becomes an erotic obsession. Like Tadzio, Venice—"half fairy tale, half snare"—combines alluring beauty with a hint of corruption. Its cultural treasures, its achievements in art, music, and architecture, have been made possible by centuries of ruthless commerce that continues in the lying hucksterism of its hoteliers and vendors. As Mann reminds us, Venice is a city founded in slime, its canals little more than sewers. At base, it is unclean. Like Aschenbach, Venice hides a secret: the plague which turns it into a city of death. The cholera, which is a product of the jungles of India, reminds us that Venice is half Asiatic, its architecture

Byzantine and its prosperity earned in piratical trade with the east, and affirms the intimate relation between the city's greatness and its corruption.

To summarize, the exoticism of Venice contributes to the element of the fantastic in "Death in Venice." As a holiday city, it provides a setting and enticements which loosen Aschenbach's grip on his impulses. In Mann's depiction of the intertwining greatness, beauty, and corruption of the city, Venice serves as a symbolic restatement of the novella's central question: What is the relationship between art and morality?

14.4 As Aschenbach's fascination with Tadzio develops into full-blown homoerotic passion, he seeks repeatedly to understand the meaning of the boy's beauty, the nature of beauty as such, and the nature of the artist—the person whose work is a striving after beauty. How do Aschenbach's opinions on these issues shift during the story?

Answer Initially, Aschenbach describes Tadzio as if the boy were a work of art. He thinks of him as a Greek statue, a "masterpiece," and compares his pale, nearly translucent flesh to Parian marble. In Aschenbach's eyes, Tadzio displays the perfect formal harmony of classical art, and Aschenbach understands his beauty according to classical aesthetics, as an individual manifestation of the universal and eternal laws of form. Accordingly, for Aschenbach, Tadzio transcends the particularity of time and place to live in all time; he becomes a creature of myth: Eros, Narcissus, Hermes, Hyacinthus.

As attractive as this image of Tadzio is, there is something dangerously partial and even dishonest about it. After all, Tadzio is flesh, not marble. By turning him into a piece of statuary, Aschenbach denies the erotic quality of his appeal. He insists overmuch on the boy's "*chaste* perfection of form" (emphasis added). As Mann points out, Aschenbach adopts the detached attitude of the connoisseur to hide from himself the truth that he is ravished by the boy. By imagining Tadzio as a perfect artifact, he deflects his own attention from the way the boy stirs his blood. However, by turning him into a problem in aesthetics and interpreting him through classical myth, Aschenbach intellectualizes his experience of the boy and denies his sensuous tangibility. Conceived alternately as inanimate artifact and ephemeral spirit, Tadzio seems to escape Aschenbach's first attempts to understand his beauty.

In a long meditative passage about two-thirds of the way through the novella, Aschenbach modifies and elaborates on his first conceptions of Tadzio's beauty. Here he concerns himself more with beauty's effect on its beholder, the way perception joins the sensual and the ideal.

Gazing rapturously at Tadzio, Aschenbach recognizes him as "beauty's very essence; form as divine thought." But, he continues, if he is thought, he is also substance, a vision that works upon the senses. In such beauty, Aschenbach asks, what is the relationship between the ideal and the sensual? The sensual, he concludes, exists only as a vehicle for the ideal. The world of substance exists only to make visible the spirit and thus to lead our minds to higher things.

Aschenbach's thinking here is in the tradition of Platonic idealism, and he goes on to reenact in his imagination the dialog between Socrates and Phaedrus in Plato's *Phaedrus* on the subject of virtue and desire. Socrates claims that beauty, though its essence is ideal, works powerfully on our senses, sending us into "shuddering and unwonted heat," driving us to a kind of madness. Yet, he continues, beauty is an aspect of the spiritual, and, unlike virtue, reason, and truth, the only aspect that we can perceive. Beauty is, he finally decides, the lover's way to the spirit, but, he cautions, only a way, a means to an end, never an end in itself.

This passage, admitting as it does that the nature of beauty is both ideal and sensual, seems more advanced than Aschenbach's first thoughts about Tadzio's beauty. However, Mann gives us to understand that by insisting on the primacy of the spiritual, Aschenbach's understanding is still inadequate to his own experience. The strong irony that undermines Socrates's insistence on sensual beauty as only a stepping-stone to the spiritual lies in the fact that Socrates, the "sly arch-lover," is even as he speaks engaged in a homosexual flirtation with Phaedrus. The clear implication is that although beauty can raise our thoughts to the ineffable, it remains a thing of the flesh. The two aspects of beauty—spiritual and sensual—are inseparably intertwined.

This is borne out when Aschenbach, at the close of his meditation, decides to write an essay with Tadzio as his inspiration, that is, to ascend to the intellectual via the physical. But like Socrates's, Aschenbach's ascent to mind is at the same time a descent to eros. His writing becomes a sensual exercise in perfect form, which leaves him exhausted, Mann tells us, as after "a debauch." Mann leaves us with a rhetorical question: "Who shall unriddle the puzzle of the artist's nature? Who understands that mingling of discipline and licence in which it stands so firmly rooted?"

The reader should recognize how far Aschenbach has come from the first exposition of his artistic credo. His humanist faith in the morality of art now seems fragile and threatened. In quick order, accomplished through a few telling incidents, "the whole cultural structure of a lifetime," as Mann calls it, is shown to be "trampled upon, ravaged, destroyed."

In the Neapolitan street singer, Aschenbach encounters a counterimage to his vision of the artist as guardian of reason and morality. The singer is coarse and by turns abject and bullying, and his songs are lewdly insinuating. His singing descends to guttural shouts and his humor to slapstick. Significantly, the singer is a huge popular success. In the performance, artist and audience seem joined in a conspiracy of indulgence; the vulgar art of the people is used to escape order, reason, and restraint. This is art solely for the purpose of pleasure. Shortly after this incident, when Aschenbach allows a cosmetician to rouge his cheeks and dye his hair, he too exploits a vulgar art in pursuit of pleasure.

As Aschenbach falls increasingly under the spell of Tadzio, the mythology of classical culture, the humanist's heritage which he has used to obscure his erotic fascination, is itself increasingly sensualized. The gods to whom he likens Tadzio become those of sexual love: Narcissus, the avatar of self-love, and Pan, the satyr. His fantasies on classical themes widen into elaborate, titillating erotic tableaux. Finally, Aschenbach has a dream in which the image of the classical world gives way to that of some more archaic, primitive realm that stands before or outside civilization. Tadzio is no longer one of the Greek deities but simply "the stranger god," a barbaric figure that presides over a mad orgy of bestial near-humans. In his dream, Aschenbach struggles to remain faithful to his old gods of dignity, self-control, work, and reason, but he finally capitulates and joins the animal rutting. This dream marks the completion of Aschenbach's degradation, his journey from classic to primitive, order to chaos, reason to madness.

Socrates, whose spirit is summoned once more in Aschenbach's delirium just before he dies, has the last word on the relationship between beauty and morality. Although beauty could lead us through the senses to spirit, is it truly possible to travel this path without going astray in sensuality? No, he concludes; eros invariably rules over beauty, and the poet is always enslaved. The artist's honorable desire to teach and to lead people is doomed by the love of beauty and sensuality that permits a person to be an artist in the first place. The artist, though striving for self-conquest and the perfection of form, is always driven by desire and so, for the sake of reason and morality, must be condemned.

14.5 Aschenbach understands his experience in terms of extremes and contraries: ironbound discipline versus total indulgence, pure intellect versus corrupt sensuality. He envisions no middle ground or dialog between these opposites. "Death in Venice" takes its structure from his black-and-white view of the world, as Aschenbach is overwhelmed by just the dark elements he has tried to eliminate from his life. The story plays out Aschenbach's worst nightmare in precisely the overwrought terms in which he has dreamed it. But does "Death in Venice" endorse Aschenbach's rigid, dualistic views of art and morality? Are Mann's views of art and morality, as embodied in "Death in Venice," different from Aschenbach's?

Answer   A significant difference between Mann and Aschenbach is that Mann is willing to confront the region of irrationality that Aschenbach rigidly excludes from his art. By writing a story about homosexual pedophilia, Mann has allowed himself to explore feelings of the most forbidden sort. This risky subject does not seem to threaten Mann or pitch him toward chaos as it does Aschenbach; rather, it appears to inspire him. Mann's novella, with its lyrical, nearly overripe prose and its perfectly crafted development, is a beautiful, sensuous object; its appeal is not unlike Tadzio's. While the story may titillate us, as Tadzio does Aschenbach, that is far from its only attraction. Mann has made Aschenbach, who could easily be repellent and laughable, into a fascinating and sympathetic figure. Tadzio, who would be in reality a bored, pouty boy on vacation with his family, becomes in Mann's fiction a creature of myth. Mann's achievement in "Death in Venice" is to have combined artistic mastery of language, form, and character with eroticism in a story about an artist who believes such a feat impossible. If successful art is a matter of negotiating a balance between seeming opposites, the sensual and intellectual, disorder and mastery, Mann has succeeded where Aschenbach has failed.

But a further question remains, which is raised implicitly by the novella itself: "Death in Venice" may be good art, but is it moral art?

If by morality we mean the kind of prescriptive morality composed of a narrow range of established judgments that Aschenbach purveys in his writings, the answer must be no. Art can serve the official values of a society only when the artist feels a part of society and shares its values. The fact that Mann has chosen to write about an artist in "Death in Venice," as he did in many of his fictions, indicates that the identity and role of the artist was not a given for him but a matter for concern and inquiry. And the artist in "Death in Venice" turns out to be a pervert and a pariah. Aschenbach embodies Mann's sense of the artist as an outsider who goes beyond the borders of conventional life. The morality of an artist, like Mann, who imagines himself at work in such a situation cannot be a matter merely of restating established values.

The conventional morality that Aschenbach embraces would require us to condemn him. But Aschenbach wins our sympathy and, quite clearly, Mann's. If we recognize this sympathy as itself a moral impulse, perhaps we can say that "Death in Venice" is moral art. But it is finally the reader, not the story, who must answer this question. Thus "Death in Venice" evades the demands of prescriptive morality and exists on more complex and ambiguous terms.

D.E.

SUGGESTED READINGS

Hamilton, Nigel, *The Brothers Mann* (1978).

Hatfield, Henry, *Thomas Mann* (1962).

Hatfield, Henry (ed.), *Thomas Mann: A Collection of Critical Essays* (1964).

Heller, Erich, *The Ironic German: A Study of Thomas Mann* (1958).

Lukács, Georg, *Thomas Mann* (1963).

Neider, Charles (ed.), *The Stature of Thomas Mann* (1947).

Reed, T. J., *Thomas Mann: The Uses of Tradition* (1974).

Stern, J. P., *Thomas Mann* (1967).

C H A P T E R   1 5

KAFKA

Cultural Background

Franz Kafka was born in 1883 in Prague, which was then the capital of Bohemia in that confusing amalgam of nationalities and states that constituted the Austro-Hungarian empire. Kafka's family was Jewish. His parents had come from the countryside, with its traditional ways of life and belief, to the city, and their outlook had become cosmopolitan, secular, and assimilationist. Kafka received a German education and wrote in German.

Each element in this rich mixture of cultures was important to Kafka. His first love was the German literary and cultural tradition; later, he learned Czech and became interested in Czech literature and the Czech nationalist movement; and he spent much of the last portion of his short life studying Hebrew and the classic texts of Judaism. Although Kafka was able to profit from all these cultural elements, he was never entirely at home in any of them, but always somehow an outsider. In Kafka's cultural situation we can recognize the plight of many of his characters, strangers to the bone who seem still to long for some place and some life that can be called home. Kafka stands as one of the great representatives of a cultural tradition—Jewish in religion, eastern European in geographic location, and German in language—that was immensely alive and fertile but also dangerously vulnerable. He is all the more significant because this culture was, just a few years after Kafka's death, annihilated.

Kafka and His Father

For Kafka, all the essential occasions of ordinary life—home and family, work, marriage—were crisis-ridden. Kafka's family was fairly prosperous; his father owned and ran a dry goods business. Hermann Kafka had all the narrowness that so often characterizes the self-made person, and his son's virtues, which were not his own, were invisible to him. Franz Kafka was made to feel that he was almost congenitally incapable of pleasing his father, and he took most of the blame for this on himself. Although fully aware of his father's shortcomings, Kafka was never able to free himself from him, and his self-lacerations often seem to be the inner expression of his father's judgment against him.

In the book-length *Letter to His Father* which he wrote at the age of 36, Kafka describes his feeling that his father has all the manly virtues—"strength, health, appetite, decision, eloquence, self-satisfaction, superiority over the world, endurance, presence of mind"—which Kafka feels he lacks. Never being able to satisfy such a father and thus being condemned from the seat of all these virtues, Kafka sees his lot as "a general load of fear, weakness, and self-contempt." He writes of his father, "From your armchair you ruled the world," and in this cruel and imperious authority (which Kafka is also able to view as slightly ridiculous), it is easy to see a partial source of the obscure but unappeasable authorities—the judges of *The Trial*, the unreachable ruler of *The Castle*—which loom over much of his writing. The remarkable *Letter*, both passionate and analytic, extreme and inconclusive (Kafka's mother tactfully refused to deliver it), stands as an emblem for Kafka's writing career.

Emergence as a Writer

Despite his achievements, Kafka's career as a writer remained only incompletely fulfilled. Although much of his writing shows clear evidence of confidence in his abilities, he was often hesitant and ambivalent about his vocation, perhaps in proportion to what he felt to be the high seriousness of the office to which he seemed called. Reluctantly and unhappily, Kafka took a degree in law in 1907 and went to work for a semigovernmental insurance company, where he remained for most of his adult life. His writing was done in the hours he could steal from the demands of the job, and only little could be coaxed out of him for publication by his friend Max Brod.

Kafka's scrupulosity about writing, his feeling that it was the only thing worth doing but almost impossible to do satisfactorily, left its mark in both the high quality of his work and its fragmentary and incomplete nature. Most of his writings are short stories, brief parables, and fragments, and Kafka's sense of the exorbitant demands of the writer's task is apparent in the way he creates expanding levels of meaning with the utmost verbal economy. The same demands seemed to make much of his work impossible to complete, for example, the unfinished novels *The Trial*, *The Castle*, and *Amerika*, which, like their characters, follow hints and promises and dangling threads of experience to no certain end.

Later Life

Kafka's inability to make a commitment, his failure of self-certainty, contributed greatly to his unhappiness in love. During his five-year engagement to Felice Braun (see *Letters to Felice*, 1967), Kafka fought again and again the inner battle between a desire for a family and fear that he could never be an adequate husband and father, between a desire for a "normal" life and fear that marriage would mean the end of his writing. After this long period of unhappiness, Kafka's engagement to Felice ended without marriage. His later, much shorter affair with Milena Jesenka ended no better (see *Letters to Milena*, 1952, and the immensely moving letters from Milena published in Max Brod's biography). It was only in the last few months of his life that Kafka was able to move from Prague, partially free himself from his parents, and manage a happy relationship with a woman, Dora Dymant, with whom he was living when he died after a long struggle with tuberculosis in 1924.

Kafka's Work

At the time of his death, Kafka had published only a few individual stories and a number of small collections, and he was unknown outside a small circle of admirers. The great body of his unpublished writings—stories, meditations, parables, diaries, and letters—was left at his death to his friend and later biographer, Max Brod, with instructions that they be destroyed. Unable to bring himself to carry out Kafka's wishes, Brod saved the works that fed the rapid growth of Kafka's posthumous reputation. Among the most important of his writings are the unfinished novels *Amerika*, *The Trial*, and *The Castle* and the stories "The Metamorphosis" (published in 1915), "In the Penal Colony," "The Great Wall of China," "A Country Doctor," "A Hunger Artist," and "Investigations of a Dog."

Perhaps the most characteristic feature of Kafka's work is his ability to write about mental and emotional events with the concreteness of description and drama that is commonly associated only with the outside world of experience, the world that we complacently call reality. By combining the palpability of this world with the complexity and inconclusiveness of thought, his writings achieve a suggestiveness that has allowed them equally to sustain religious, political, biographical, philosophical, and psychological interpretations.

Given the facts of his brief, unhappy life, the personal elements apparent in much of his writing, and the disturbing quality of many of his fictions, it is easy to understand how Kafka has gained a reputation for morbid and unhealthy wallowing in self. Following this line, the critic Edmund Wilson has accused him of leaving the reader nothing more encouraging than "the half expressed gasp of a self-doubting soul trampled under." But any view of Kafka is damagingly one-sided if it fails to take into account the hardheaded, relentless logic with which he works out his stories; his loving commitment to the exact, detailed description of the stuff of everyday life; and the way in which his self-mockery often yields a kind of comedy that allows him, even in pain, to jump free of himself.

Kafka and the Kafkaesque

Kafka has the distinction of being one of the few writers, like Dickens and Dostoevsky, whose names have entered everyday speech as the emblem for a special zone of experience. To call something Kafkaesque is to describe a predicament that is at once hopeless, cruel, and absurd, imposed from above by some remote, unassailable authority that acts with a pretense of unquestionable rationality. Perhaps the most Kafkaesque of Kafka's heroes is Joseph K. in *The Trial*. In this novel, Kafka takes the criminal trial, one of the modern world's proudest attempts to subjugate experience to the forms of rationality, and suffuses it with absurdity. Although Joseph K. is arrested and must defend himself, he is never told of what he is accused, he has no forum in which to make his defense, and his conviction is foreordained. Kafka's popular reputation as in some ways the quintessential twentieth-century writer rests largely on such depictions of a world where bureaucracy has gone mad, turning the average person into the victim of anonymous forces which cannot even be identified, much less defeated.

ESSAY QUESTIONS WITH ANSWERS

"The Metamorphosis"

15.1 "As Gregor Samsa awoke one morning from uneasy dreams he found himself transformed in his bed into a gigantic insect."* The famous first sentence of "The Metamorphosis" lands the reader abruptly and rather ruthlessly in the midst of a crucial interpretive problem. Is the transformation of Gregor real, or is it merely a metaphor? Or should the story be understood as a pure fantasy along the lines of, for example, Lewis Carroll?

Answer　There is nothing in the story which will allow the reader to deny the fact of Gregor's metamorphosis. On the contrary, Kafka does everything he can to impress us with its literalness. Here, as in so many of Kafka's stories, the fantastic event is presented in the most matter-of-fact manner and surrounded with the most ordinary details of everyday life: "His room, a regular human bedroom, only rather too small, lay quiet between the four familiar walls." Gregor's waking thoughts are the vague, familiar worries of any weekday morning: Have I time to sleep a bit longer? What is the weather? I had better get up or I will miss my train. Gregor's transformation strikes him merely as odd, drawing his attention only a bit more than his other mundane preoccupations. It is an inconvenience that makes it a bit harder to get out of bed.

Not only does Gregor's metamorphosis remain unexplained, it is treated as if it required no explanation. Unlike science fiction, where the fantastic is first sensationalized and then given a (pseudo) scientific explanation, the mystery here is both unacknowledged and undispelled. Kafka's spare, direct prose goes on evenly, as if to imply that everything is in order. But no matter how realistically and plausibly Kafka describes this fantastic event, it is difficult for the

*Translated by Willa and Edwin Muir in *Franz Kafka: The Complete Stories*, ed. Nahum N. Glatzer, New York, Schocken Books, 1971. All references to "The Metamorphosis" in this chapter are to the Muir translation.

reader to accept it as simply true. It continues to unsettle the reader, demanding an explanation that is never given.

The critical problem is that Gregor's metamorphosis blurs the usually distinct boundary line between the real and the unreal. This impossible metamorphosis even lends an air of unreality to the perfectly normal events around it. Gregor's parents' nagging, ordinary enough in itself, seems comically absurd when Kafka shows us their son on the other side of the bedroom wall bravely struggling to master his new anatomy. When the impossible is presented as true, the certainty that allows us to use words such as "real," "normal," and "true" is undermined. By combining the fantastic with the realistic, "The Metamorphosis" occupies a special fictional space where the confident use of these words is suspended.

If the story were more fantastic, as *Alice in Wonderland* is, it would be easier to come to terms with; the reader would understand that it takes place in the special province of fantasy, where the improbable happens as a matter of course. In *Alice in Wonderland*, we are not surprised to find talking rabbits and invisible cats, because the story consistently follows the rules and conventions of fantasy, which allow for such creatures. Similarly, we never find Mickey Mouse and Donald Duck odd, because the humanized animal is simply a convention of the animated cartoon. By contrast, "The Metamorphosis" keeps us off balance, and the abiding problem in reading it is deciding how to deal with our desire to make it simpler and less unsettling, and to force from it an uncomplicated explanation.

15.2   From what point of view is "The Metamorphosis" told? Why did Kafka choose that point of view, and how does it augment the peculiar quality of the story?

Answer   "The Metamorphosis" is told in the third person, from the point of view of an omniscient narrator—one of the most traditional narrative techniques, of course. However, we need to qualify the word "omniscient." Although the narrative voice gives us access to the minds of all the characters, it is perhaps more remarkable for what it withholds than for what it tells. We are never told what to think about any of the characters or how to evaluate any of the happenings. The narrator never comes to our aid with answers to any of the questions posed by the story. Instead, the story unfolds in the most neutral, nearly clinical manner possible. This reluctance to explain or to direct our sympathies or understanding contributes to the story's unsettling, enigmatic quality.

Yet the way in which Kafka tells the story unobtrusively influences our feelings about the characters. Not only is the story concerned primarily with Gregor, it often adopts his point of view. Very often, the impersonal voice of the narrator mingles with Gregor's, representing his thoughts in indirect speech. In the following sentences, we can see the omniscient point of view slide into one that seems to coincide with Gregor's own thoughts, with the last sentence sounding as if it could have been spoken by Gregor:

> In the left-hand room a painful silence followed this refusal, in the right-hand room his sister began to sob.
>
> Why didn't his sister join the others? She was probably newly out of bed and hadn't even begun to put on her clothes yet. Well, why was she crying?

At other times, we are made literally to see things from Gregor's point of view, as when his father lifts what seem to be enormous shoes to crush him. The effect is to heighten our sense of Gregor's feelings. We feel his isolation, and we know that he understands what is going on around him, even when his family comes to think he does not. However, we know no more than Gregor, and we can be no less perplexed by his condition than he is. Kafka's mingling of omniscient and first-person narrative modes lends special drama to our perception of Gregor's predicament. At first we see Gregor from the outside—alone, afflicted, incomprehensible—and then suddenly we see from his perspective and feel what it means to be so offensively incomprehensible.

15.3 In what way are the personality and social position of Gregor related to the meaning of the metamorphosis he has experienced?

Answer The first place in Gregor's mind is occupied by his work and his family. The two are deeply associated. He works as a commercial traveler to pay off his family's debts, and his greatest concern seems to be that he properly fulfill the responsibilities of the loyal employee and dutiful son. However, a close reading of the first portion of the story reveals some ambivalence in Gregor's feelings about both work and family. He works hard, but he is afraid that he may be thought a malingerer; he seems to pride himself on being the provider for his family, but at the same time he looks forward to being able to quit his job. His otherwise unexplained fear of losing his job almost seems a product of his desire, as he says at one point, "to cut [himself] loose."

A sense of the contradictions in Gregor's feelings emerges from his thoughts as he lies listening to his sister sobbing outside his door:

> Well, why was she crying? Because he wouldn't get up and let the chief clerk in, because he was in danger of losing his job, and because the chief would begin dunning his parents again for the old debts? Surely these were things one didn't need to worry about for the present. Gregor was still at home and not in the least thinking about deserting the family.

This train of thought moves rapidly from a minor transgression (not getting out of bed), to failure (being fired), to rebellion (desertion of his family). Gregor's mind moves so quickly from one idea to the next that the ideas seem tied together for him by some necessity. Kafka's use of indirect speech here virtually puts us inside Gregor's mind. When Gregor states that he is "not in the least thinking about deserting his family," he is plainly contradicting himself; his anxiety has brought him precisely to this idea, even if only to deny it.

Gregor's mind turns on the Ixion wheel of guilt. His work is demeaning, but since any complaint would be disloyal to his parents, he works twice as hard and sacrifices himself for his family. From this brave self-sacrifice comes pride in duty fulfilled, but pride swells the dutiful son into the self-important son and provider who could think of deserting his family. Since the very thought of such desertion is a baseness which deserves to be punished, no work is too demeaning a punishment for so ungrateful a son. Gregor's conflicting feelings leave him turning in circles, stuck and helpless. The reader can virtually see his frustration when he is turned on his back, frantically waving his legs in the air, unable to move or get out of bed.

In many ways, Gregor's metamorphosis seems to be a palpable realization of his unhappy and ambivalent state of mind. He is trapped by felt obligations that he can neither fulfill nor free himself of; the harder he struggles, the more he disables himself with failure and self-contempt. Gregor's life seems something—like his metamorphosis—which has befallen him rather than something to be freely lived.

15.4 In what way is Kafka's technique of combining the fantastic and the realistic related to Gregor's psychological and social problems?

Answer Gregor's metamorphosis violates the logic by which we live a great portion of our lives, the logic that says that object A is definitively and eternally distinct from object B, that effect C must have cause D. The logic of definition and of cause and effect and the sciences that have developed out of this logic are, of course, only one way of making sense of the world. They leave to one side the different logic of the imagination and emotions. It is this logic which holds sway in "The Metamorphosis." One of its ruling principles, which one finds in religion, ethics, and psychology, is that to wish something is in a significant way to realize or enact it. For example, a person who only wishes to commit some violence, a psychologist might point out, may suffer all the grief of the person who actually commits it. In the metamorphic zone of imagination, wishes become acts, and the innocent person, without striking a blow, becomes a murderer. Identity is unstable, cause is unhinged from effect, and guilt can precede any crime. Gregor Samsa lives under some such dispensation, according to which a lazy reluctance to get out of bed in the morning is almost indistinguishable from deserting one's parents and where, to oversimplify a bit, to feel oneself a contemptible insect is to be an insect.

15.5 Although its psychological realism makes "The Metamorphosis" a highly serious work, it is also very funny. What are the sources of its humor?

Answer Insofar as humor grows out of the varieties of inappropriateness—discrepancy, disproportion, mismatched expectations and outcomes—"The Metamorphosis" is comic in its very conception. In Gregor's transformation, Kafka has created a circumstance to which every reaction seems inappropriate. The presence of the gigantic insect in the story seems to redraw the scale of normality so that almost every possible reaction to it seems outlandish. One example would be the reaction of the three lodgers to Gregor. They seem to consider him simply as a particularly grievous lapse of rooming house hygiene. This is at the same time an example of Kafka's use of what might be called a kind of written deadpan: a too-flat response to a wild improbability. Kafka also uses another comic technique in this scene. His mixing of the fantastic and the realistic provides access to a subtle territory where he can present the slightly improbable: These three lodgers with their identical beards, walking in tandem and talking in unison, seem just a bit peculiar, by turns silly and sinister.

However, Kafka's greatest comic achievement in "The Metamorphosis," as in much of his best work, is really part and parcel with his psychological realism. This might be called a comedy of neurosis, as in the scene in which Gregor finally struggles out of the bedroom and pleads in his twittering insect voice with the supervisor, who has rather improbably turned up at his home:

"I'll put my clothes on at once, pack up my samples and start off. Will you only let me go? You see, sir, I'm not obstinate, and I'm willing to work; traveling is a hard life, but I couldn't live without it. . . . I'm loyally bound to serve the chief, you know that very well. Besides, I have to provide for my parents and sister. I'm in great difficulties, but I'll get out of them again."

Here the absurdity is all Gregor's, and the humor is at his expense. In this cruelly funny speech, Kafka seems to mock his hero's ardor to do the good that is expected of him. The willing worker is exposed as the unctuous underling, and the pieties of the dutiful son sound ridiculous coming from the insect.

The comedy of Gregor's situation grows from the fact that he cannot win. On the one hand, Kafka sustains the judgment against Gregor because he is unable to satisfy the strong inner and outer authorities that demand that he be a good worker and a loyal son. But on the other hand, in this scene Kafka makes fun of the humiliating self-abasement that comes from even wanting to satisfy these authorities. The irony is that a certain kind of struggle is always a struggle against oneself, and once one has started to fight, one has lost. We can see the same paradoxical humor in some of Kafka's aphorisms, such as "In the war between yourself and the world, back the world," and in this vertiginous self-appraisal: "I have scarcely anything in common with myself."

15.6 How do Gregor and his relationship with his family change during the story?

Answer The metamorphosis itself is an action without an agent. No decision or will is behind it; it happens of itself, and nearly the whole story unfolds as a consequence of it. Gregor subsides further and further into his insect nature: He begins to prefer spoiled food to fresh, comes to enjoy crawling over the walls and ceiling, and allows his room to be emptied of the objects that serve to remind him of his human self. His ties to his family grow more attenuated. At first they call Gregor "he" and "him," but then only "it."

As Gregor sinks, however, his family rises. His father also undergoes a metamorphosis. The man who had seemed too old and broken to be able to work is rejuvenated. Gregor's father reclaims his role as provider and head of the family, and his new job at a bank puts him in a uniform which increases his dignity. He is even able to reveal the fact that unbeknownst to Gregor, some money had been saved from the wreck of his business. The family is not so badly off after all, and Gregor's earnings had not been so badly needed. The sister, Grete, seems to profit directly from Gregor's strange misfortune; by caring for him, feeding him, and cleaning his room, she develops a new sense of pride and self-sufficiency, becoming as important to the family as Gregor once thought himself to be. Gregor, who had hoped to earn enough money to send his sister to the conservatory, is reduced to depending on her for rotten food and leavings.

Each of these developments in the life of his family seems to be a humiliating refutation of Gregor's sense of filling an important place in their lives. Each of the three sections of the story ends with an encounter between Gregor and the family. In the first, Gregor is shooed back into his room by his shocked and angry father. In the second, his father attacks him with apples, leaving one lodged in his side. The last thing Gregor sees as he drags himself back into his room is his mother embracing his father, "in complete union with him." He is increasingly excluded as the family draws together to face the problem he poses. At the end of the story, Gregor, dead, is swept out with the garbage, not by his family but by the charwoman. His death is a liberation for his family; the story that began in winter ends in March, with a symbolic hope of spring. At the end, the family is hopeful and united, and Grete, grown to a young, attractive woman, seems to promise them a happy future.

15.7 Does the insect in "The Metamorphosis" carry a particular symbolic meaning? If so, what is it?

Answer It is probably a mistake to assume that a symbolic meaning underlies and explains "The Metamorphosis." In insisting that the insect or the story yield a single meaning, one is working under the assumption that every fact and experience is naturally and unvaryingly connected to a single, universally available meaning, an assumption that "The Metamorphosis" plainly puts in doubt. If the world were so naturally full of meaning, no one would suffer a fate as unhappy and issueless as Gregor's, and there would be no need for Kafka to write his stories. To assume that there is some code by which to "translate" the story is to insist that the world and our minds are simple, rational, and sensible in a way that "The Metamorphosis" plainly tells us they are not.

"The Metamorphosis" has inspired a great deal of useful critical exegesis. Some critics have seen Gregor as the Oedipal son of Freud's psychoanalytic theories, who suffers from a guilty desire to supplant his father. Others have viewed the story in its social and historical context as a parable of the precarious situation of eastern European Jews between the wars and a dark portent of their future. Still others have assimilated "The Metamorphosis" to a view of Kafka as a religious writer who was in the painfully alienated situation of writing about the desire for faith from a position of essential unbelief. However, as these interpretations become more abstract and philosophical, they seem to diminish the story. They lose credibility and pale beside the palpable fact of Gregor scuttling across the floor, the rotting apple lodged in his side, trailing dust and filth behind him.

In one of his short meditations, Kafka describes the wisdom of the wise man as "something unknown to us, something that he too cannot define more precisely, and therefore cannot help us here in the least." The sense of Kafka's stories lies in their undiminished entirety; they are themselves the meaning that Kafka could not possibly "define more precisely."

D.E.

SUGGESTED READINGS

Benjamin, Walter, *Illuminations* (1969). See the two essays on Kafka.

Brod, Max, *Kafka: A Biography* (1947).

Flores, Angel (ed.), *The Kafka Problem* (1963).

Flores, Angel, and Homer Swander (eds.), *Franz Kafka Today* (1958).

Gray, Ronald (ed.), *Kafka: A Collection of Critical Essays* (1963).

Greenberg, Martin, *The Terror of Art: Kafka and Modern Literature* (1968).

Janouch, Gustav, *Conversations with Kafka* (1971).

Politzer, Heinz, *Franz Kafka, Parable and Paradox* (1967).

Tauber, Herbert, *Franz Kafka* (1968).

Wilson, Edmund, *Classics and Commercials* (1950). See the chapter "A Dissenting Opinion on Kafka," also reprinted in Ronald Gray, *Kafka*.

CHAPTER 16

BRECHT

Early Years and World War I

Eugen Berthold Friedrich Brecht was born in 1898 in the provincial city of Augsburg in Bavaria, Germany. His father was an official in a paper mill who eventually rose to the position of director, and his mother was the daughter of a civil servant. Thus, the origins of Brecht, who was to be politically of the left, artistically of the avant-garde, and emotionally identified with the working class, were bourgeois and respectable.

At the time of World War I, Brecht was in Munich, aimlessly studying medicine at the Ludwig Maximilian University. In 1918, he was drafted and assigned to serve as a medical orderly behind the lines. In later years, Brecht somewhat exaggerated the extremity of the conditions to which he was exposed, but there is no doubt that his wartime experiences helped form his political beliefs and identity as a writer. Although Brecht was already a pacifist, the war helped him identify his enemies early. The most hated figures in his plays are the political leaders and generals who, safe themselves, lead their people to slaughter, and the profiteers who grow fat on death.

In Brecht's early disgust for the nationalistic cant that buoyed the German war effort, one can see the beginnings of his skepticism, distrust of lofty ideals and sentiment, and quickness to spot the official lie. In a poem from this period, "The Legend of the Dead Soldier," Brecht describes the German army's need for cannon fodder as being so urgent that a corpse is dug from the grave, pumped full of brandy, given a clean bill of health, and marched back into battle with a martial flourish. In its satirical exaggeration and willingness to shock, this early work strikes notes that were to become typical of Brecht's writing.

From the first, Brecht's approach to literary art focused on performance. During his wartime days and after, he would appear in bars and coffeehouses and sing ballads such as "The Legend of the Dead Soldier," accompanying himself on guitar. Like his later work as an organizer and director of theater troupes, Brecht's cabaret singing brought him into intimate contact with audiences, other performers, and critics (often rather rough and ready ones). Brecht's was always very much a career pursued in public.

Early Works

The first of Brecht's plays to be performed was *Drums in the Night*, which was staged in Munich in 1922. It tells the story of a soldier, Kragler, who returns from the war to a corrupt society. Kragler is no better than his surroundings. Instead of leaving his fiancée (who has betrayed him) and supporting a revolutionary uprising, Kragler cynically chooses personal and political accommodation. But he has no illusions: he admits, "I am a swine, and a swine goes home." Although Kragler's antirevolutionary stance is at odds with Brecht's evolving political beliefs, his cynicism and instinct for self-preservation reveal him as a true anti-heroic Brechtian "hero."

In its staging too, the play points toward Brecht's later aesthetics. The theater was hung with banners inscribed with phrases from the play, and the setting was intentionally stylized and artificial in appearance. For this play, Brecht was awarded the annual Kleist prize for new dramatists of note, thus beginning his career as a highly visible member and sometime *enfant terrible* of the avant-garde German theater.

In 1924, Brecht moved to Berlin, where he met, among other leaders of the German theater, Erwin Piscator (1893–1966), whose theory of "epic" drama greatly influenced him. Piscator put the theater in the service of Marxist polemics as a tool to educate and incite the masses. Formal unity and aesthetic effect were subordinated to the communication of politically significant information. Piscator's plays were actually episodic revues that might combine newsreels, projected photographs and newspaper headlines, songs, and speeches, all presented with an abruptness and discordance meant to embody the shock and disorder of postwar city life.

Brecht's *Man Equals Man*, performed in 1926, is the first of his plays to display his characteristic vision of the individual in society. The setting is a colonial India derived in equal parts from Kipling and from Brecht's imagination. Galy Gay is a meek Irish dock worker who is seized by three British soldiers and forced to replace a missing member of their squad, Jeriah Jip. Through a kind of brainwashing they convince Galy that he is Jeriah, and he assumes the latter's identity as a fearless, bloodthirsty fighting machine. Brecht offered the play as "proof" of the thesis that a person's individuality is so fragile that it can be easily dissolved by the social forces that play upon that person's fears and desires:

> You can do with a human being what you will.
> Take him apart like a car,
> Rebuild him bit by bit.
> As you will see, he has nothing to lose by it.

In 1928, Berlin's Theatre am Schifferbauerdamm was the setting for the debut of *The Threepenny Opera*, the play that for American audiences is Brecht's signature piece. Like so many of his plays, it is a melange of literary borrowings animated by Brecht's distinctive if not entirely consistent view of social relations. It was based on John Gay's *The Beggar's Opera*, a biting musical satire that had been a success on the London stage 200 years before. To Gay's plot, Brecht and his musical collaborator, Kurt Weill, added bold new songs, many based on François Villon's fifteenth-century French ballads and Kipling's *Barrack-Room Ballads*. The most famous of these is undoubtedly "Mack the Knife."

Brecht and Weill's operetta, via Gay, of London lowlife—robbers, beggars, prostitutes, and corrupt police—was meant as a satire on Berlin society, a critique of the commercial spirit, and a plea for social justice. However, the play is far less successful as a satire than as a celebration of the anarchic energies of the gangster Macheath and his bordello companions. To Brecht, dynamism and audacity were always attractive whether found in criminals, capitalists, or revolutionaries, and this often led to contradictions between Brecht's didactic intentions and the actual dramatic tenor of his plays. As a result, *The Threepenny Opera* has rarely been viewed as a coherent political satire. In its cynicism and bawdiness, its depiction of a played-out and corrupt society, the operetta has generally been received by latter-day audiences as a window on history, a vivid glimpse of Berlin between the wars as the feverish 1920s reached their culmination in economic collapse and Nazism.

During the later 1920s, Brecht became increasingly committed to Marxism, and his plays began to reflect this commitment. At this time he wrote a number of didactic plays, or *Lehrstuecke*, which have as their theme the need for the individual to subordinate his or her individuality to the collective purpose. *The*

Flight of the Lindberghs, He Who Says Yes, and *The Measures Taken* all preach self-abnegation in the name of collective progress, and their aesthetics display a corresponding spareness and austerity. Their function was wholly utilitarian—to educate and persuade for the purpose of political change—and they read like the lessons they were meant to be (some were written for schoolchildren). While these are far from Brecht's finest plays, they represent a rare moment when his political thinking and his aesthetics converged in practice as well as theory. Both the "scientific" Marxism which Brecht favored at the time and his didactic dramaturgy were characterized by austerity, impersonality, and a wholly objective approach to human issues.

Exile and Major Plays

Once the Nazi party rose to prominence, Brecht, as an avowed communist and antimilitarist, was in jeopardy. When Hitler gained absolute power in 1933, Brecht's sense of political realities and instinct for self-preservation prompted him to flee Germany for Denmark. From his new home in Copenhagen, Brecht turned out antifascist plays such as *The Roundheads and the Peakheads* (1937) and *Fear and Misery in the Third Reich (1935–1938)* along with a great number of more ephemeral writings. During this period of self-imposed exile, which was to last until 1948, Brecht also wrote four plays that are central to his reputation. In *Galileo* (1938), Brecht portrays the great astronomer as an unscrupulous and cowardly man who allows his scientific findings to be subjugated by the authoritarianism of the Church. *Mother Courage and Her Children* (1941) tells the story of a trader and camp follower during the Thirty Years War, which devastated Germany during the seventeenth century. Mother Courage is one of Brecht's ambiguous protagonists, a callous profiteer who sacrifices her children but whose suffering takes on an epic quality that elevates her in our eyes. *The Caucasian Chalk Circle* (1945) is a charming reworking of an ancient legend and a parable on the subject of property, justice, and self-sacrifice.

With the outbreak of World War II in 1939, Brecht moved to a safer haven in Sweden, and in 1940 he moved to Finland. In May 1942, Brecht left Finland, traveling eastward through Moscow and across the Soviet Union and the Pacific until he arrived in California in June. A number of émigré German artists, among them Thomas Mann, had settled in California; Brecht hoped that with their aid and the proximity of the American entertainment industry, he might earn his living as a screenwriter while reestablishing his career as a dramatist. However, Brecht was able to find little work in film. Those in the American theater world who became his champions were largely academics, such as Eric

Bentley, who could be of little help in finding him the popular audience he desired to reach. What American successes Brecht had, such as the 1947 staging of *Galileo* with Charles Laughton in the title role, were critical rather than popular.

Perhaps Brecht's greatest theatrical success in America came in 1947 with his testimony before the House Un-American Activities Committee (HUAC). Fascism, this time in the guise of McCarthyism, had, it seemed, followed Brecht halfway around the world. Brecht's testimony was a masterpiece of simple cunning that took full advantage of his inquisitors' ignorance of his writings and politics. Like many of his characters, Brecht used the appearance of acquiescence to dodge a blow that would have crushed a more "principled" person. At the close of his testimony, the committee thanked Brecht and praised him as an exemplary witness.

Return to Germany and Last Years

Between Brecht's lack of success in getting his plays staged and the increasing conservatism of the American political atmosphere, the United States had become an uncongenial home. In 1948, Brecht returned to a divided Germany. With some anxiety, as evidenced by his first securing an Austrian passport, he decided to settle in East Berlin. This choice suited his artistic ambitions as well as his political convictions, since the German Democratic Republic was willing to put considerable theatrical resources at his disposal. By settling in East Germany, Brecht entered into what was not always a very comfortable bargain. In exchange for a situation in which to live and work as a dramatist, he had to satisfy his patrons with works of the proper political stripe; the East German authorities saw in Brecht, a writer of international reputation, an opportunity to enhance their image.

Brecht served his patrons sometimes willingly, sometimes cynically, and sometimes not at all. He was better at preaching the subjugation of the individual to the class struggle than at practicing it. The exact nature of the relationship between Brecht and the East German establishment has been the focus of much critical examination, and Brecht has not always emerged from this inquiry as a person of complete integrity.

In any case, Brecht did prosper artistically. He was allowed to form and direct a large and talented repertory company, the Berliner Ensemble, which was given its own theater, the Theatre am Schifferbauerdamm, which had been the scene of some of Brecht's early triumphs. This company gave some of his plays—especially *Mother Courage* and *The Caucasian Chalk Circle*—their definitive productions both in East Berlin and in other European capitals.

During these years, Brecht was feted as a hero of the Communist countries, although his relations with the East German bureaucracy remained strained, and he took every opportunity to travel in the non-Communist world. In August 1956, while preparing the Berliner Ensemble for an engagement in London, Brecht, then 58 years old, collapsed and died.

Epic Theater

In the years immediately after Brecht's death, his reputation rested as much on his theory of theater as on his plays. Brecht's theory of epic drama (the term was borrowed from Piscator) was a reaction against conventional realist drama, which bent all its efforts toward creating the illusion that the lives and actions on stage were as real as those of the audience. By creating this sense of a common reality, in which the audience is induced to identify with the characters on stage, the realist drama gains its distinctive emotional power.

Brecht felt that realist theater worked like a narcotic on the members of the audience, playing on their feelings, manipulating their responses, and keeping them from thinking clearly about what they were seeing. He also pointed out that the fixed narrative pattern of realist drama, moving inexorably from exposition to crisis to denouement, casts a pall of inevitability over its depiction of human experience. Brecht felt that these features of realist theater prevented an understanding of the human condition as something created anew in each age, the product of dynamic social and material forces. Brecht intended his epic theater to inspire thought and dialog that would foster the development of a society which could rationally control these forces.

Brecht sought to free the audience to think by the use of devices he called *Verfremdungseffekten*, often translated as "alienation effects" or "distancing effects." For example, the audience often knows from the start how a Brecht play is going to end, either because the play is based on a historical episode or a well-known fable or simply because Brecht contrives some way of informing them. Suspense, one of the realist theater's classic means of manipulating the audience, is thus destroyed.

Instead of dominating theatergoers by playing on their fears and anxieties, the epic theater frees them to think about what they are seeing. Unlike the realist drama, which always appears to be taking place in the present, the completed or past quality of the events in epic drama allows the theatergoer to contemplate the play as though it were history and to draw from it all the lessons history can teach. The epic theater encourages the audience to ask, Could things have turned out differently? How must people live together if suffering is to be avoided? To the same end, the wide-ranging, episodic structure of epic drama, which is unlike the unified, building action of realist drama, also creates the sense that history is complexly determined and contingent rather than inevitable, open to the influence of human endeavor.

Other *Verfremdungseffekten* concern acting technique, setting, and the use of music, dance, and other art forms within the play. All tend to emphasize the nature of the play as an artifact, something made by a particular group of people for a particular audience at a particular moment in history. Here too the intention is to heighten the audience's historical sense.

Brecht's theory of epic drama is precisely that: a theory. It is difficult to say to what degree the theatrical devices he championed produce the effects he sought. Certainly his plays, which sometimes bear little resemblance to the epic theater of his theories, deliver many of the traditional pleasures of realist drama. By the same token, the anti-illusionistic plays of other modern playwrights cannot be said to have created an audience that is any more politically conscious than the audience Brecht meant to awaken from its aesthetically induced slumber.

Poetry

Ironically, the aspect of Brecht's literary career that has been drawing the most attention in recent years is neither his dramatic theorizing nor his theater craft but his poetry. Brecht wrote poetry throughout his life, generally on the political and social themes that animate his plays. This attention to Brecht's poetry has highlighted what may be his most enduring achievement: the fashioning of a unique personal idiom. Although not always evident in translation, Brecht's language has a rough beauty all its own. It has been said to combine widely diverse levels and sources of diction: the vigorous energy of Luther's translation of the Bible, the earthiness of peasant talk, and the "vulgarity" of city speech. It is Brecht's language that gives his works vitality. It is this distinctive, demotic language that, whatever our feelings about Brecht's politics, makes him such a persuasive witness on the turbulent history of our times.

ESSAY QUESTIONS WITH ANSWERS

The Caucasian Chalk Circle

16.1 What theme, which is later developed in the story of Grusha and Michael, is introduced in the "Prologue" to *The Caucasian Chalk Circle*?

Answer The "Prologue" to *The Caucasian Chalk Circle* takes place in a village in the Caucasus mountains of the Soviet Union. World War II has just ended, and the members of two collective farms are meeting to decide a dispute concerning their lands, which they have recently defended against the Nazis. The members of the fruit-growing collective Galinsk propose that they be allowed to take over the land of the dairy-farming collective Rosa Luxemburg, which had temporarily moved its goat herds eastward as the German army advanced. The members of Galinsk argue that this land has been overgrazed so that it is no longer suited for dairy farming. They explain that with an irrigation scheme they have developed, the land could serve much better for fruit growing.

At first, the dairy farmers resist. This valley is their home, and home is, simply and irrationally, home: the place where "bread tastes better . . .the air smells better, voices sound stronger, the sky is higher, the ground is easier to walk on."* The Delegate from Moscow who has come to help the two collectives decide their dispute neatly summarizes the problem: "It's true we have to consider a piece of land as a tool to produce something useful, but it's also true that we must recognize love for a particular piece of land."

In this case, utilitarian reason (greater productivity) prevails over sentimentality (love of home) as the dairy farmers concede that their land could indeed be better used for orchards. As one of the collectivists proclaims, quoting Mayakovsky, the poet of revolutionary Russia, "The home of the Soviet people shall also be the home of Reason!"

The dispute between the two collectives concerns in essence the idea of

---

*Translated by Eric Bentley and Maja Apelman, New York, Grove Press, 1966. All references to *The Caucasian Chalk Circle* in this chapter are to this translation.

property—who should own (or have the use of) what, and why. It is settled according to a first principle of communism: Property shall be distributed to those who can best use it for the common good. In the body of *The Caucasian Chalk Circle*, the issue of property reappears in the story of Grusha and Michael. However, the property at issue in that case is not real property, and its possession is not determined so simply and rationally.

16.2   The "Prologue" introduces the narrative means by which the Tale of the Chalk Circle will be told. What are these means, and how do they contribute to the distinctive form of the play?

Answer   The two collectives celebrate the resolution of their dispute with a presentation by the Story Teller Arkadi Tscheidse and his musicians. Apparently, the Soviet economy has a place for this bardic figure from an earlier day. As one of the collectivists says, if the Soviet state can "arrange the redistribution of vines and tractors, why not of songs?"

The Story Teller introduces the Tale of the Chalk Circle as an old one, taken from the Chinese and rendered in a new version. He sits on the floor holding an old notebook, at which he occasionally glances. The musicians sit at his side, and the collectivists who are his audience also become the chorus which from time to time comments upon the action or sings. As the Story Teller proceeds, the stage comes alive with the Governor, his wife, their sycophantic doctors, the Fat Prince, the pushing mob, the bullying soldiers, and later, Grusha and Simon.

Brecht puts the device of the Story Teller to numerous uses. At times, the Story Teller is silent and the play is carried forward by means of the dialog. At other times, the stage is empty or nearly empty, the characters fall silent, and the Story Teller speaks. Often, the Story Teller provides exposition and sets the scene, as in the opening lines of his story: "In olden times, in a bloody time, there ruled in a Caucasian city . . ." Sometimes he comments on the action or points a moral. He may praise the characters, warn them, chastise them, or predict their fate.

Perhaps the most striking use to which Brecht puts the Story Teller occurs when he tells us the thoughts of the characters as they stand silent on stage. When Grusha and Simon meet again at the end of Scene iii, the Story Teller's narration of their silent unshared thoughts adds to the pathos of this brief reunion.

The Story Teller and his narration are meant to produce the distancing effect described in Brecht's theory of epic drama. His presence reminds us that the Tale of the Chalk Circle is precisely that: a tale. Unlike illusionistic art, it does not hide its artificiality, pretending to be as natural and real as nature itself. It is an artifact, and as such it has an origin and a history. The Tale of the Chalk Circle is an old Chinese legend. It exists in many versions, including, as we recognize at its conclusion, a biblical version.

Now it is being revised and retold to the Soviet collectivists by the Story Teller as the story of Grusha and Michael. The problems of justice, property, and self-sacrifice at the heart of the tale are thus presented by Brecht as continuing human problems, expressed in both the ancient Chinese legend and the revision of the legend told to the collectivists at the later historical moment described in the "Prologue." By putting the collectivists into his drama as an audience within the play, Brecht tacitly reminds us of our own status as audience, at yet a further historical remove from both the original legend and this Soviet retelling of it. Thus, our own time may appear to us in historical perspective, and we may be moved to consider the special meaning this tale has to us, given the specific ways in which our age has chosen to deal with these moral and social problems. Viewed as history, our present may be examined with the enhanced perception that, ideally at least, the historical perspective can bring: with objectivity and clarity, a critical sense of human possibilities and limits, and an aspiration toward a more just and humane future.

16.3   The narrative device of the Story Teller reminds the audience that this is a story we are watching unfold. But does this necessarily mean that the audience will maintain its special relationship to the play—unemotional, thoughtful, skeptical—as required by Brecht's theory of epic theater? Take, for example, the episode at the end of Scene i, in which Grusha sits all night by the side of Michael, the Governor's abandoned child, and agonizes over whether to run off with him and save him from his father's enemies. Is an audience likely to be cool and unemotional while watching this scene?

Answer   This scene, which pits Grusha's desire to help the child against her fear for her own safety, is naturally a dramatic one, and Brecht uses setting, action, and narration to heighten the emotional pitch. On the wall above Grusha hangs the severed head of Michael's father; the Story Teller describes the city around her as "full of flames and crying." As the day wanes, Grusha visibly wrestles with her conflicting emotions; she approaches Michael, hesitates, walks away. She listens to the child's breathing and for the tread of approaching

Ironshirts. The Story Teller puts into words the plea and admonition that Grusha hears in the child's crying:

> "Woman," it said, "help me."
> And it went on, not whining, but saying quite sensibly:
> "Know, woman, he who hears not a cry for help
> But passes by with troubled ears will never hear
> The gentle call of a lover nor the blackbird at dawn
> Nor the happy sigh of the tired grape-picker as the Angelus rings."

The epic function of the Story Teller's narration here is not to reduce the emotionality of this scene so that we may simply think about it but rather to broaden and generalize its significance. The child's appeal to Grusha states a general moral proposition: When we let our fearful instincts for self-preservation diminish our capacity for charity, we risk a kind of death in life. Although Grusha is terrified by the mortal danger that threatens her if she helps the child, she also knows she faces a moral danger by hardening her heart to him. In a single, powerful phrase, Brecht makes plain that in a dangerous world, goodness is a dangerous proposition: "Fearful is the seductive power of goodness!"

By invoking the abstraction "goodness," Brecht helps the reader see Grusha's problem as a particular instance of a problem all people face at times in relation to their fellow human beings. But Brecht's dramatization of this scene ensures that the problem cannot be solved abstractly, on the level of good intentions. Grusha must actually choose now, in these dangerous times, when it takes all one's courage and energy merely to save oneself. When Grusha picks up the child, her action is broadened—made epic—by our feeling that charity has won a battle with fear. This epic quality is made possible precisely by the heightened emotionality of the scene—the fact that we are stirred by Grusha's dilemma and recognize in her choice our own aspiration.

The political aim of Brecht's epic theater is in part a hortatory one—to change people's behavior by awakening their sympathy and outrage—although Brecht might have objected to so preacherly a description. In this scene, his ambition is served by fostering the audience's emotional identification with Grusha, in direct contradiction to the theory of epic theater. While this contradiction may diminish one's faith in Brecht's theories, the power of this scene can only increase one's respect for his theater craft. As in so much of his literary and political life, Brecht's theorizing falls short of describing his more complicated and subtle practice.

16.4 When asked to name some classic examples of traditional drama, the titles people come up with tend to have something in common. Many are proper names: *Oedipus Rex, Hamlet, Phaedra, Hedda Gabler*. This is not surprising, since the essence of traditional drama lies in the depiction of character. The main development of each play is toward a more complete delineation of the unique identity of its central character. Hamlet, for example, is a mystery at the start of Shakespeare's play. As the play unfolds, our understanding of him grows. This is not to say that we finally understand Hamlet completely and exhaustively. Instead, our understanding of him grows in complexity. In some ways, Hamlet may seem more mysterious at the end of the play, but his is a mystery we have somehow grasped. Are the characters, major and minor, in *The Caucasian Chalk Circle* similarly mysterious and complex? Do they develop or change? Does our understanding of them deepen?

Answer   The minor characters in *The Caucasian Chalk Circle* are more like puppets or caricatures than fully realized characters. Each has only one or two qualities, and these are wildly overdrawn. In the first scene, the Governor is the personification of kingly arrogance, his wife is all vanity and false motherly regard, the two doctors who attend their child outdo each other in terrified obsequiousness, and the Fat Prince is a fawning sycophant whose insolence is hidden from the Governor only by the latter's blind arrogance. There are no depths or mysteries to these characters; the audience knows them completely from the moment they open their mouths.

In dealing with a major character such as Grusha, Brecht's characterization is equally simple and direct. Grusha is kind, motherly, loyal, loving, and courageous (though not unafraid). We learn these things about Grusha by the end of her first important scene, when she runs off with Michael. Although her qualities are tested and proved, she does not change in any significant way during the course of the play. Although our affection for her may grow, she does not seem more complicated or mysterious. She is the same good-hearted, simple woman we met in Scene i. If there is any mystery about her, it is one that runs beyond the bounds of her individuality: How can some people preserve their humanity when terror rules?

The simplicity of Grusha's character and the directness of its depiction are also in keeping with the overall tone of the play, in which simplicity is both an aesthetic organizing principle (as in the stylization of the minor characters) and a valued human quality. This virtuous simplicity can be seen at its most poignant in the courtship of Grusha and Simon. The two lovers address each other with a sweet formality that makes their scenes together touching and beautiful. Their speech is plain yet poetic, filled with proverbs and metaphors drawn from the everyday experiences of people who live close to nature. Their bond is based on qualities that are likewise simple and beautiful: loyalty, tenderness, mutual respect. In Brecht's depiction of Grusha and Simon, simplicity becomes both the key to a code of human relations and an aesthetic touchstone that gives the play moments of true charm and beauty.

16.5 How does Brecht's conception of character serve his political intentions?

Answer We know Brecht's characters by what they do, in particular by how they treat other people. Of each character (with the exception of Azdak), it can be said that he or she either oppresses or respects other people; each is either a friend or an enemy to human dignity. It is a truism to say that one understands dramatic characters through their actions and relations with others, but this proposition carries double weight in Brechtian drama, since Brecht is less interested in the uniqueness of the individual than in the fabric of human relations. This is an appropriate focus for a playwright of avowedly political intent, especially one who felt that human relations in modern industrial society are in need of drastic change.

The real drama of a character like Grusha arises not from a progressively deepening elaboration of who she is but from watching her choose among the modest possibilities for action that life has brought her. Grusha, true to the epic theory of character, is free to make real choices, such as her crucial decision to save Michael.

This aspect of Brechtian character may be illustrated by a comparison with classical tragedy, which in many ways is the antitype to epic theater. Consider Sophocles's *Oedipus Rex*. At the start of the play, all the significant action has already ended. Oedipus has long before slain his father and married his mother. The action of the play consists only of Oedipus's discovery of these truths and their enormity. Oedipus comes to know who he is. He is Oedipus, the man who killed his father and married his mother. Action and identity define each other in a way that cancels choice and possibility. Being who he is, he could have done nothing else; having done what he has, he can be none other than Oedipus, the cursed. In classical tragedy, character and fate are one and the same.

If Grusha is less complex and resonant a character than Oedipus, at least she has a small degree of freedom. And her freedom to choose to save Michael allows her to create her character as a moral being. This belief in the possibility of choice is essential to a playwright of political intent. If such a playwright is to persuade us to rearrange our social relations, we must believe that we can choose to do so.

16.6 Like the "Prologue," the end of the Tale of the Chalk Circle concerns the determination of ownership; instead of rights to land, this case involves the right of Grusha to keep Michael as her child. Do the same rules of rationality govern both distributions of "property"? What of Azdak, who decides the case? Is he bound by rules of reason and justice?

Answer Both decisions are at odds with traditional legal concepts of private property and ownership. As Michael's natural mother, the Governor's wife has the law on her side in her claim to him. And she desires him quite literally as property; only by regaining Michael can she perfect her claim to her husband's estate. In Azdak's decision, however, the good of the child is considered more important that the vindication of mere legal rights, and Grusha is given the child. This decision parallels that of the "Prologue"; in both cases, legal rights of ownership are subordinated to the wider good. At the close of his recitation in Scene v, the Story Teller explicitly draws the moral that links the beginning and end of Brecht's play:

> . . . what there is shall go to those who are good for it,
> Children to the motherly, that they prosper,
> Carts to good drivers, that they be driven well,
> The valley to the waterers, that it yield fruit.

However, the means by which these distributions are effected are quite different. The collectivists of the "Prologue" make their decision by talking rationally together. They can reach an agreement that is felt by all to be just because their interests are bound together. In a state in which private property has been abolished, the work of each contributes to the good of all. In the reasonableness, trust, and unselfishness that characterize the political process of the Georgian collectivists, Brecht offers a utopian vision of human relations, which, it seems safe to say, has never been fully realized in any modern state.

The decision to give Michael to Grusha takes place in the decidedly unutopian world of Grusha's adventures, a world where each person's survival depends on individual success in the war of all against all. Azdak, the instrument of this decision, though he does justice in this one case, is wholly a creature of this inherently unjust world.

Azdak is no ordinary judge. A poor village scrivener of radical sympathies, a poacher, a cynic, a man who lives by his wits, Azdak owes his judgeship to the chaos of the times. The Ironshirts clothe Azdak in judge's robes as a joke on the very idea of justice, and Azdak plays the role to the hilt. He takes bribes, seduces litigants, and generally abuses his position, indulging every opportunity for wit and whim. As the Story Teller says, "The judge was a rascal; now the rascal shall be a judge."

Azdak commits every sin of arbitrariness and injustice, except hypocrisy—he is too boldfaced for that. His one positive principle is to favor the poor, as a kind of vengence on their oppressors. He may thereby do some justice, but that is incidental; he has no overriding commitment to justice or to any other ideal. He is a realist before all else, and his first commitment is to survival. As he readily admits, he is a coward; if he does some good, it will not be at the expense of his hide.

Azdak achieves justice through cunning and opposition, not by means of reason in the ordinary sense. This comes as a sudden comic reversal rather than an assertion of rule; it banishes for a moment the codified injustice of civil law and creates a human order where true mother and child, lover and beloved, are reunited, where the good are rewarded and the bad punished. However, this is not a lasting reign of justice. The turmoil which has given Azdak this moment of power also assures its transience. As the Story Teller says, the time of Azdak's judging was remembered "as a brief golden age, almost an age of justice."

Brecht has been criticized for what some have felt to be excessive idealization of the Soviet state in the "Prologue." However, Brecht's biographers have made it clear that he never believed that the Soviet Union had achieved anything like this state of reason and fairness. It is perhaps more accurate to think of the "Prologue" as a consciously fashioned depiction of a political ideal, an aspiration set at a realistically gauged distance from our own historical moment, a realm where, as Azdak demonstrates, justice must still be won by cunning and luck.

D.E.

SUGGESTED READINGS

Demetz, Peter, *Brecht: A Collection of Critical Essays* (1962).
Esslin, Martin, *Brecht: The Man and His Work* (1971).
Gray, Ronald, *Bertolt Brecht* (1961).
Hill, Claude, *Bertolt Brecht* (1975).
Lyons, James, *Brecht in America* (1980).
Willett, John, *The Theatre of Bertolt Brecht* (1968).

C H A P T E R   1 7

BECKETT

Beckett and Modernity

Samuel Beckett is an uncompromising writer whose every word appears to have been written in the service of his powerfully idiosyncratic sensibility. That such a writer is "difficult" is not surprising. What is surprising, perhaps more to Beckett than to anyone else, is that he is popular or, more accurately, notorious. Beckett's play *Waiting for Godot*, first produced in English in 1955, transformed an unknown Irish expatriate into the public personification of literary avant-gardism. Theater columns all over the world were filled with articles and debates about this "new kind of drama," and everybody knew the "joke" of the play—that two characters and an audience should be made to wait so long for a character who never arrives.

Since then, Beckett, an intensely private man who has always fled publicity, has had a prominent place in the collective cultural consciousness. The respect accorded his novels and plays has continued to grow. He has become one of the most written-about writers of the twentieth century. In 1969, he was awarded the Nobel prize for literature.

Through it all, Beckett's themes and methods have remained what they were from the first. His fictions are filled with characters lingering on the verge of extinction. The key word is "lingering." Beckett's strange characters—clownish tramps (*Godot*), a tripartite consciousness which is finally reduced to a nameless disembodied mind (the trilogy of novels *Molloy*, *Malone Dies*, and *The Unnamable*), an old man in solitary dialog with tape recordings of himself (*Krapp's Last Tape*), a woman buried up to her neck (*Happy Days*), people immured in pots, dwelling in garbage cans, crawling eternally through some Dantean muck—approach ever closer to death and silence without getting there. Their common refrain is, "I can't go on. I'll go on."

One might ask why this poet of the endlessly drawn out last gasp is one of the handful of writers whom our age has identified as modern in an exemplary way. For many critics, Beckett has succeeded, perhaps uniquely, in capturing the fears and doubts peculiar to our times. Yet if Beckett has succeeded in this respect, it is by the purest inadvertence. The last thing Beckett set out to become was a social prophet. Throughout his writing career, he has chosen to pursue a narrow range of themes with an absorption that gives them the appearance of private obsessions. Yet Beckett's continuing ability to fascinate a popular audience seems to indicate a genuine correspondence between his private obsessions and our common condition. That Beckett's solipsistic craft has so unintendingly struck this representative note makes it a subtler feat than any social prophecy and contributes not a little to the power and authenticity of his vision.

Early Years and Friendship with Joyce

Beckett was born in Dublin in 1906. His family was Protestant and traced its origins to French Huguenots who had immigrated to Ireland in the seventeenth century. William Beckett, Samuel's father, was a successful quantity surveyor, and the family lived comfortably, moving to successively grander houses until they built Cooldrinagh, the suburban manor in which Samuel was raised.

Beckett was educated at Portora Royal School, where he distinguished himself in languages and athletics, and at Trinity College, Dublin, the alma mater of Jonathan Swift and Laurence Sterne. At Trinity, Beckett read French and Italian; he was graduated in 1927 with the school's most prestigious award in modern literature. He spent the following year unhappily teaching at Campbell College in Belfast, and in October 1928 he went to Paris as an instructor at the École Normale Supérieure.

Paris between the wars was the cultural capital of the world and indisputably the center of literary innovation. In Paris, Beckett moved among the two groups which figured most significantly in the city's cultural life: the patrons, including Peggy Guggenheim and Nancy Cunard, both of whom took an amatory interest in him, and the artists, notably his fellow expatriate James Joyce. Beckett allied himself with the group publishing the self-conscious experimental magazine *transition*, and it was there that he published his first work, "Dante . . . Bruno. Vico . . Joyce," an essay on Joyce's "Work in Progress," which was ultimately published as *Finnegans Wake*. Beckett was one of the admirers who surrounded Joyce and were habitually called upon to help him in his perpetual practical difficulties, financial and otherwise. Beckett served as an unpaid secretary and factotum and often read to Joyce, whose eyes were failing badly. Although Joyce and Beckett appear to have genuinely admired each other, Joyce, the older by twenty-four years, seems to have intentionally kept some distance between them, as he did with all his friends, and their friendship was never what Beckett might have hoped.

Beckett's literary work during this period amounted to, in addition to the Joyce essay, a short story called "Assumption," some poems in French, a long poem on Descartes entitled *Whoroscope*, and an essay on Proust. In 1930, he returned to Ireland to take the position of lecturer in French at Trinity. However, he soon resigned this post and embarked on several unhappy aimless years of traveling in England, Germany, and France. During this time, Beckett read philosophy, notably Arnold Geulincx, a seventeenth-century Belgian who developed a distinctive and eccentric extension of Descartes's formulations on the relation of mind and body. He also completed his first novel, *Murphy*. *Murphy* remained in manuscript for two years and made the rounds of forty-two publishers before finally being accepted by Routledge in 1937. Many such difficulties preceded the "overnight" fame which *Godot* brought Beckett nearly twenty years later.

Also in 1937, Beckett settled permanently in Paris, where he and his wife still reside. This move gave Beckett some stability and, equally important, lead him toward the choice of French as the language in which he would do most of his future writing. French gave Beckett a means of expression purged of the metaphorical riches and personal associations which made English unsuitable for his austere fictions. Subsequent to the novel *Watt* (written 1942–1944), nearly all of his work has been written in French and later translated into English by the author.

War Years and Major Works

In June 1940, Beckett fled Paris as the German army moved relentlessly toward the city. He traveled south and then, in October, returned to Paris, where he joined the Resistance. Beckett played a valuable role in the anti-German intelligence network until his group was betrayed in October 1942. He barely escaped with his life, and he was forced to spend the remainder of the war in hiding in the Vauclause. In typical laconic and modest fashion, Beckett has dismissed his Resistance activities, for which he was decorated by the French government, as "Boy Scout stuff."

At the close of the war, Beckett returned to Paris and there wrote (1947–1950) the trilogy of novels which he regards as his most significant work: *Molloy*, *Malone Dies*, and *The Unnamable*. In 1952, *En Attendant Godot*, only the second play Beckett had written and the first to be staged, received its first production, in French.

Later Works

Most of Beckett's subsequent work has been drama of one form or another, including radio plays (*Embers*, 1959; *Words and Music*, 1962), a film featuring the comedian Buster Keaton (*Film*, 1964), and a television play (*Eh Joe*, 1966), as well as theater pieces (*Endgame*, 1957; *Happy Days*, 1961). In his most recent work, the stage has become barer and the characters more immobilized, with story reduced to a plane geometry of actions and language to muttering and mime. But this is the logical conclusion of Beckett's lifelong preoccupation with deliquescence. Like his characters, Beckett's texts have always lingered on the verge of silence. His language is spare, direct, and precise in timing and tone, although at times it is hauntingly poetic. It seems to exist in a dialog with silence, a nothingness which surrounds the word. This dialog on the subject of human finitude and suffering often passes into the grim comic register called black humor. Ultimately, it is Beckett's wit, his eye for the silly resiliencies that complicate our pain, which turns his death's-head vision into art. As Nell tells us from her garbage can (*Endgame*), "Nothing is funnier than unhappiness."

ESSAY QUESTIONS WITH ANSWERS

Waiting for Godot

17.1   Chekhov advised that the playwright who hangs a gun over the mantel in Act I must fire it in Act IV. One assumption implicit in Chekhov's rule—which Chekhov himself did not always obey—is the belief that experience is teleological; that is to say, it moves continuously and inevitably toward some definite end (the gun shot, Oedipus's self-discovery, Tartuffe's downfall, Phaedra's death). This belief is the enabling assumption and justification of all storytelling. The end, whatever it may be, is the most meaningful and essential part of any story. Does *Waiting for Godot* obey Chekov's rule, or does the play illustrate some other pattern of experience in time?

Answer   In a sense, Beckett has hung a gun over the mantel: Godot and the expectation that he will arrive. But Beckett's gun never fires, since Godot does not come. Instead, it appears that Godot will never come, that Didi (Vladimir) and Gogo (Estragon) have endured an eternity of waiting and must continue to wait, that Godot, whoever or whatever we imagine him to be, may not exist.

Rather than progressing sequentially from beginning to middle to end, *Godot* goes nowhere. The first words tell the audience what to expect. "Nothing to be done," says Gogo, pausing for a moment in his endless struggle with his boots. Indeed, nothing of any consequence happens in the play. As they wait, Gogo continues to wrestle with his boots while Didi pothers with his hat; they talk aimlessly to pass the time, usually missing each other's point. Their friendship cycles from private sulking to gloomy commiseration to affirmations of loyalty to pouty disagreement to wheedling reconciliation and back to sulking. They eat. Pozzo and Lucky pass through, astonishingly but uneventfully. The Boy arrives, bearing Godot's regrets and his promises. At last, the pointless day ends in disappointment, leaving only the smallest hope that the next day may be different. Perhaps tomorrow Godot will come. So ends Act I.

Act II, which occurs on the next day, virtually repeats the first act, varying only in the details. We get the sense that these are two of an endless series of identical empty days stretching back toward some remote past and ahead toward some unimaginable future, with their promised culmination, the arrival of Godot, endlessly deferred, cast unreachably ahead like a walker's shadow.

Stories usually move in what seems like a straight line, from some beginning through an unfolding sequence of events to an end. In *Godot*, the end is never reached so that the play seems to move, by means of repetition, in a circle. *Godot* is shaped like the tune Didi sings at the start of Act II:

> A dog came in the kitchen
> And stole a crust of bread
> Then cook up with a ladle
> And beat him till he was dead.
>
> Then all the dogs came running
> And dug the dog a tomb
> And wrote upon the tombstone
> For the eyes of dogs to come;
>
> A dog came in the kitchen
> And stole a crust of bread. . . .*

Like the play as a whole, this ditty tells a story (or mock story) without an ending. The result of eliminating the ending is that the song ceases to make ordinary sense. As it circles back on itself, it destroys its own meanings. The events recounted in the first stanza have only a moment's credibility before they become a fiction produced by the second stanza, which is in turn swallowed up by the first. This disconcerting effect depends on the "Then" at the beginning of the second stanza. It is a bogus "then" in the sense that it does not point to a second event that follows sequentially upon an earlier event. If it did, we would have a story—this happened, and then that happened—and the sense of the song would be stable and clear. Instead, the word "then" destroys sequence; it merely functions as a pivot around which the song swerves back on itself, turning into a conundrum rather than a true story.

Something similar happens in *Godot* as a whole. Like Didi and Gogo, the reader or the audience may feel that if Godot would only arrive, some sense would emerge out of this strange play. One would be able to look back from this ending and arrange it all into a story, a satisfying explanation of all that

---

*Translated by the author, New York, Grove Press, 1954. All references to *Waiting for Godot* in this chapter are to this edition.

has gone before. However, by denying us this ending, the play frustrates the order-making principle of teleology, and experience becomes confusing for both its audience and its characters.

Didi and Gogo have lost all capacity to understand their experience in time. They are stumped by such questions as: What day is today? and What happened yesterday? They have no sense of continuity and sequence so that the same place encountered on two successive days seems like two different places. Without the capacity to understand the order of events, virtually all questions become unanswerable, since the ability to link an antecedent cause to a subsequent effect is essential to rational explanation. Gogo is beaten nightly as he sleeps in his ditch, but he cannot say why; all he knows is that he has done nothing to deserve it, and that is no explanation at all. Pozzo, when he finally fixes his mind on the question, simply cannot say why Lucky never puts down his bags or why Lucky never leaves him. And of course, the play's imponderables—Who or what is Godot? Why must Didi and Gogo wait?—seem beyond even the hope of an answer. Thus, *Godot* not only violates Chekhov's rule, it eliminates the cause and effect principle of rational explanation embodied in that rule.

17.2 In realist literature, characters are typically endowed with a measure of free will. This freedom to act is a modest one, much limited and qualified by the circumstances, the ordinary obstacles and obligations, that make up one's situation in life. Action arises from a struggle between the individual and the individual's circumstances, and it is this struggle which makes the action morally significant, the stuff of drama. Do Didi and Gogo ever act? Are they either absolutely free or absolutely bound? Or do they possess some limited freedom, qualified by their circumstances, like characters in a realist text?

Answer Didi and Gogo never act in the sense of having an effect on their world or changing their circumstances in even the smallest measure. Their one purpose—to wait for Godot—is a commitment to inaction, and a hopeless one at that. Their fitful resolutions—to leave, to help Lucky, even to hang themselves—dissolve in talk and indecision. The smallest tasks, like managing their boots and hats, seem beyond their capacities. Reasoning and remembering are lost arts. Their only efficacy is on the level of pure biology, as their sores fester energetically, their feet and breath stink unremittingly, and their flatulence blows like the simoom. Yet this, of course, is just another aspect of their powerlessness; even their bodies have the upper hand over them.

Why are Didi and Gogo so incapable of action? They are not like Hamlet, for example, who is made helpless by his situation, by desires and compunctions produced by conflicting relations with others. Didi and Gogo *have* no situation. They are unbound by family, work, or any of the other duties and limitations imposed by life in society. They stand alone, outside society. They are incarnations of perfect freedom standing by that symbol of perfect freedom, the open road.

Yet Didi and Gogo feel unfree, bound to wait for Godot. Whenever they try to leave, they seem physically incapable of doing so; they are flung back on stage like punchy boxers shoved back into the ring.

At one point, Gogo asks if they are "tied" to Godot. Didi answers: "To Godot? Tied to Godot! What an idea! No question of it. (*Pause.*) For the moment." Lurking in Didi's pause is the realization that they are indeed tied. But they are not actually enslaved to Godot any more than they are bound to punch a clock in the morning or come home to suburban families at night. It is not the world that binds Didi and Gogo but their minds. They are bound to wait for Godot not by Godot himself but by their expectation that he will come. It is their hope which traps them. It seems reasonable to think that if they gave up their hope for Godot, they would be able to give up their vigil. Yet perversely, after an eternity of disappointment, they continue to hope. They present the paradox of free people manufacturing their own chains. They are free to imagine the possibility of some Godot, but they cannot free themselves from their imaginations.

In a sense, *Godot* reverses the terms of freedom and unfreedom that typify the realist text. Didi and Gogo are free of the circumstances of the world but "tied" by mind.

17.3 Chekov's statement (see Question 17.1) involves another assumption about literary representation: the belief that plays should be filled with such things as guns and mantelpieces, that is, the stuff of the material world. Does *Godot* accord with this assumption about the role of the material world in drama? What sort of setting and objects figure in the play? Do they figure significantly in the play's action, as Chekhov implies they should?

Answer The setting of *Godot* consists of a country road, a mound, and an unidentifiable tree, all in an unnamed land. These are the rudiments of place, but of no place in particular. The spot is so essentially featureless that Didi and Gogo cannot decide whether they have never been there before or have been there forever.

In *Godot*, the material clutter of the world of guns and mantelpieces has been pared down and purified. Isolated, removed from associations with other objects which could together create some identifiable place such as "home," or "Ireland," or "an apartment in Paris," the few objects in *Godot* take on a strange autonomy and abstractness. The solitary tree is not a familiar feature from a real landscape but a puzzlement. Is it a willow, or is it not? Maybe it is actually a shrub or a bush. When it suddenly sprouts overnight, this does not seem like the ordinary recurrence of a seasonal process but an ominous effusion. It seems less an ordinary tree than an emissary from nature, which is otherwise absent from the play. Perhaps the tree is nature itself.

Similarly, Gogo's boots and Didi's hat are not the ordinary accoutrements we would expect but implacable enemies of comfort. The tenacity with which they pinch and bind suggests that they have a life of their own, as indeed they seem to when Didi and Gogo, in a classic vaudeville turn, juggle their identical bowlers back and forth, unable to decide which hat belongs on whose head. These fractious articles seem less like human implements than brute matter that is inimical to human purposes.

While the objects in *Godot* carry considerable metaphysical freight, appearing as incarnations of nature or matter, they seem oddly drained of ordinary meaning. Unlike Chekhov's gun, which is pregnant with dramatic significance—suspense, moral decision, violence—the things in *Godot* are dead and silent. A kind of detritus, they signify as little about human motives and events as the miscellaneous rubbish which Didi finds in his pocket instead of a note from Godot. Things are rubbish in *Godot*. They offer no satisfaction, create no home, serve no purpose. Didi and Gogo, two tramps dressed in rags, are men on the rubbish heap.

The material world has gone dead, in part because action is impossible in *Godot*. Ordinarily, objects are meaningful to people because they shape and are shaped by the things people do. When this active connection between people and the world is broken, things no longer make human sense. Caught up in events, the tree could have taken on a familiar identity as, say, "the tree from which Didi spotted Godot coming across the field." But untethered by action, it takes on a distant, absolute identity as "the tree" or "nature." Broken off from the texture of ongoing life, the tree becomes a fragment that is connected to nothing but itself.

One finds this fragmentation throughout *Godot*. The play is sprinkled with place names: the Pyrennes, Paris, the Macon Country, the Eiffel Tower, the Rhone. However, the audience is given no idea how to use them to create a coherent past for Didi and Gogo, some explanation of how or from where they have come to their present impasse. In fact, it is hard to picture Didi and Gogo anywhere but this spot, waiting for Godot. The places they name seem literally a world away from their nameless habitation. Coming from them, the words "Paris" and "the Rhone" seem like shards of the real world, a world not continuous with, but merely adjacent to, the strange, inhospitable setting of the play.

By isolating the *Godot*-scape from the real geographic world and populating it with a mere residue of the objective world, Beckett manages the minimalist trick of changing less into more. The lack of features and names in the setting unmoors our imagination, which, unrestrained by familiar physical reference ("Oh, it looks like the South of France"; "My Granpa had a maple like that one"), goes spiraling off toward metaphysical reference. Just as the tree becomes nature and boots and hats become matter, the *Godot* noplace becomes everyplace, the wasteland of human existence. Didi and Gogo become symbols of all humanity at the point of exhaustion, and Godot becomes much more than some bloke who cannot be depended on.

Throughout *Godot*, Beckett demonstrates how the reduction of dramatic elements to bare bones—whether setting, story, character, or language—can lead to an immense inflation of meaning. This is the essential paradox of Beckett, a writer who is devoted to the exploration of nothing but whose writings have produced a volume of interpretation matched by few modern authors. We may think of *Godot* and Beckett's other writings as an empty room; the barer it is, the greater the echoes. As for who is doing the shouting, Beckett or his readers, that is impossible to say.

17.4 *Waiting for Godot* departs from most of the canons of literary representation and thus becomes something other than the kind of realist drama that holds a mirror up to our world. If *Godot* is not about the problems of particular people in a particular place and time, what is it about?

Answer Because of the title, we may conclude that the play is about Godot. But if we approach the text with this assumption, the play deftly steps aside, and we go blundering past. Godot is not the answer to any question but a cipher, the catalyst for further unanswerable questions. No more than Didi or Gogo can we answer the who or what, the why or when, of Godot.

We may take the obvious hint given in the name and conclude that this is a play about God. But this answer merely substitutes a Mystery for a mystery. Clearly, the play does not present God as a spiritual fact of life, a knowable presence who commands faith. If, as some critics argue, the play presents God as existent but absent, hidden from Didi and Gogo, how are we to tell one absence from another?

His absence is just the point of Godot. In his absence, we can imagine him to be anything. Beckett has been careful to allow any number of inferences while sanctioning none. The play is dotted with Christian and biblical references, but they tease at meaning rather than establish it, and they vanish without comment almost as soon as they appear. When Gogo calls himself Adam, Pozzo does not even hear him, and when Pozzo is identified as both Cain and Abel, "all humanity," Gogo quickly changes the subject, irrelevantly pointing to a little cloud. It is almost as if this sparest of plays were embarrassed by these references to the richest vein in western cultural history.

Early in Act I, however, the play does offer an extended if irreverent discussion of the Bible. Didi is perturbed by the fact that the four Evangelists each give different accounts of the passion and the fate of the two thieves who were sentenced to be crucified alongside Jesus. Why, he asks, if all four were there, does "only one of the four say that one of the two [thieves] was saved?" Why should one believe Luke instead of the other three? Didi is no naive believer. He approaches the Bible not as the undisputed word of God but as a problematic text which, rather like the play Godot, suggests multiple interpretations but endorses no one of them. Didi wonders that even under these uncertain conditions people choose to believe the more optimistic account of Luke. Here indeed is a mystery considerably greater than the identity of Godot: the mystery of hope. For belief maintained without knowledge or some authority to command faith is no more than hope. In this theme appears something one might settle on as the subject of Godot: not a God who is to be doubted or believed in, but hope, or belief without faith. Accordingly, the emphasis in the title should fall on Waiting, not on Godot, since Didi and Gogo's long wait presents the phenomenon of hope in all its aspects: high aspiration, comic victimization, mindless habit, a kind of damnation, and a pathetic mistake.

As a play absorbed with the issue of hope, Godot does not have a subject in the ordinary sense. It is not about something; instead, it enacts its subject. Didi and Gogo's waiting, which is the entirety of Godot, enacts the phenomenon of hope. The activity of hoping is doubly brought home to us because we are likely to share Didi and Gogo's hope. As we read the play or watch it in performance, we long for Godot, for some relief from the monotony and uncertainty, just as fervently as the characters do. This experience of hope in time is the play's subject and infuses itself into every bit of the play's unfolding duration. What Beckett said of Finnegans Wake is true of Godot: "It is not about something, it is that something itself."

17.5 Beckett has said, "I am interested in the shape of ideas even if I do not believe in them." Can it be said that the idea of hope presented in *Godot* has a particular shape? How does the shape of hope relate to the structure of the play as a whole?

Answer Binary opposition is the shape which dominates the structure of *Godot*. The play is strewn with pairs, most of them opposites. It is a two-act tragicomedy which spans two days in the lives of two characters (temperamental opposites) who twice encounter a second pair (Pozzo and Lucky, master and slave) as they wait for their situation to be transformed into its opposite—Godot's absence into his presence.

The pair of contraries which, more than any other, haunts *Godot* is the one which Didi mentions early in Act I: "Two thieves. One is supposed to have been saved and the other . . . (*He searches for the contrary of saved.*) . . . damned." These are the contraries which define the drama. Didi and Gogo live in a condition we recognize as fallen, and they wait for some salvational possibility—Godot—which will reverse the unhappy dispensation under which they live. No text or prophecy or faith authorizes their hope, but the formal capacity of mind to imagine contraries does: If one thief was saved, the other must have been damned; if one can conceive of damnation, one must at least be able to imagine the possibility of salvation.

Godot demonstrates the capacity of mind to shape a metaphysical entity (hope, Godot) from nothing. Take Didi's phrase "No lack of void." This is Beckett's version of the Creation as three nothings ("no," "lack," "void") combine to create an intimation of something. Of course, Beckett's joke is that what results is more void, an extra helping of nothing. But we have something beyond that: the flickering apprehension of presence in absence, like Godot himself.

The phrase "no lack of void" recapitulates in small the paradoxical habit of mind which characterizes the entire play. Like the play, which pares story, action, and the material and social world down to nearly nothing, it strains toward negation. But willy-nilly it brings into being a ghostly presence, a Godot, an augmented void. Even our negations tempt us back toward being and belief. As Gogo says, their talk may be insignificant, but it is not insignificant enough.

The shape of *Godot*, as Bert States has recently described it, is the shape of paradox. Didi and Gogo's hope is built precisely on the hopelessness of their situation and their groundless capacity to imagine its opposite, just as their expectation of Godot is motivated solely by his absence. In *Godot*, mind gives us both too much and too little, like the word "Godot," whose extra syllable is too much to affirm our hope and too little to extinguish it.

17.6   With virtually no action to distract us, the language of *Godot* commands our attention; in large part, it *is* the action of the play. What are the distinguishing features of the language in *Godot*? If language takes the place of action, are the characters any more successful in their use of language—to describe their experience and comprehend their situation—than they are in their attempts to act?

Answer   The language of *Godot* is very noticeable indeed. Although the characters' speech is generally simple and colloquial, Beckett stylizes its delivery so that it moves prominently into the foreground. Beckett has a comedian's knack for timing, from the perfectly executed punch line to delayed reaction, rapid counterpoint, and comic simultaneity. The rhythms of *Godot*'s language give the play some of the appeal of music. The sense of Didi and Gogo's speech is so subordinated to its tempo and form that their talk often seems less a conversation than a well-scored duet. In Act I, for example, they converse in stichomythia, or the rapid exchange of single lines:

Estragon: What exactly did we ask him for?
Vladimir: Were you not there?
Estragon: I can't have been listening.
Vladimir: Oh . . . Nothing very definite.
Estragon: A kind of prayer.
Vladimir: Precisely.
Estragon: A vague supplication.
Vladimir: Exactly.
Estragon: And what did he reply?
Vladimir: That he'd see.
Estragon: That he couldn't promise anything.
Vladimir: That he'd have to think it over.
Estragon: In the quiet of his home.
Vladimir: Consult his family.
Estragon: His friends.
Vladimir: His agents.
Estragon: His correspondents.
Vladimir: His books.
Estragon: His bank account.

Vladimir: Before taking a decision.
Estragon: It's the normal thing.
Vladimir: Is it not?
Estragon: I think it is.
Vladimir: I think so too.

This is language driven solely by its own momentum, with one response automatically eliciting the next. None of it is based in any reality concerning Godot. It seems instead to be generated entirely by the rhythmic capability of spoken language and its profligate capacity to engender an infinite number of phrases of a certain form: his friends, his agents, his correspondents, his books. These are forms freed from the obligation to signify or communicate. Just as objects in *Godot*, when separated from human action, take on a strange autonomy, so language, failing its intended purposes, is freed to go off on its own. Unweighted by meaning, Didi and Gogo's aimless nattering hangs in midair, spinning idly around its own axis, referring to nothing but itself.

Early in Act I, the two of them try once more to clarify their hopelessly uncertain arrangements with Godot:

Vladimir: Let's wait and see what he says.
Estragon: Who?
Vladimir: Godot.
Estragon: Good idea.
Vladimir: Let's wait till we know exactly how we stand.
Estragon: On the other hand it might be better to strike the iron before it freezes.
Vladimir: I'm curious to hear what he has to offer. Then we'll take it or leave it.

In case we have missed the point, the muddled "strike the iron before it freezes" makes it clear that they are trading clichés: "wait and see," "how we stand," "take it or leave it." Clichés are linguistic forms from which meaning has faded, language approaching the condition of pure structure without sense. These formulas allow Didi and Gogo to chatter away about Godot despite not having the faintest idea what they are talking about. Their speech is not a way to say something but an end in itself. Talking soothes them; a kind of whistling in the dark, it is a way to hide their ignorance and dread.

The impotence of language in *Godot* is particularly evident whenever anybody tries to name or identify something. Didi and Gogo cannot pin a definite name on the tree or assign a color—black, brown, gray, or green—to Gogo's boots. They find that Pozzo answers to both "Cain" and "Abel." In Godot, however, they have not a thing that cannot be named but a name without a thing or person to attach to it. "Godot" is a complex of suppositions fastened to the name of someone who exists in name only.

Language fails just as miserably whenever the characters try to communicate their inner experience. Their speech is rarely natural or spontaneous. They never simply speak their minds; instead, they seem to listen in on themselves and revise their thoughts to correspond to what they have "overheard." Here, for example, is Pozzo, who in Act I fancies himself an orator. He begins what he means to be a hymn to the beauty of the twilight sky, only to find that his speech takes him in a direction he never meant to go:

> What is there so extraordinary about it? Qua sky? It is pale and luminous like any sky at this hour of the day. (*Pause.*) In these latitudes. (*Pause.*) When the weather is fine. (*Lyrical.*) An hour ago (*He looks at this watch, prosaic.*) roughly (*Lyrical.*) after having poured forth even since (*He hesitates, prosaic.*) say ten o'clock in the morning (*Lyrical.*) tirelessly torrents of red and white light it begins to lose its effulgence, to grow pale (*Gesture of the two hands lapsing by stages.*) pale, ever a little paler, a little paler until (*Dramatic pause, ample gesture of the two hands flung wide apart.*) pppfff! finished! it comes to rest. But— (*Hands raised in admonition.*) —but behind this veil of gentleness and peace night is charging (*Vibrantly.*) and will burst upon us (*Snaps his fingers.*) pop! like that! (*His inspiration leaves him.*) just when we least expect it. (*Silence. Gloomily.*) That's how it is on this bitch of an earth.

This marvelously funny speech is built like a cartoon bridge. Beginning at one edge of the abyss, Pozzo must simultaneously build his bridge of words and scramble across it as it collapses and falls away at his heels. Pozzo must get across any way he can; when he does, he finds out that his lyrical nightfall has become a metaphor for extinction.

In classical oratory, language and feeling build together, creating a powerful, unified impression. Here, language and feeling go their separate ways, or rather, language leads and feeling is forced to follow unhappily behind. Without mutual support, both seem impoverished, arbitrary, and inauthentic.

Here is Didi in Act II, giving a speech like Pozzo's, which gets the better of him. Notice what happens to the bold intention announced in his first sentence:

Let us not waste our time in idle discourse! (*Pause. Vehemently.*) Let us do something, while we have the chance! It is not every day that we are needed. Not indeed that we personally are needed. Others would meet the case equally well, if not better. To all mankind they were addressed, those cries for help still ringing in our ears! But at this place, at this moment of time, all mankind is us, whether we like it or not. Let us make the most of it, before it is too late! Let us represent worthily for once the foul brood to which a cruel fate consigned us! What do you say? (*Estragon says nothing.*) It is true that when with folded arms we weigh the pros and cons we are no less a credit to our species. The tiger bounds to the help of his congeners without the least reflexion, or else he slinks away into the depths of the thickets. But that is not the question. What are we doing here, *that* is the question. And we are blessed in this, that we happen to know the answer. Yes, in this immense confusion one thing alone is clear. We are waiting for Godot to come—

This is language striving to stretch beyond itself into action and instead getting caught up in its own processes. Didi's hackneyed imitation of the grand style, his clichés, and the familiar thesis-antithesis ("the pros and cons") structure all suggest that this is language stuck in well-worn grooves. In fact, the whole speech is an imitation, the first part sounding like a rallying speech from one of Shakespeare's histories and the second half, of course, echoing *Hamlet*. Thus the speech moves from the possibility of significant action (history), to vacillation, to defeat (tragedy), and finally, despite Didi's brave beginning, back to the impasse which allows neither action nor defeat: they are waiting for Godot. Didi's speech represents language itself as a kind of waiting. It merely fills time eventlessly, helping to pass time that, as Gogo says, would have passed anyway.

Overall, language in *Godot* fails at its usual purposes of description, communication, and expression. By emphasizing the formal aspects of language—from the tempo of spoken language to the meaningless structures of clichés and rhetorical posturing—Beckett creates a language in which form itself is the most significant feature. In *Godot*, language is driven by an imperative toward form, not sense; it seems bent only on ceaselessly reproducing out of itself timeworn forms and phrases that impede understanding and action rather than furthering them. Seen this way, language becomes a realm unto itself, independent from the world it is meant to describe and the experience it is meant to master. In *Godot*, we get the distressing sense that language is both absolute and absolutely useless; the characters are condemned to do nothing but talk endlessly without the possibility of truly saying anything.

17.7 The suspense of waiting is broken only twice in *Godot*, by the appearance in each act of Pozzo and Lucky. Travelers along the road, they are strangers to the purgatorial noplace that Didi and Gogo inhabit. Do Pozzo and Lucky seem to live under the same dispensation as Didi and Gogo—endless waiting; featureless time without action, event, or end; and the eradication of society and history—or do they live under different conditions?

Answer Pozzo and Lucky restore to the play much of what has otherwise been eliminated. Their master-slave relationship reintroduces in condensed and simplified form all of society. The rope which binds Lucky to Pozzo is the visible equivalent of the impalpable constraints which give society its coercive force. Pozzo himself is the embodiment of the social animal at its worst. All pose and manner, he is practiced at the arts of ostentation, from oratory to bullying.

Apparently some sort of local grandee, Pozzo is on his way from his manor to the market to sell Lucky, his carrier. As a feudal remnant, he restores the historical dimension to the play. Indeed, Pozzo represents the intrusion of the linear march of time into the timeless, circular waiting of Didi and Gogo. His prized possession is his pocket watch, his "half-hunter with deadbeat escapement." All his significant speeches deal with time, from his disastrous paean to nightfall to his last maddened outburst, "Have you not done tormenting me with your accursed time!"

Most important, though, is Pozzo's own career through time. Although we see Pozzo only twice, we can make out the trajectory of his life in time: a rise to the "greatness" he displays in Act I and a catastrophic fall, the blindness which afflicts him in Act II. The Pozzo "plot" restores to the play the element of story, for it suggests a path traveled from beginning to end. More specifically, Pozzo travels the path of tragedy, that most teleological of narrative forms, whose power depends on the remorselessness of fate and the utter finality of endings.

Admittedly, Pozzo is no Theban king, and his silliness is an absurd substitute for tragic *virtú*. But *Godot* could not accommodate such grandeur, and in Pozzo we have a tragic hero redrawn to the scale of Beckett's play. Pozzo commits the classic sin of tragedy, hubris (overweening pride), and is punished with blindness, the affliction of Oedipus and the Earl of Gloucester (*King Lear*). Typical of tragedy, Pozzo's punishment is not finely meted out; instead, it is a blow dealt by Fortune, excessive and unreasoned, so arbitrary that it strikes Lucky, the unoffending man, as well as his offending master.

The title page of *Godot* advertises the play as a tragicomedy. The play mingles the tragic and comic in ways that are easier to sense than describe. However, it may be useful to think of *Godot* as divided between the Didi-Gogo comedy and the Pozzo-Lucky tragedy.

Didi and Gogo live under the conditions of comedy. The comic hero wants only happiness. His aim is modest, merely the life one ought to be able to live. The comic hero's strategy is not to wrest this life from the world but to have it in spite of the world, a private victory enjoyed privately. But his small ambitions are bedeviled by small obstacles: stubbed toes, banana peels, pinching boots, and irritating hats. The same mishaps befall the comic hero again and again because the distance between the comic hero and his modest desire is permanent, something essential in the nature of things. Thus the comic hero is doomed to a life of repetition, forever taking the same pratfall and getting up to take it again. Like Falstaff, such a hero is never down for good; he resists the finality of final things. Accordingly, the ending of comedy is insignificant; its life lies in the comic moment, the instant of the pratfall or the punch line. Comedy is built from these repeated moments, and so it moves in circles, in "routines," simple eddies of time. And if within comic time Didi and Gogo, as comic heroes, never move any closer to their desire, neither are they forced to renounce their hope.

Pozzo lives under the conditions of tragedy. The tragic hero desires greatness, which must be pursued actively, because greatness lies in the hero's willful assertion of self against the world and against human limitations. Since it tests the limits of human possibility, this pursuit must be a public act, measured against lesser ambitions and the failures of lesser people. Conceived in all-or-nothing terms, the life of the tragic hero takes its meaning entirely from its end, either complete success or utter failure. Unlike the life of the comic hero, the significance of the tragic hero's life lies not in the moment but in the completed biography. The tragic hero's life is a headlong dash toward the last moment which will illuminate all that has gone before. When it arrives, the hero's defeat is absolute. Having lived in linear time, where the consequences of actions are cumulative and inescapable, the tragic hero is finally crushed by time. Like Hotspur rather than Falstaff, such a hero stays down for good. This hero's fate, like Pozzo's blindness, is final and irreversible. The hero's course through time is so end-haunted that death seems to rush up to seize the hero. Pozzo's last words compress this life course into a single grim thunderclap of time: "They give birth astride of a grave, the light gleams an instant, then it's night once more."

Thus, it is possible to see in the Didi-Gogo plot and the Pozzo-Lucky plot two ideal and antithetical visions, comic and tragic. The first exists outside the flow of time, is immune to the harder blows of causation and circumstance, and reaches no end. The second is entirely the creature of linear time, cruelly punishes the actor with the consequences of his actions, and locates its fullest amplitude of meaning in its ending. Once again, we see Beckett's penchant for paired opposites and his ability to adduce generic forms of life—comedy as such, tragedy as such—by presenting their essential, purified structures.

17.8   If two different forms of life—the comic and the tragic—coexist in *Waiting for Godot*, do they significantly intersect, or do they simply spin past each other, merging into the general eventlessness of the play? Do Lucky and Pozzo have any effect on Didi and Gogo?

Answer   Lucky confronts Didi and Gogo with the tragic fact of suffering. In Lucky, there is at least the germ of a dramatic element that is otherwise absent from the play: a moral dilemma. On their first encounter with Lucky, Didi and Gogo's reaction alternates between horror, gawking fascination, and complacency ("It's inevitable"). Finally, Didi gets up the courage to protest to Pozzo in the name of humanity:

> Vladimir: (*Stutteringly resolute.*) To treat a man . . . (*Gesture towards Lucky.*) . . . like that . . . I think that . . . no . . . a human being . . . no . . . it's a scandal!

But Didi has too little determination, and Pozzo is too impervious to moral suasion. "I am perhaps not particularly human, but who cares?" Pozzo tells us. When Gogo tries to wipe Lucky's tears and gets a swift kick for his pains, Didi and Gogo's limited fund of sympathy is quickly exhausted. When Pozzo complains histrionically and improbably about the hard lot of a master, their sympathies shift absurdly to him. In this encounter, Didi and Gogo hardly display the goodness of the Samaritan.

In Act II, they do little better. The now blind Pozzo and the dumb Lucky come cantering on stage, collide, and fall to the floor, with Pozzo bleating piteously for help. Didi and Gogo temporize and bargain with Pozzo for their assistance, and Gogo takes the opportunity to revenge himself by putting the boot to Lucky now that he is down. Finally, they help the pair to their feet and on their way. Throughout these comic doings, Didi and Gogo feel the faint stirring of some moral imperative—they see in the stricken Pozzo both Cain and Abel, the epitome of suffering humanity—but this leads to no significant action. However, Didi does attain a sudden access of consciousness which amounts to a momentary revolution in his feelings. It is prepared for by his astonished discovery that Lucky has been struck dumb. Didi reacts with genuine shock and horror, an outburst of spontaneous emotion that is perhaps unmatched in the play.

Here the tragic plot involving the violence of time has penetrated the timeless world that Didi and Gogo inhabit. Lucky's being struck dumb is a blow delivered in time, final, absolute, and irreversible. What shocks Didi is the brutality of life in time—"Dumb! Since when?"—a reality from which his waiting existence has shielded him. He perceives the reality of the end and the horrible possibility that it may be arbitrary and accidental. Didi's moment of recognition is not unlike the illumination suffered by the tragic hero at the final discovery of his or her fate. In this moving and beautiful speech, Didi demonstrates for the first time in the play the possibility of self-transcendence as he imaginatively grasps the suffering of others. He is able to see his life whole and consider the consequences of having lived it as he has, and he is able to admit the awful possibility that, deadened by the habit of waiting, his life has been wasted and will not be redeemed:

> Was I sleeping, while the others suffered? Am I sleeping now? To-morrow, when I wake, or think I do, what shall I say of to-day? That with Estragon my friend, at this place, until the fall of night, I waited for Godot? That Pozzo passed, with his carrier, and that he spoke to us? Probably. But in all that what truth will there be? (*Estragon, having struggled with his boots in vain, is dozing off again. Vladimir looks at him.*) He'll know nothing. He'll tell me about the blows he received and I'll give him a carrot. (*Pause.*) Astride of a grave and a difficult birth. Down in the hole, lingeringly, the grave-digger puts on the forceps. We have time to grow old. The air is full of our cries. (*He listens.*) But habit is a great deadener. (*He looks at Estragon.*) At me too someone is looking, of me too someone is saying, He is sleeping, he knows nothing, let him sleep on. (*Pause.*) I can't go on! (*Pause.*) What have I said?

Godot is thought of as a play that has daringly abandoned the traditional conventions of drama, from story to setting. Yet at this crucial moment, the play draws its energy from a brush with tragedy, that most traditional dramatic form. The world of *Godot* is suddenly pierced with the undeniable reality of suffering, failure, and death, the exigencies that are the heart of conventional drama. This intrusion gives Didi a moral dimension; for the first time, he truly suffers, and the entire play takes on a new resonance. We understand waiting not only as a metaphysical or theological problem but as a moral condition, a deadening habit that deafens us to the cries around us.

However, this is just a moment's perception. The play seems embarrassed and skeptical about all its important themes, moral as well as theological, and can rest with none of them. Didi's insight flickers and goes out. He and Gogo return to their waiting, and the play moves quickly to its inconclusive end.

D.E.

SUGGESTED READINGS

Bair, Deirdre, *Samuel Beckett* (1978).
Coe, Richard, *Samuel Beckett* (1968).
Cohn, Ruby (ed.), *Casebook on Waiting for Godot* (1967).
Esslin, Martin (ed.), *Samuel Beckett* (1965).
Fletcher, John, *The Novels of Samuel Beckett* (1970).
Kenner, Hugh, *Samuel Beckett: A Critical Study* (1968).
Kenner, Hugh, *A Reader's Guide to Samuel Beckett* (1973).
Pilling, John, *Samuel Beckett* (1976).
States, Bert O., *The Shape of Paradox: An Essay on Waiting for Godot* (1978).
Tindall, William York, *Samuel Beckett* (1964).

INDEX

INDEX

ABOUT THE AUTHORS

David Engel received an M.Phil. and a J.D. from Columbia University, where he has taught courses in English literature, writing, and the humanities. He has published a number of articles and reviews on various literary and critical topics. Mr. Engel is an attorney who lives and works in New York City.

Ruth Hoberman is an assistant professor of English at Eastern Illinois University. She received a B.A. in French from Oberlin College and a Ph.D. in English and Comparative Literature from Columbia University. Dr. Hoberman's current research interests include the relationship between modernist fiction and biography in England between the two world wars; her book on the subject will be published by Southern Illinois University Press.

Frank Palmeri is an assistant professor of English at the University of Miami in Florida. He received an M.A. in American literature and a Ph.D. in comparative literature from Columbia University. He has taught literature courses at several American universities, and in 1982–1983, he taught at Anhui University in the People's Republic of China. Dr. Palmeri has published several critical articles; among his special fields of interest are satiric and apocalyptic literature.